Atlas of the Senseable City

Atlas of the Senseable City

Antoine Picon and Carlo Ratti

Yale
UNIVERSITY PRESS
New Haven and London

Yale University Press books may be purchased in quantity for educational, business, or promotional use. For information, please e-mail
sales.press@yale.edu (U.S. office) or sales@yaleup.co.uk (U.K. office).

Graphic design project by:
studio FM milano
Tom Benson

Printed in Slovenia.

Carlo Ratti's Editorial team: Daniele Belleri (Lead Editor), Michael Baick, Melanie Erspamer
Special thanks to: Vincent Leung, Stela Karabina, Giulia Maccagli,
Carlotta Sillano

Proofreading: Melanie Erspamer
Indexing: MLM Indexing Service

Library of Congress Control Number: 2022931186
ISBN 978-0-300-24751-0 (hardcover : alk. paper)

A catalogue record for this book is available from the British Library.

This paper meets the requirements of ANSI/NISO Z39.48–1992
(Permanence of Paper).

10 9 8 7 6 5 4 3 2 1

CONTENTS

MIT Senseable City Lab

The Senseable City Lab (SCL) is a multidisciplinary research group at the Massachusetts Institute of Technology that focuses on innovation in the built environment. Founded in 2004 by Carlo Ratti and Assaf Biderman, it combines academic rigor with industry expertise–synthesizing analysis and speculation, critique and proposition, science and design.

Transcending the methodologies of a single field, the Lab takes an omnidisciplinary approach, having engaged over 400 collaborators across the academic spectrum and across different geographies (all continents have been represented, apart from Antarctica). Project teams fuse the expertise of designers, planners, engineers, physicists, biologists, social scientists, and more–all united behind a shared desire to innovate.

At the Lab, professors, research scientists, post-doctoral researchers, research fellows and assistants, and visiting scholars and students collaborate with industry partners, nonprofits, trusts and foundations, governments, disadvantaged communities, and citizens. To further scale the work's impact, the Lab has opened satellite labs in Stockholm, Amsterdam, and Singapore–with more in the pipeline.

The Lab's work is guided by impact, whether in the form of publication of new knowledge, physical interventions, or visionary proposals. In under two decades, the Lab has chalked up four start-ups, 15 patents, 70 exhibitions, 100 real-world projects, 100 prizes, over 500 papers, and 5,000 media mentions. Academic citations firmly put the Lab in the world's top ten urban research centers.

On the cusp of turning 20, the Lab is looking at new opportunities looming on the horizon: the layering of digital information across urban space has become so fine-grained that the way we study, describe, and understand cities is being radically transformed–as are the tools we use to design them. At the same time, the very pervasiveness of the digital world can help us better understand its own limits.

In an accelerating future, it is becoming urgent to explore the application of ever-greater technological sophistication to ever-more pressing challenges.

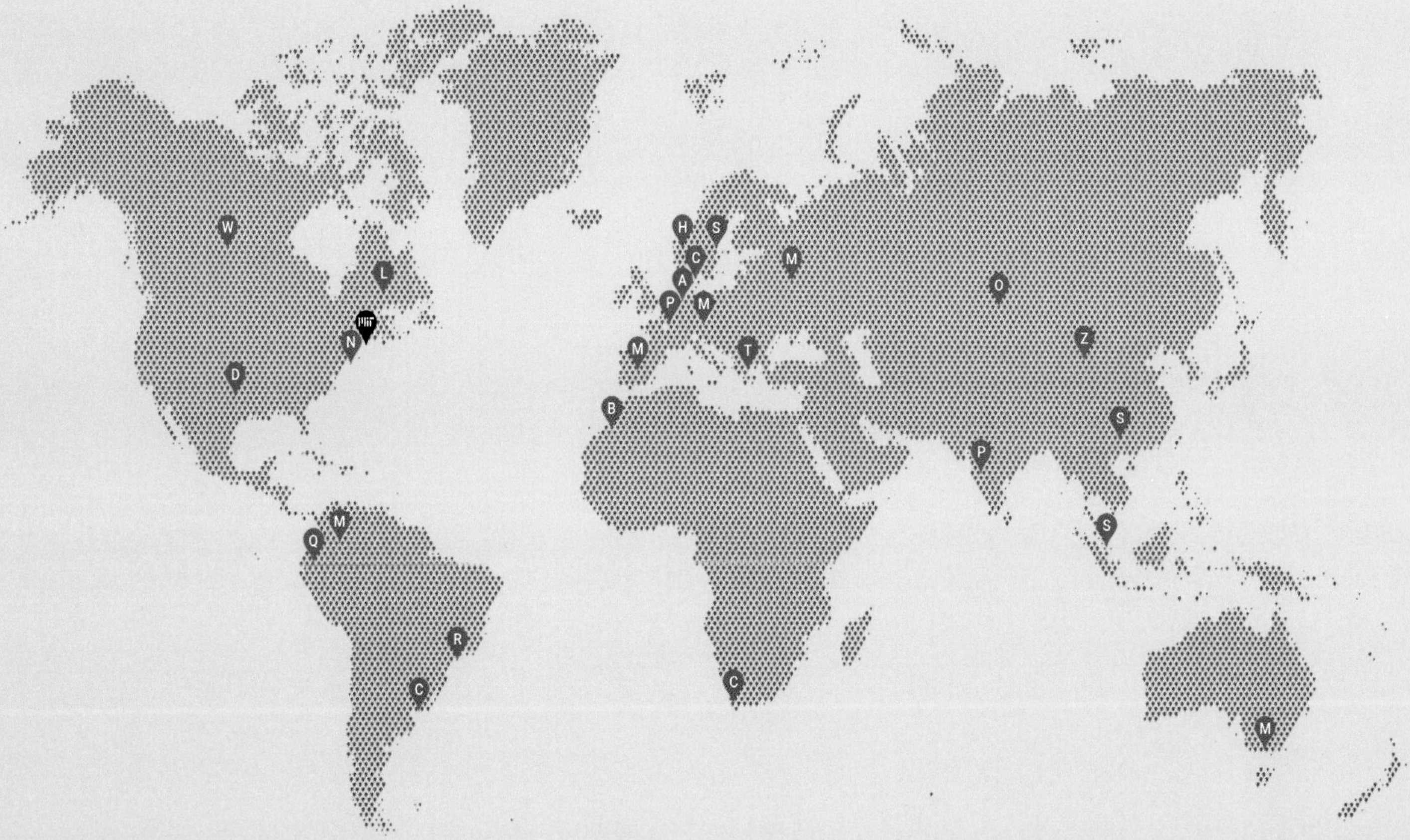

Municipalities that have
collaborated with the
MIT Senseable City Lab.

Atlas of the Senseable City

Introduction: Mapping the Future of Cities

Digital urban maps are everywhere. They are not limited—far from it—to geographic information systems used by professional cartographers and planners. They punctuate city life for everyone, popping up on individual computer and smartphone screens. They provide car drivers with current traffic conditions and the best itinerary to go from one place to another. They inform people of the presence of nearby monuments, shops, and restaurants. By clicking on the icons that represent these venues, one can access all kinds of information, from historical overviews to special offers, from menus to customer reviews. Digital maps are gradually replacing printed city guides. Meanwhile, features like Snapchat's Snap Map enable us to know the locations of our friends, as well as what they are doing. Other maps offer profiles of people whom we might want to meet—or date.

Digital mapping amounts to a true revolution—one that goes hand in hand with the far more general shift involving the advent of a new city based on both atoms of matter and bits of information, on the pairing of places and websites, a city often characterized as "smart."[1] With this atlas, we reveal the emergence of a new, pervasive urban reality, which digitally augments the planned corridors and designed buildings that we see with our unaided eyes. (Are we even still able to see without our digital protheses, starting with our smartphones?) We hope to reveal here an urban landscape of not just spaces and objects, but also motion, connection, circulation, and experience. The path we will follow will thus lead us from the materiality of cities to the various aspects of urban life that used to appear less immediately tangible. Digital urban maps actually expand the realm of the tangible. Whereas traditional urban maps were perceived as abstractions from the city's everyday physical existence, the cartographic documents discussed here appear to be inseparable from it, as if digital cities were now inseparable from their physical twins.

1 See, for example, Anthony Townsend, *Smart Cities: Big Data, Civic Hackers, and the Quest for a New Utopia* (New York, London: WW Norton & Company, 2013); Antoine Picon, *Smart Cities: A Spatialised Intelligence* (Chichester: John Wiley & Sons, 2015). See also the conclusion of this book.

A Revolution in Urban Cartography

One measure of the present cartographic revolution is the diversity of maps that have become available. Thanks to increasing amounts of tracking data (from GPS [Global Positioning System] units recording latitude and longitude over time), we can plot all sorts of phenomena, from environmental pollution levels to the movements of car and bicycle traffic. All around the world, urban research laboratories, including the Massachusetts Institute of Technology's Senseable City Lab (SCL), which is directed by one of this book's authors, are exploring new ways to visualize these data in the hopes of enabling a better understanding and management our cities. The SCL Trash Track project, for instance, with its spectacular maps that reveal the final journeys of a number of discarded everyday objects, is a contribution to the streamlining of our recycling infrastructure and practices.[2]

Not only are experts in research laboratories using tracking data to invent new maps, so are amateur cartographers. By using free software platforms such as Google Maps, CartoDB, and OpenStreetMap, individuals and businesses can produce maps that are suited to their or their clients' needs. In 2010, such democratization led the French sociologist Patrice Flichy to celebrate "the consecration of the amateur," in contrast to the absolute rule of professionals that previously characterized sectors from tourism to journalism.[3] When more people are able to participate, collaborative efforts can quickly establish shared information resources that are real competitors to official geographic institutions, such as Britain's Ordnance Survey or France's Institut Géographique National. These efforts can prove crucial in times of crisis. For instance, OpenStreetMap's Japanese contributors were instrumental in answering the mapping challenges raised by the 2011 Sendai earthquake and tsunami.[4] For the first time in history, cartography is no longer the exclusive domain of specialized institutions and professionals. For a number of people, it has become a mode of expression and even a means of socialization, as shown by the multiplication of mapping parties all over the world that gather participants around cartographic as well as urban issues and serve as forums for meetings and exchanges.[5]

"The consecration of the amateur" should not, however, lead to the erroneous conclusion that we no longer need professional cartography or the institutions that produce it. Though it often competes with official geographic institutions, OpenStreetMap cannot carry out the complex geodesic operations that are necessary to provide an entirely reliable basis to the various cartographic layers piled onto it. It should be conceived as a new level of, rather than a substitute for, traditional cartography. This idea could very well be a fundamental characteristic of many emerging technologies that are currently transforming our world. Just as OpenStreetMap will never replace scientific cartography, the self-driving car should be envisaged as complementary to traditional modes of transport, beginning with public transit, rather than as a replacement for them.

2 See Dietmar Offenhuber, *Waste Is Information: Infrastructure Legibility and Governance* (Cambridge, MA: MIT Press, 2017).

3 Patrice Flichy, *Le Sacre de l'amateur: Sociologie des passions ordinaires à l'ère numérique* (Paris: Le Seuil, 2010).

4 See for instance Pradyumna P. Karan and Unryu Suganuma, eds., *Japan After 3/11: Global Perspectives on the Earthquake, Tsunami, and Fukushima Meltdown* (Lexington, KT: University Press of Kentucky, 2016).

5 Gwendoline l'Her, Myrian Servières, Daniel Siret, "La Cartopartie, une nouvelle forme de balade urbaine déployée par les villes," *Les Cahiers de la recherche architecturale, urbaine et paysagère*, no. 3 (2018).

Though hard to replicate in a printed book, digital mapping also allows us to visualize and interact with evolving situations. Real-time maps of road traffic are now so commonplace as to be unremarkable. Sanitation, sewage, and other types of urban infrastructure can be tracked in the same fashion. Furthermore, countless maps can be generated by plotting the positions of connected devices, such as smartphones, onto background maps. These dynamic maps are disturbingly blurring the distinction between surveillance on the one hand and cartography on the other. Also fading away is the dividing line between reality and simulation, since numerous apps allow extrapolation from recorded data in order to develop scenarios and test hypotheses of the urban system's evolution.

Because of their capacity to transcribe in real time what is happening and to serve as starting points for systematic explorations of what is possible, maps are becoming diagnostic and decision-making tools for politicians, administrators, and technicians. But they also allow more subjective kinds of information to be recorded—from the emotions people feel in front of a monument to their opinions on a shop or restaurant. Apps such as Foursquare have capitalized on this new capacity of cartography to allow experiences to be shared. They have been joined by almost all the major players in the social media world, from Facebook to Twitter, who have also developed and deployed geotagging features.

At the same time, a whole host of tensions have cropped up: not only between objectivity and subjectivity, but also between a top-down view of management that risks veering toward technocracy and a bottom-up approach in which individuals and groups are all given a voice. On the one hand, there are projects such as IBM's Operations Center for the municipal authorities of Rio de Janeiro, a constant stream of maps and surveillance-camera recordings that provides real-time tracking of city life, from meteorological events and disease outbreaks to policing and trash collection.[6] On the other hand, there are a multitude of sites, from Yelp to Google Earth, that allow individuals to express themselves by sharing information.

The ubiquity of maps and the strategic issues related to their production and use reflect a profound transformation of digital culture that could be described as a "spatial turn," to use the expression coined by the American geographer Edward Soja in relation to the evolution of the social sciences from the 1980s onward after the rediscovery of the importance of space as a determining dimension of the social.[7] A digital spatial turn—to fully appreciate the meaning of this expression, it is useful to remember the ambition that accompanied the rise of the digital in the early 1990s: that it would be a pervasive reality distinct from the mere development of information technologies.[8]

When it first emerged, digital culture tended to claim that it would lead to the disintegration of physical space, with the Internet set to overcome the former's limitations, such as distance and the lack of connection that this often implied.[9] This claim explains why the architect and urban theorist William J. Mitchell felt justified in predicting the inexorable decline of physical mobility in urban settings in his 1995 book *City of Bits: Space, Place,*

6 Natasha Singer, "Mission Control, Built for Cities: IBM Takes 'Smarter Cities' Concept to Rio de Janeiro," *New York Times*, 3 March 2012, http://www.nytimes.com/2012/03/04/business/ibm-takes-smarter-cities-concept-to-rio-de-janeiro.html?pagewanted=all&_r=0.

7 Edward W. Soja, *Postmodern Geographies: The Reassertion of Space in Critical Social Theory* (London: Verso, 1989).

8 On the key differences between the information age and the digital era, see for instance Nicholas Negroponte, *Being Digital* (New York: Knopf, 1995).

9 See Vincent Mosco, *The Digital Sublime: Myth, Power and Cyberspace* (Cambridge, MA: MIT Press, 2004), 119.

and the Infobahn.[10] This was not the first time that people had dreamed of overcoming space and distance. From the telegraph to the telephone and the radio, the rise of telecommunications in the nineteenth and early twentieth centuries was accompanied by similar expectations. For the toastmaster of a banquet held in New York in 1868, Samuel Morse's telegraph had "annihilated both space and time in the transmission of intelligence."[11]

Yet the final outcome proved quite different than what had been imagined initially. The telegraph and the telephone did not abolish physical space. Similarly, space has not disappeared because of the digital revolution; rather, it has been transformed. Under the influence of technologies such as wireless networks and geolocation, physical space and digital content have increasingly hybridized. The current popular description is "augmented reality," because atoms and bits are joining forces rather than remaining strangers.[12] Both physical space and online space are in a sense enhanced by being ever more intricately interwoven. Anyone who is walking along the street looking at their smartphone screen is in a situation of augmented reality. The astounding boom in connected objects, collectively referred to as the Internet of Things, is taking us in the same direction: toward a digital culture that is proving to be profoundly spatialized. In this context, maps are acquiring a new dimension. It is not enough for them to plot out positions in space; they must also fix the points of convergence between the physical and the digital world. This convergence will be one of the main factors in the transformation of cities over the coming decades.

Ultimately, this transformation is what the present atlas is all about. Whether they involve flow visualization, data exchange, urban metabolism, or the physical experience of cities, the maps and projects included in this book are intended as explorations of possible future scenarios for cities. This is not a case of assigning fixed characteristics to the future, once and for all, in the way that earlier utopias attempted to define the traits of ideal cities and societies. What follows here does not set out to paint a finished portrait. Rather, it is a sketch of a shifting landscape, revealing the existence of escape routes that could lead toward various horizons. Atlases have always had the power to make us think and dream. Indeed, they enable us to explore places we have never been to, places that sometimes do not even exist in the time we live in. This is what we have tried to do here, portraying what we are just beginning to discover, a city that still partially belongs to the future rather than the present.

10 William J. Mitchell, *City of Bits: Space, Place, and the Infobahn* (Cambridge, MA: MIT Press, 1995).

11 Tom Standage, *The Victorian Internet: The Remarkable Story of the Telegraph and the Nineteenth Century's On-Line Pioneers* (New York: Walker, 1998), 90.

12 *Augmented reality* is often used in a narrower sense, defined as those digital devices that overlap digital information onto the physical world for our eyes to see. Here we use the term in a broader sense: the augmentation of the physical world with digital information.

From Data to Maps

Have we not all at some point drifted into a daydream upon looking at a map? Cartography shares this power with other visual forms, but unlike other types of images, maps are rooted in the world of data. Sensors, meters, and smartphones have led to an exponential growth in the production of data, especially in cities.[13] The new sensed urban realm can be compared to a digital El Dorado, one that ever more companies are setting out to exploit: alongside giants like Cisco Systems, IBM, and Siemens, there are myriads of small and medium-sized businesses capitalizing on this opportunity, such as startups seeking to commercialize innovative means of transport or biomedical companies offering new techniques for biologically monitoring individuals and populations.

A whole range of political and economic issues are surfacing around big data. Perhaps most importantly, to whom does this information belong? There are several possible answers, as the data may have been produced directly by city governments or collected by the private companies that supply water, energy, or telecommunications. And what degree of free rein should be given to specialist businesses that are seeking to put data to productive use? These problems are currently subject to keen debate. While certain cities insist on the need to remain in charge of urban data, others do not hesitate to envision data's privatization. In addition to these first couple of questions regarding the ownership of data, there are others to be asked about access to those data—that is, about the subject of "open data." How far is it acceptable to go when communicating information that may prove sensitive?[14] It is worth remembering at this stage that information can often provoke unwanted consequences. When apps like Waze provide alternative itineraries so car drivers can avoid congestion, for example, they may divert traffic to the usually quiet streets where schools are located, thus endangering the lives of children who cross them.[15] As a favored tool for data visualization, mapping stands at the heart of all these concerns.

Moreover, how should the information be displayed? With a change of color or a different way of subdividing space to make the data relate to it, the message can alter dramatically. Crime maps are typical of these distortions. The conclusions that they suggest are highly dependent on not only the data collected but also the spatial frame employed. A decision as simple as the use of physical versus institutional divisions of space, like city blocks or districts, can convey a very different impression depending on the choice of contour lines, thus leading to divergent interpretations of the situation. This is equally true of political maps that indicate voting tendencies and results. Maps are never neutral. They are always the result of data manipulation, even if digital tools may seem to make them objective.[16]

One of this atlas's ambitions is to render these manipulations visible and thus encourage critical reflection on the subject. Alongside political and economic issues, or rather in relation to these, there is no shortage of scientific questions either. Is a new science of cities being born as a result of this increase in data, as urban-modeling specialists such as Michael Batty and Marc Barthelemy have suggested?[17] This new science would give

13 Cisco Systems, *Cisco Annual Internet Report (2018–2023)*, 9 March 2020, https://www.cisco.com/c/en/us/solutions/collateral/executive-perspectives/annual-internet-report/white-paper-c11-741490.html.

14 See Brett Goldstein and Lauren Dyson, *Beyond Transparency: Open Data and the Future of Civic Innovation* (San Francisco: Code for America, 2013).

15 Such a case recently arose in the French city of Lyon. The municipality negotiated with Waze to preserve the peacefulness of some streets. See Antoine Courmont, "Plateforme, big data et recomposition du gouvernement urbain: Les Effets de Waze sur les politiques de régulation du trafic," *Revue française de sociologie* 59, no. 3 (2018): 423–449.

16 See Laura Kurgan, *Close Up at a Distance: Mapping, Technology, and Politics* (New York: Zone Books, 2013).

precious information on key questions, such as the factors that truly govern urban growth and welfare. Might it also enable better management of cities, having allowed entire sectors of the economy to evolve? The debate is far from closed.

Dashboard, Logbook or Commons?

Different types of urban mapping offer different perspectives on the city. Some set out to give an account of the current state of the environment, what is happening within infrastructures, streets, and buildings, in much the same way as an observatory or a dashboard would. In the future, this type of map will also allow monitoring of city residents, their health, and even their moods. This is likely to raise tough questions about privacy.

Dashboard maps are inextricably linked to the desire to manage cities better, as if the management process were somehow a matter of steering. By the same token, the development of new tools for visualization and simulation of the urban realm is often linked to a temptation to exercise top-down control. This could be described as neocybernetic, taking after the cybernetics of the 1950s and 1960s. A multidisciplinary approach initiated by the mathematician Norbert Wiener of the Massachusetts Institute of Technology (MIT), cybernetics posited that the complex systems of human beings and their organizations could be better steered when studied from an information processing and exchange perspective.[18]

"Logbook" maps, by contrast, serve to pinpoint individual or collective experiences and to superimpose life trajectories on the fabric of the city, whether with a view to achieving a greater sense of ownership over it or to sharing the curiosities and emotions to which it gives rise. From this perspective, maps are comparable to a sort of navigational logbook that mingles urban space with life experiences. Artists such as Daniel Belasco Rogers and Christian Nold have contributed to explorations of this new type of use for maps. While Rogers used a GPS to map all his journeys in Berlin, generating a work that he displayed under the revealing title *The Drawing of Our Lives*, Nold has sought to reveal the emotional content of certain locations, in line with the "psychogeographical" investigations of the Situationists (see chapter 4).[19]

Alongside dashboard maps and logbook maps, we see activist maps: the iSee mapping app, for instance, which allows users to evade the surveillance video cameras installed in Manhattan, and maps with a more reflective purpose, such as those that the architect Laura Kurgan has dedicated to the urban impact of American policies on imprisonment.[20] Her maps, which reveal the dramatic extent of the United States penitentiary system and the spatial and social inequalities that it helps to reproduce, are more telling than any text.

Within this varied group, it is worth highlighting the particular importance that maps are assuming as common property based on the collaborative

17 Michael Batty, *The New Science of Cities* (Cambridge, MA: MIT Press, 2013); Marc Barthelemy, *The Structure and Dynamics of Cities: Urban Data Analysis and Theoretical Modeling* (Cambridge: Cambridge University Press, 2016).

18 On the cybernetic approach, see, e.g., Steve Joshua Heims, *Constructing a Social Science for Postwar America: The Cybernetics Group, 1946–1953* (Cambridge, MA: MIT Press, 1991).

19 Daniel Belasco Rogers, *The Drawing of Our Lives*, plan b (website), accessed 10 September 2015, http://planbperformance.net/works/lifedrawing/; Christian Nold's website, accessed 23 July 2015, http://www.christiannold.com/.

20 "Million Dollar Blocks," accessed 13 June 2019, http://spatialinformationdesignlab.org/projects/million-dollar-blocks.

accumulation of data or the exchange of information among people living in the same city. The success of initiatives such as OpenStreetMap has already been mentioned above: such platforms have created truly shared resources of geographic data, whose quantity increases day by day through tens of thousands of voluntary contributions. Nowadays, maps also serve the purpose of gathering urbanites' suggestions regarding the future of their cities. The products of the Carticipe (now Debatomap') platform, for example, which has been used in a series of French cities—including Laval, Marseille, Saint-Étienne, and Strasbourg—are entirely representative of a new generation of participatory maps. One of the challenges of urban cartography lies in combining highly structured data with less-structured information produced by the public.

From dashboards to logbooks to digital commons, contemporary uses for cartography definitively reflect the existing diversity of approaches to cities and of the projects associated with them. We may well set out to make cities more efficient, like well-oiled machines, but this is not the same as seeking to record and share the emotions that they arouse. In the end, it is possible to favor the construction of a shared resource of information and ideas over one that better aids rationalization or the subjective experience of the urban realm. By allowing all of these projects to take shape, cartography enables them to be compared, letting cities find and adopt the best policies. For it is likely that cities of the future will be partly regulated through neocybernetically inspired monitoring and management tools. That should permit the optimization of some types of heavy infrastructure, such as rapid transit systems or networks for water distribution and sanitation. At the same time, cities of the future will accord more and more importance to individuals, who will be connected through their smartphones and maybe soon—who knows?—through smart clothing or implants. Such cities, relying on participation and collaboration, are only just beginning to appear.

Beyond Data and Their Representation: Maps as Infrastructure for the Future

Urban futures and mapping are ever more closely linked. Their relationship should lead to a profound transformation of how maps are perceived. Traditionally, maps were placed under the umbrellas of two major paradigms: the database and the pictorial representation. Revealingly, these both appeared at around the same time—during the Renaissance—through the pioneering contributions of Leon Battista Alberti and Leonardo da Vinci in the field of urban mapping. In his *Descriptio Urbis Romae* (*Description of the city of Rome*), written in the 1440s, the humanist and architect Alberti noted the coordinates of a series of significant places in the papal city, such as major monuments and the corners of the Roman wall, instead of indicating their whereabouts in a plan, implying that, in his eyes, a map constituted the graphic expression of a set of geographic data.[21] According to him, before being visual, cartography was based on the careful recording of a series of figures. With his plan of the Italian town of Imola, produced some sixty years later, Leonardo suggested, on the contrary, that the map was none other than a bird's-eye view. His use of realistic colors—red for the tiled roofs of the houses, blue for the water in the moats surrounding the fortified town and for the river meandering nearby—testifies to this intention.[22]

Database or pictorial representation? This Renaissance dichotomy might not be relevant today, as we are creating an increasingly precise digital copy of our physical world. As a result, several factors enable the list of possible interpretations of maps to broaden. The first is related to the new solidarity between digital maps and a complex set of devices and tools: sensors, all manner of meters, wired and wireless networks, computers, cell phones, information-processing algorithms, automated databases. The second is the role that maps play within institutions and as foundations for social relationships, whether in distributing competencies among municipal technical services departments or binding individuals together on collaborative platforms. Finally, referring to maps has become so commonplace that it often goes unremarked. On this front, it is hard not to be reminded of the Xerox PARC pioneer Mark Weiser's observation that "the most profound technologies are those that disappear. They weave themselves into the fabric of everyday life until they are indistinguishable from it."[23] Digital mapping appears self-evident, whether the map is displayed in large scale in a control room or in miniature on a cell phone screen, appears static or animated, is consulted in real time or after the fact.

These three characteristics of digital mapping—its intimate connection with the complex technological background that enables its production, its role as a foundation for social relationships, and its self-evident character—are very similar to the properties of infrastructure in our modern world. What if, instead of interpreting digital cartography from the traditional perspectives of the database and the picture, one considered it as an infrastructure, a quintessentially urban infrastructure?

The term *infrastructure* first appeared during the second half of the nineteenth century, in French, to describe engineering realizations that constituted the material basis of technological systems such as road or railway networks. Bridges and tunnels were thus considered infrastructure. After passing into English at the dawn of the twentieth century, the word kept the same meaning, closely associated with civil engineering, for decades. It was only after World War II that it acquired the broader sense of the technological layers that undergird activities ranging from physical circulation to telecommunication and from the deployment of armed forces to economic development.[24] Today, infrastructure is even more extensively associated with the notion of a fundamental level of support without which we would not be able to carry out many of our day-to-day activites that seem to go without saying. Infrastructure is also inseparable from the various practices of the professionals in charge of its design and maintenance, as well as from the behavior of its users. Another way to put this is that it constitutes the basis of a series of social competences and social relations.

21 Mario Carpo and Francesco Furlan eds. *Leon Battista Alberti's Delineation of the City of Rome (Descriptio Urbis Romae)* (Tempe: Arizona Center for Medieval and Renaissance Studies, 2007).

22 Carlo Pedretti, *Leonardo: Il Codice Hammer e la mappa di Imola* (Florence: Giunti Barbera, 1985).

23 Mark Weiser, "The Computer for the 21st Century," *Scientific American* 265, no. 3 (September 1991): 94.

24 Ashley Carse, "Keyword: Infrastructure: How a Humble French Engineering Term Shaped the Modern World," in *Infrastructures and Social Complexity: A Companion*, Penny Harvey, Casper Bruun Jensen, and Atsuro Morita, eds. (New York: Routledge, 2017), 27–39.

Finally, infrastructure is often massive but at the same time almost invisible, seeming to disappear behind the everyday practices that it allows. Quasi disappearance is one of the characteristics of infrastructure, inasmuch as it constitutes the medium for so many activities—a medium that seems so self-evident that its presence is not normally perceived.

Railway lines, freeways, telephone cables, and satellites clearly belong to the infrastructural realm. But in addition to these technological artifacts and systems, our modern world has seen the rise of another type of infrastructure, "knowledge infrastructure," which the science historian Paul Edwards defines as "robust networks of people, artifacts, and institutions that generate, share, and maintain specific knowledge about the human and natural worlds."[25] According to Edwards, the Internet and the global meteorological system, with its weather stations and computers, fall into the category of infrastructure that does not merely organize the world but also informs our perception of it, from our everyday online activities to our understanding of the effects of climate change.

Why not interpret digital maps of cities—or rather, the system they constitute today, at once vast and differentiated—as a knowledge infrastructure? Indeed, they are the most visible part of the "robust networks of people, artifacts, and institutions that generate, share, and maintain specific knowledge about" cities. As such, they form a fundamental layer of urban life without which many activities could not be carried out. This infrastructural quality could well explain the frequent references by those scrutinizing recent cartographic production to the famous text where Jorge Luis Borges writes of "a map of the Empire whose size was that of the Empire, and which coincided point for point with it," or to a slightly lesser-known passage from Lewis Carroll's *Sylvie and Bruno Concluded,* in which the country itself is used "as its own map."[26] The relationship between the city and its maps is not based solely on the idea of an extraction of information, or of representation. A deeper link seems to be at play, as though mapping now constituted one of the preferred vectors of urban dynamics—a function that goes far beyond the performative role that Valérie November, Eduardo Camarcho-Hübner, and Bruno Latour assign it in an article that calls into question its representation of reality.[27] According to them, too much attention has been devoted to mapping's mimetic dimension and not enough to how it is actually used to navigate space. In fact, maps still do represent reality, and this is all the more reason that they tend to become inseparable from it. But in addition to the traditional interpretations (databases and pictorial images, as noted above), maps can be considered from an infrastructural viewpoint, and the implications of this are worth exploring. The performative character of maps ranks high among those implications. Indeed, it is not a coincidence that its in-depth study began when digital maps and GPS units, those powerful spatial navigation aids, were becoming quite common.

Considering contemporary digital maps as urban infrastructure not only puts their performative character into a broader frame but also enables a rethinking of the meaning of "digital twin." Indeed, united to the physical through the various mapping practices that we have evoked above, from dashboards to digital commons, cities of bits no longer appear as extensions

25 Paul Edwards, *A Vast Machine: Computer Models, Climate Data, and the Politics of Global Warming* (Cambridge, MA: MIT Press, 2010), 17.

26 Jorge Luis Borges, "On Exactitude in Science," in *Collected Fictions*, trans. Andrew Hurley (New York: Penguin, 1999), 325; Lewis Carroll, *Sylvie and Bruno Concluded* (London: Macmillan, 1893), 169. For references to these works, see, e.g., Gilles Palsky, "Borges, Carroll et la carte au 1/1," *Cybergeo: European Journal of Geography*, Document 106 (September 1999), http://cybergeo. revues.org/5233.

27 Valérie November, Eduardo Camarcho-Hübner, and Bruno Latour, "Entering a Risky Territory: Space in the Age of Digital Navigation," *Environment and Planning D: Society and Space* 28, no. 4 (2010): 581–599.

or mirrors of cities of brick and mortar—they are part of the same augmented urban reality. One of the challenges of contemporary city planning lies in this hybridity without true equivalent in the past. How to make plans that address it is a question that has not been fully answered to this day.

Beyond the subcategory of knowledge infrastructure, infrastructure in general can be approached from three perspectives, or rather as a three-tiered reality.[28] First, as noted above, it possesses a physical basis. Roads and railroads but also the Internet are inseparable from a series of material artifacts: causeways, rails and railway stations, cables and servers. From this physical basis, the second level unfolds, of professional organization and stabilized sociotechnical practices. This level concerns more than administrators, designers, and operators of infrastructure—users also participate in its production and reproduction. Moreover, this second level corresponds to what the French technological historian Konstantinos Chatzis calls the "regulation" of infrastructure, obviously in reference to the idea of social regularity, one of the main avenues for its interpretation by the social sciences.[29] Finally, the third level is constituted by a social imaginary, distinct from but not above the first two. Instead, it is located at the point where they meet; it helps them to adapt while infusing them with a more general significance than the sort that is born of services provided by day-to-day infrastructure. Just like the roads and railways of the First Industrial Revolution, the Internet has given rise to powerful socially shared images—in other words, to an imaginary that has oriented its development and use.[30]

This last dimension may seem paradoxical at first: how can infrastructure be at once almost invisible and inseparable from a pervasive imaginary? The answer is actually quite simple, for it is found in the everyday experience of infrastructure, which tends to recede into the background because of this familiarity but also reappears vividly as something that frames so many moments of our lives. For instance, the Internet that is almost invisible with a good connection that enables its users to concentrate on what they are looking for online regains visibility as an infrastructure that organizes large parts of social life. From the latter perspective, it is associated with various images of social interaction.

Digital urban maps fit well within this tripartite frame. They are inseparable from a series of artifacts and systems—sensors, cameras, cables, servers, computers, smartphones—which are almost identical to those that constitute the Internet's physical basis. From their professional use by Uber and Waze employees to their use by different platforms' clients, digital urban maps rely on regulated social behaviors. Last but certainly not least, they appeal to a powerful imaginary while being almost invisible when used on an everyday basis—to navigate a city, for instance. Their multiplication connects them even more to many contemporary urban issues. Beyond the pictures that they present to our eyes, they always end up opening a path to new collective images of the city and what it might become in the near future. To envisage maps as infrastructure is not only to recognize their key role in supporting all sorts of activities in our contemporary cities. It is also to realize that maps are not just databases, representations, or navigational tools. They offer glimpses into the future, collective visions that enable still

28 For an introduction to this three-tiered approach, see Antoine Picon, "Urban Infrastructure, Imagination and Politics: From the Networked Metropolis to the Smart City," *International Journal of Urban and Regional Research* 42, no. 2 (March 2018): 263–275.

29 Konstantinos Chatzis, *La Pluie, le métro et l'ingénieur: Contribution à l'histoire de l'assainissement et des transports urbains, XIXe–XXe siècles* (Paris: Harmattan, 2000).

30 See, e.g., Patrice Flichy, *The Internet Imaginaire*, trans. Liz Carey-Libbrecht (Cambridge, MA: MIT Press, 2007).

undefined aspirations to take a more precise form. They are instrumental in shaping our cities' destinies.

As mentioned earlier, we have chosen to follow four thematic threads in this atlas: motion, connection, circulation, and experience. They correspond to four essential aspects of contemporary digital urban maps envisaged as infrastructure: physical, professional, sociotechnical, and imaginary layers.

Motion captures the switch from the static recording of geographic data to the dynamic tracking of the movements of objects—above all, people—which the generalization of GPS and mobile terminals, first and foremost smartphones, has made possible. It carries with it the notion of an intensified urban reality in which movement represents far more than a series of discrete trajectories. Dense clouds of flickering and moving geospatial points constitute a constantly changing tapestry that offers the most powerful image of contemporary urban life.

Connection is about all the messages that we exchange over space and time using telecommunication networks. It is above all about the intersection between data and human sociability, which maps enable us to chart in innovative ways. From such a perspective, new spatial structures appear that force us to rethink and sometimes challenge existing boundaries.

As for circulation, it addresses the metabolic dimension of urban life, which digital tools can track and model in far greater detail than traditional surveying and recording instruments. These tools make visible the granular data of crucial activities such as trash removal, as well as the evolution of urban ecologies or the global sanitary state of populations. Circulation offers insights into what urban monitoring may mean very soon, at the intersection of environmental concerns and biopolitics.

Finally, maps can capture not only the various material and other objective phenomena involved in the lives of cities but also more subjective and "immaterial" aspects such as the impressions made by our discoveries as we explore them or the memories they generate—in other words, experience. Maps also allow an almost seamless passage from the individual to the collective, from individual feelings to the constitution of collective emotions. Of our four categories, experience is probably the most fundamental for understanding how maps and the social imaginary are intimately related today.

There are of course many overlaps among these four approaches to digital urban mapping. Motion and circulation, for instance, are closely related, as are connection and experience in our digitally permeated world, in which we seldom say or feel something without leaving a trace in a database somewhere. The picture of the city of the future that emerges from this overview is full of both promises — of greater efficiency, of healthier and richer lives — and substantial threats, because of the constant monitoring and surveillance it may entail. All this is to say that the political question is unavoidable at this stage. In which cities do we want to live, and how? Contemporary digital maps throw new light on these crucial questions.

Maps, Cities, and Politics: From the "Right to the City" to the Right to See

Throughout this evocation of the rise of digital urban maps, the political dimension of the phenomenon has made repeated appearances. The connection between maps and infrastructure represents an additional incentive to deal in a more direct way with this dimension, insofar as nothing is more political than urban infrastructure.[31] The imaginary character of maps in particular allows for their population with political themes and preoccupations, from the neocybernetic ambition to govern the city as efficiently and smoothly as possible to the opposite dream of disrupting existing power in order to achieve a greater degree of individual and collective freedom.

The political dimension of digital urban maps can be approached from different angles. To start with, digital maps do not represent mere substitutes for traditional urban cartography but instead complement it. From this perspective, the question arises of how to organize this coexistence in a genuinely productive way. How should one envisage, for example, the complementarity between official geographic surveys and enterprises like OpenStreetMap? Such a query is inseparable from the more general issue of how to bring harmony to the coexistence of traditional infrastructure and services and the new platforms that have so far mostly disrupted them.[32] What kind of equilibrium should one seek between taxi fleets and Uber? How should self-driving cars support public transportation instead of competing with it? The importance of maps in the new platform economy is striking, in fact—think of their essential role in Uber's operations. The French political scientist Antoine Courmont has convincingly argued that the time is ripe for a "new deal" between established institutions in charge of traditional infrastructure, starting with municipal authorities, and platforms.[33] Digital urban maps will definitely appear in the practical aspects of such a deal.

The issues raised by big data—who owns it, who is allowed to use it and how—will also be inseparable from this deal. As we have seen, digital maps are a key mode of visualizing and otherwise using big data, which reinforces their political character. Again, complex questions of governance are at stake in their multiplication. Their production and use might need to be regulated at some point, despite their "consecration of the amateur" and the freedom that implies. To understand this, simply imagine how sensitive geolocated social and racial information could lead to the creation and diffusion of "hate maps," just as hate sites and posts have proliferated on social networks.

Important as they are, questions of urban governance like those we have evoked may not be as meaningful for the general public as issues of privacy and surveillance or the opposition between top-down and bottom-up models for the digital city to come. As we have seen, maps are inseparable from the detailed tracking of physical and electronic motions and circulations. Geolocation, the basis for this detailed tracking, gives insights into our lives that we may not wish to be available: by accessing the data related to the

31 For a classic example of how infrastructure can be political, see Langdon Winner, "Do Artifacts Have Politics?," *Daedalus* 109, no. 1 (1980): 121–136. For a more recent take, see, e.g., Lisa Björkman, *Pipe Politics, Contested Waters: Embedded Infrastructures of Millennial Mumbai* (Durham, NC: Duke University Press, 2015).

32 Nick Srnicek, *Platform Capitalism* (Cambridge: Polity Press, 2017).

33 See, e.g., Antoine Courmont, "Plateforme, big data et recomposition du gouvernement urbain," *Revue française de sociologie* 59, no. 3, (October 2018): 423–49. https://doi.org/10.3917/rfs.593.0423.

trips I make, a stranger might infer, for instance, which doctor I see and draw conclusions about my health. Of course, most of the data produced by individuals are anonymized. But the risk of a substantial privacy breach always looms in the background. Even when created with the best intentions, maps are inseparable from what the American social psychologist Shoshana Zuboff has described as "surveillance capitalism."[34] Indeed, this drawback is generally counterbalanced by the benefits produced by extensive digital mapping, but vigilance—and fundamentally political vigilance—is required.

The opposition between top-down and bottom-up models for the city is equally political. Not a single day goes by without op-eds and news articles supporting democracy and participation against the technocratic leanings of the various powers that be within the spread of digital systems and tools. Top-down versus bottom-up: this tension has been present for a very long time in cartography. On the one hand, maps have generally been produced by institutions, in a decidedly top-down manner: until recently, only administrations and large corporations could handle the various tasks required to make a reliable map. On the other hand, maps have often been used in ways that escape the control of authorities. Even if a government endorsed a map, the latter could be used to literally find ways to subvert the former's policies—all the more so if the map revealed its makers' agenda, thus enabling their opponents to counter it more easily. Indeed, maps are never neutral, especially in the urban field: they always bear the mark of underlying intentions. In other words, maps are both instruments of established power and means of empowerment and emancipation.[35]

A similar dichotomy is at work in contemporary digital mapping. However, similar does not mean identical. On-screen maps may be far more interactive than traditional ones, but their malleability is often more restricted than those of traditional cartographic documents, on which one could scribble and draw at will. Uber does not give you much leeway in the use of its maps. At the same time, the existence of the dashboard, logbook, and digital commons genres indicates that nothing is written in stone. As an ever-expanding field offering multiple possibilities, digital urban mapping may be mobilized in strikingly different ways: to track as well as to roam freely, to control but also to empower. Are these possibilities mutually exclusive? The fundamental question of the digital city to come may have to do, again, with the way it combines top-down policies, such as those concerning the management of large urban infrastructure, with bottom-up collaborative and emancipatory perspectives. The politics of the city will depend to a large extent on the ways that maps are mobilized to steer, guide, and at the same time empower residents.

Last but certainly not least, maps constitute an essential component of both what can be seen and what can be understood of the vast amounts of data that surround us and determine who can see and understand those vast amounts. Again, maps are among the privileged ways of visualizing and communicating information to large audiences. Without them, many datasets would not make sense to nonspecialists. Already, the world in which we live tends to reveal many of its features only to those who can understand the coding of information, leaving those who can't in a state

34 Shoshana Zuboff, *The Age of Surveillance Capitalism: The Fight for a Human Future at the New Frontier of Power* (New York: PublicAffairs, 2018).

35 Daniel Buisseret, ed., *Envisioning the City: Six Studies in Urban Cartography* (Chicago: Chicago University Press, 1998).

of relative blindness. Contemporary conspiracies thrive on the feeling that essential information remains hidden from the eyes of the public. Maps are one of the few efficient antidotes to this pressing contagion, provided of course that their making—how the data are collected, aggregated, and spatialized—is explained to their users. Indeed, one of the ambitions of this atlas is precisely to share with its readers, through detailed discussion of the SCL's cartographic production, how urban visualizations are obtained.

The ability to see is very unequally distributed. Class, culture, and social and professional status exert profound influence on what people can actually perceive and pay attention to. In a penetrating book, the French philosopher Jacques Rancière introduced the notion of "aesthetic regimes" to better approach what he has termed "the distribution of the sensible"—namely, how and to whom objects, people, and information are made visible in a given society.[36] Never before has the distribution of the sensible proved so crucial as in our information-driven society, in which perceiving, being aware, and knowing have become absolutely essential. Politics envisaged as the various power relations that structure society depends to a large extent on such a distribution. In the digital era, urban maps have become a favored expression of the prevailing "aesthetic regime" that conditions this distribution. As such, they are eminently political. One of our deepest wishes is that they will ultimately contribute to a more evenly spread capacity to see, reflect, and act accordingly.

Another way to put it, this time referring to the seminal work of Henri Lefebvre, is that his famous "right to the city"—the possibility offered to every inhabitant of the city to participate fully in its life and the debates and decisions that shape its future—now depends on the ability to see what is out there and what is going on, very often by using maps.[37] Indeed, how can one be a complete city dweller today without having access to information and being able to interact with others? As we have seen, digital maps help shape social interaction—thus, they condition a new right to see. From the right to the city to the right to see, digital maps are inseparable from this important shift in our understanding of contemporary urban democracy. They should remind us that beyond technology, the future of the city remains first and foremost a political question.

36 Jacques Rancière, *The Politics of Aesthetics: The Distribution of the Sensible*, ed. and trans. Gabriel Rockhill (London: Continuum, 2004).

37 See Łukasz Stanek, *Henri Lefebvre on Space: Architecture, Urban Research, and the Production of Theory* (Minneapolis: University of Minnesota Press, 2011).

Selected Bilbliography

In the following chapters you will see twenty-four maps created by the SCL, organized around four themes and explained in brief captions. Big data made these maps possible—and with them, new insights into the emerging space of city science. For those who might be interested in the more analytical aspects of the Lab's work, the selected publications below—each of which corresponds to a few of the maps in this atlas and is freely accessible on the SCL website—are an excellent place to begin. A picture may be worth a thousand words, but we still hope that you will pursue further reading.

Calabrese, Francesco, Giusy Di Lorenzo, Liang Liu, and Carlo Ratti. "Estimating Origin-Destination Flows Using Mobile Phone Location Data." *IEEE Pervasive Computing* 10, no. 4 (April 2011): 36–44.

Dong, Lei, Carlo Ratti, and Siqi Zheng. "Predicting Neighborhoods' Socioeconomic Attributes Using Restaurant Data." *Proceedings of the National Academy of Sciences* 116, no. 31 (July 2019): 15447–15452.

Girardin, Fabien, Francesco Calabrese, Filippo Dal Fiore, Carlo Ratti, and Josep Blat. "Digital Footprinting: Uncovering Tourists with User-Generated Content." *IEEE Pervasive Computing* 7, no. 4 (October–December 2008): 36–43.

Li, Xiaojiang, and Carlo Ratti. "Mapping the Spatial Distribution of Shade Provision of Street Trees in Boston Using Google Street View Panoramas." *Urban Forestry and Urban Greening* 31 (April 2018): 109–119.

Nyhan, Marguerite, Sebastian Grauwin, Rex Britter, Bruce Misstear, Aonghus McNabola, Francine Laden, Steven R. H. Barrett, and Carlo Ratti. "'Exposure Track'—The Impact of Mobile-Device-Based Mobility Patterns on Quantifying Population Exposure to Air Pollution." *Environmental Science and Technology* 50, no. 17 (August 2016): 9671–9681.

O'Keeffe, Kevin P., Amin Anjomshoaa, Steven H. Strogatz, Paolo Santi, and Carlo Ratti. "Quantifying the Sensing Power of Vehicle Fleets." *Proceedings of the National Academy of Sciences* 116, no. 26 (June 2019): 12752–12757.

Picon, Antoine. *Smart Cities: A Spatialised Intelligence.* New York: John Wiley and Sons, 2015.

Ratti, Carlo, Dennis Frenchman, Riccardo Maria Pulselli, and Sarah Williams. "Mobile Landscapes: Using Location Data from Cell Phones for Urban Analysis." *Environment and Planning B: Planning and Design* 33, no. 5 (October 2006): 727–748.

Ratti, Carlo, Stanislav Sobolevsky, Francesco Calabrese, Clio Andris, Jonathan Reades, Mauro Martino, Rob Claxton, and Steven H. Strogatz. "Redrawing the Map of Great Britain from a Network of Human Interactions." *PLoS ONE* 5, no. 12 (December 2010): e14248.

Reades, Jon, Francesco Calabrese, Andres Sevtsuk, and Carlo Ratti. "Cellular Census: Explorations in Urban Data Collection." *IEEE Pervasive Computing* 6, no. 3 (July–September 2007): 30–38.

Santi, Paolo, Giovanni Resta, Michael Szell, Stanislav Sobolevsky, Steven H. Strogatz, and Carlo Ratti. "Vehicle Pooling with Shareability Networks." *Proceedings of the National Academy of Sciences* 111, no. 37 (September 2014): 13290–13294.

Szell, Michael, Sebastian Grauwin, and Carlo Ratti. "Contraction of Online Response to Major Events." PLoS ONE 9, no. 2 (February 2014): e89052.

Tachet, Remi, Paolo Santi, Stanislav Sobolevsky, Luis Ignacio Reyes-Castro, Emilio Frazzoli, Dirk Helbing, and Carlo Ratti. "Revisiting Street Intersections Using Slot-Based Systems." *PLoS ONE* 11, no. 3 (March 2016): e0149607.

Vazifeh, Mohammad M., Paolo Santi, Giovanni Resta, Steven H. Strogatz, and Carlo Ratti. "Addressing the Minimum Fleet Problem in On-Demand Urban Mobility." *Nature* 557 (May 2018): 534–538.

Yoshimura, Yuji, Stanislav Sobolevsky, Carlo Ratti, Fabien Girardin, Juan Pablo Carrascal, Josep Blat, and Roberta Sinatra. "An Analysis of Visitors' Behavior in the Louvre Museum: A Study Using Bluetooth Data." *Environment and Planning B: Planning and Design* 41, no. 6 (December 2014): 1113–1131.

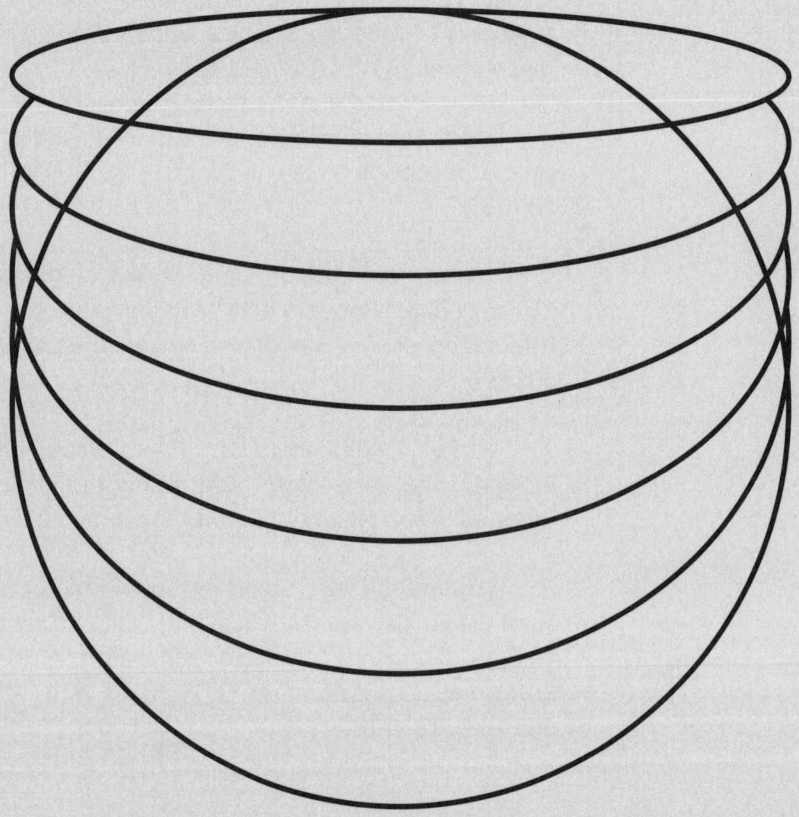

MOTION

CHAPTER — 1

Motion

"Un bon croquis vaut mieux qu'un long discours" (a good sketch is worth more than a long speech): so Napoleon Bonaparte, one of history's greatest military strategists, is reported to have said.[1] In an ironic twist of fate, a very good sketch indeed captured his great undoing: the French civil engineer Charles Joseph Minard's map of Napoleon's fatal march to Moscow and back, drawn in 1869.[2] The document shows not only geographical space but six "data dimensions": the number of troops, the distance they traveled, the temperatures they faced, their latitude and longitude, their direction of travel, and key dates. With this project, Minard pioneered a new field of concise data visualization: the modern information graphic, or "infographic." Minard's work continued with his near-contemporary Jacques Bertillon, who refined the infographic genre with a host of innovative subjects and methods.

Minard had found a way to represent large-scale flows, but it was not until the twentieth century that the resolution increased from the aggregate to the individual, allowing the map to become a document of personal movement. In 1957, Paul-Henry Chombart de Lauwe approached cartography from the perspective of a sociologist with such studies as *Trajets pendant un an d'une jeune fille du XVIe arrondissement*, which maps a year of movement within Paris by a young woman living in the city's 16th arrondissement.[3]

Later, with the introduction of the Internet, the miniaturization of computing, and the ubiquity of telecommunication networks, a new dimension in individual cartography emerged. What Chombart de Lauwe spent a year painstakingly recording with analog tools can now be immediately generated, and on a more massive scale. Starting in the 1990s, the deployment of GPS-enabled devices made early experiments possible—such as Laura Kurgan's installation *You Are Here: Information Drift* or the WAAG's bicycle mapping in Amsterdam.[4] These studies were limited by the necessity of deploying unwieldy devices, but beginning in the early 2000s, the diffusion of smartphones placed a high-resolution sensor in virtually every pocket. With that decisive turn, millions of people could be tracked simultaneously, revealing the natural behavior of new "urban cyborgs" — humans equipped with phones that improved or replaced biological communication, memory, and sense of direction.

To explore human movement in urban landscapes, the SCL has taken advantage of cell phones, a growing network of mobile sensors with an unprecedented ability to map the contours of human life. In Graz, Austria, real-time cell phone datasets helped us understand the dynamics of cell phone activity.[5] A later project, run in Rome, used cell network activity to reveal where people moved and how they communicated across the Italian capital during the final match of the 2006 World Cup. Measurable data captured the collective euphoria at Italy's victory.[6] Since then, studies have matured, encompassing

1 Napoleon Bonaparte, quoted in Claudi Alsina and Roger B. Nelsen, *Icons of Mathematics: An Exploration of Twenty Key Images* (Washington, DC: American Mathematical Society, 2011), 91.

2 Charles Joseph Minard, *Carte figurative des pertes successives en hommes de l'armée française dans la campagne de Russie 1812–1813*, in *Tableaux graphiques et cartes figuratives de Mr Minard* (Paris: École Nationale des Ponts et Chaussées, 1869), fol. 10975, tabl. 28.

3 Paul-Henry Chombart de Lauwe, *Trajets pendant un an d'une jeune fille du XVIe arrondissement*, in *Paris et l'agglomération parisienne* (Paris: Presses universitaires de France, 1952), vol. 1, 106.

4 Laura Kergan, "You Are Here: Information Drift," Assemblage 25 (1994): 15–43; Aske Hopman, "Amsterdam Realtime," in *Art & D: Research and Development in Art* (Rotterdam: V2_NAi, 2005), 52.

5 Carlo Ratti, Andres Sevtsuk, Sonya Huang, and Rudolf Palier, "Mobile Landscapes: Graz in Real Time," in *Location-Based Services and TeleCartography* (Berlin: Springer, 2007), 433–444.

6 Francesco Calabrese, Massimo Colonna, Piero Lovisolo, Dario Parata, and Carlo Ratti, "Real-Time Urban Monitoring Using Cell Phones: A Case Study in Rome," *IEEE Transactions on Intelligent Transportation Systems* 12, no. 1 (2011): 141–151.

larger and more varied datasets. The maps in the SCL's LIVE Singapore! project, for example, combine information from diverse fields, ranging from the nation's transportation system and weather patterns to cell phone activity, taxi routes, energy consumption, container ship schedules, and aircraft flight paths.[7]

Today, as computation becomes ubiquitous and digital tags suffuse the environment, more and more geospatial data points flicker and fly across the planet. Nearly every material movement—whether of people, vehicles, or goods—can be tracked and tagged in real time, creating, in the aggregate, an unprecedented amount of "urban big data." An emerging paradigm of high-resolution, mobile "computers" calls for a new cartography regime—one that dynamically plays out in the temporal dimension—to show how our society and its artifacts move through digital and physical spaces. There is a broad spectrum of possible applications, spanning from real-time corporate logistics management to making friends in a new neighborhood. In the pages that follow, data reveal the motions that animate a city. They imagine how a suite of new tools—ride- and vehicle-sharing apps, predictive algorithms, and autonomous vehicles—could revolutionize New York City traffic. We also consider public transportation—buses and trains remain more efficient and sustainable than anything else people have dreamed up. The routes in a morphological map of France's rail system stretch and shrink based on travel time, revealing how the modern meaning of distance cannot be captured in meters (or miles) alone. Finally, one of the SCL's most recent projects on motion shows that human mobility around the world—whether on foot or in a vehicle, in Boston or Dakar—follows similar, near-universal rules, forming patterns that help us understand the nature of urbanity itself.

7 Kristian Kloeckl, Senn Kristian, and Carlo Ratti, "Enabling the Real-Time City: LIVE Singapore," *Journal of Urban Technology: Street Computing* 19, no. 2 (2012): 89–112.

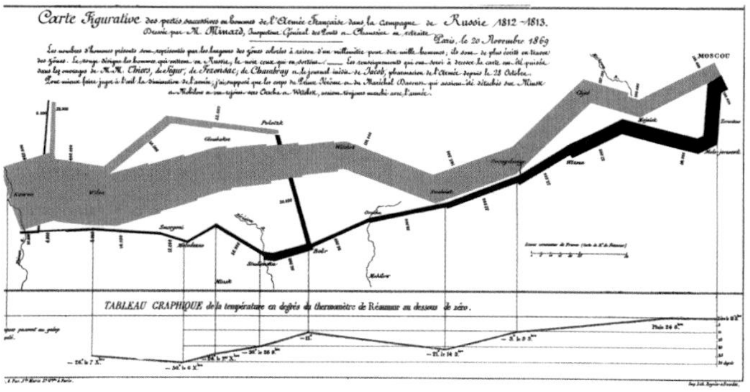

01

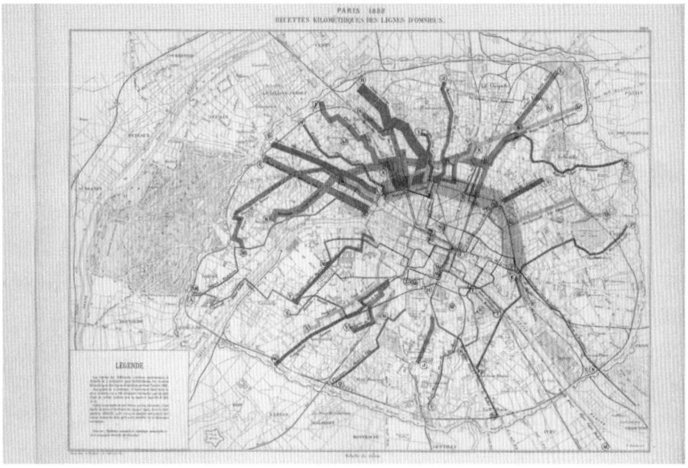

02

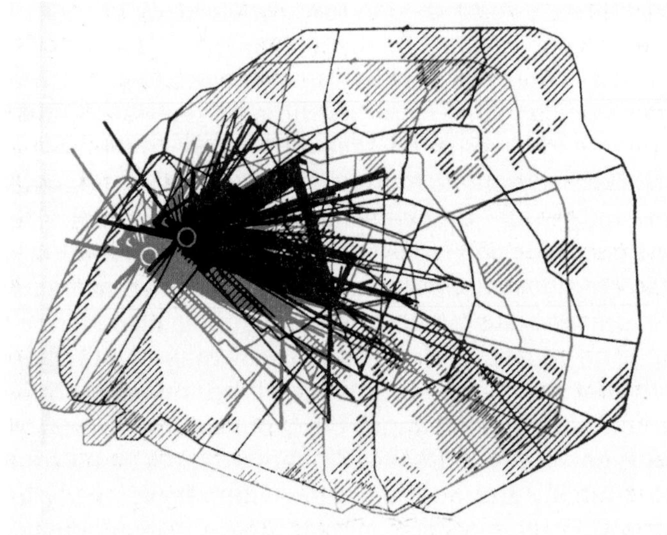

03

01. CHARLES MINARD, FIGURATIVE MAP OF THE SUCCESSIVE LOSSES IN MEN OF THE FRENCH ARMY IN THE RUSSIAN CAMPAIGN, 1812-1813, 1869.

This map, realized by Charles Joseph Minard, gives an immediate sense of Napoleon's ill-fated Russian campaign of 1812–1813, tracing the French Army's advance into and retreat from the Russian Empire. It combines various data dimensions, pioneering what would later become the field of data visualization. In fact, Minard unites six datasets: the number of troops, their location on certain dates, the army's direction of travel, the distance traveled, the army's latitude and longitude, and the temperature. Condensing all of this into a single two-dimensional image, Minard illustrates the army's overwhelming human losses—without ever mentioning Napoleon. On entering Russia, the army had 422,000 men; they were only 100,000 on reaching Moscow and a meager 10,000 by the time they crossed back over the border. The thickness of the band visualizes the number of troops, with a ratio of one millimeter to 10,000 men. In the unprecedented enormity of Napoleon's Russian campaign, the emperor's supposed adage about the value of a good sketch is extraordinarily clear. Leo Tolstoy committed nearly 600,000 words to depicting this period in *War and Peace*, yet Minard tells the story in a single picture.

02. ACQUES BERTILLON, KILOMETRIC REVENUES OF BUS LINES, 1888.

Jacques Bertillon, who succeeded his father, Louis-Adolphe Bertillon, as the head of Paris's Municipal Statistics Department in 1883, was a key player in the development of infographics, following in the footsteps of Émile Cheysson, an engineer fifteen years his senior who had published an authoritative *Album de statistique graphique*. Bertillon employed his training as a physician to generate epidemiological infographics about the city of Paris. In 1888 and 1891, he expanded his repertoire by publishing a two-volume *Atlas of Graphical Statistics of the City of Paris*, whose contents far outstrip his initial interest in medicine. In this map of the revenues of Paris's bus routes in 1889, the thickness of the lines shows how much money per kilometer each earned. Bertillon's work was the culmination of his predecessors', refining Minard's technique of representing flows in maps and guiding the work of subsequent centuries. This bus map is a clear prequel to the data-driven methods that public transit services now use to optimize cost efficiency and public benefit when allocating resources.

03. PAUL-HENRY CHOMBART DE LAUWE, MAP OF A YOUNG WOMAN'S MOVEMENTS IN PARIS, 1957.

In the early 1950s, the French sociologist Paul-Henry Chombart de Lauwe made this map of the movements within Paris of a young woman who was studying political science there. Her repeated journeys describe a triangle with vertices at her residence, her university, and the home of her piano teacher. Chombart de Lauwe's map has fewer data dimensions than Minard's, but it still reveals how patterns emerge from data. It also prioritizes personal, individual movement, one of the first maps to do so. Chombart de Lauwe was an advocate of participatory planning and the involvement of city dwellers in the creation of urban space. His map stirred up the French theorist Guy Debord, who claimed that everyone should feel "outrage at the fact that anyone's life can be so pathetically limited."[8] Chombart de Lauwe's data inspired Debord and the Situationist International, an antiauthoritarian intellectual and artistic movement that Debord cofounded and led, to research psychogeography, an exploration of urban environments based on the emotions and behaviors, both conscious and unconscious, of individuals. The Situationists' then-radical theories helped lay the groundwork for an idea that has since become mainstream, albeit from a more utilitarian perspective, in urban studies: personal movement can provide great insight into how people use their city, and therefore on how it can be planned.

8 Guy Debord, "Theory of the Dérive," *in Situationist International Anthology*, ed. and trans. Ken Knabb (Berkeley, CA: Bureau of Public Secrets, 1981), 50.

04

04. WAAG, ESTHER POLAK, AND JEROEN KEE, AMSTERDAM REALTIME, 2002.

The possibilities that GPS offers for large-scale mapping were explored in the early 2000s by Waag, an Amsterdam-based creative research institute that investigates technology and society. Members developed a project to represent the individual movements of people in the city by equipping volunteers with portable GPS units. For two months, these units collected data on the volunteers' geographic positions, which the researchers aggregated to create a map of Amsterdam that emerged in real time. The data, plotted against a black background, formed a network of lines and patterns that corresponded to the city's layout without the researchers ever having to explicitly define streets or housing blocks. Waag's map was among the first experiments in using GPS to visualize a city solely by means of people's movements. It was presented at the exhibition *Maps of Amsterdam, 1866–2000*, revealing its role as a new step in cartography. When the *Amsterdam RealTime* map was created in 2002, the iPhone was still five years away and Nokia was one of the most popular phone brands. Today, with the ubiquity of smartphones, maps like this can be drawn with the GPS devices that we all carry in our pockets.

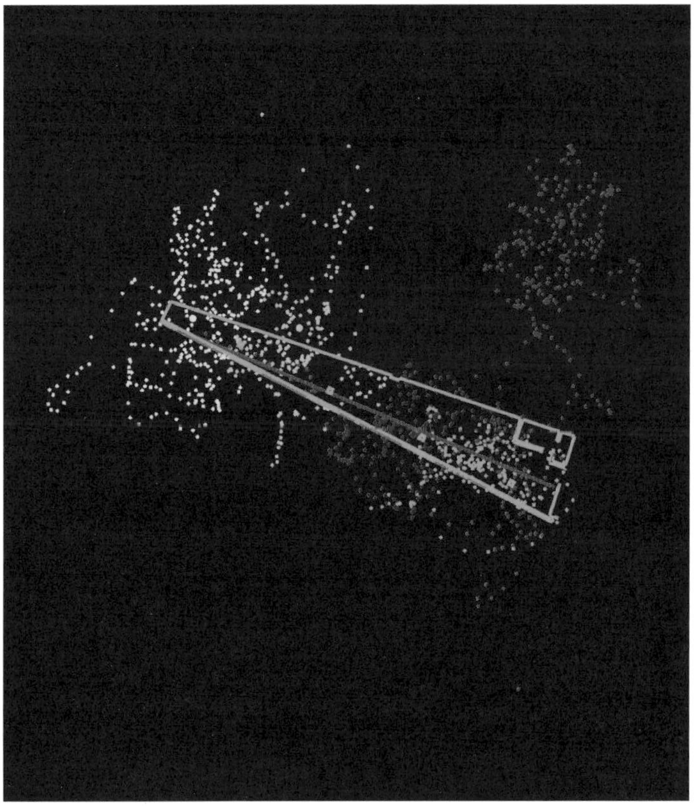

05

05.LAURA KURGAN, 50 MINUTES, 5 POINTS (STOREFRONT), FROM YOU ARE HERE: INFORMATION DRIFT, 1994.

Laura Kurgan was among the first cartographers to experiment with GPS and to take the visualization of movement from the static to the dynamic. In the 1990s, she explored new technologies that had been developed primarily for the military, such as satellite-based real-time mapping and early versions of GPS and head-up display (HUD) programs. After fixing a position sensor on the roof of the Storefront for Art and Architecture in New York City, she showed the (accidental) unceasing drifting of the GPS signal—as if the gallery were moving around. The GPS receiver never, in fact, mapped the building's position with unwavering precision, instead creating a phantom geography of locations that did not correspond to the gallery's actual site. The resulting map, part of the ironically titled *You Are Here* installation, hints at a new cartographic paradox ushered in by digital technologies: a layout created not by objects in physical space but by the presence of imprecise sensors in a kind of virtual space. Today, the maps we use most frequently—those in Google Maps—are based on signals from the kinds of digital devices that Kurgan used, even if they have achieved a higher precision. Such maps allow us to move through urban environments by showing us not the static city but a shifting, imperfect estimation of where we are.

CHAPTER • 1

Motion ↓
MIT Senseable City Lab Projects

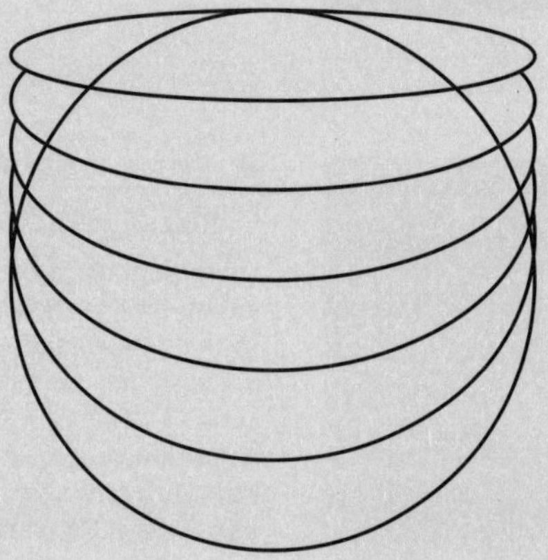

01.
Real Time Graz and Real Time Rome — 2006

02.
LIVE Singapore! — 2010

03.
Touching Bus Rides — 2012

04.
SNCF Trains of Data — 2011

05.
HubCab — 2014

06.
Minimum Fleet — 2018

07.
Light Traffic — 2014

08.
Wanderlust — 2021

01.
Real Time Graz and Real Time Rome — 2006

Real Time Graz and Real Time Rome were two of the SCL's first investigations into how large-scale datasets from mobile phones can be aggregated to better understand the movement of people in urban space. Previous experiments in visualizing cities based on such movements, like Waag's *Amsterdam RealTime*, used GPS units. In the SCL's projects, however, for the first time, data were collected through the cell phones that people were already carrying.

In today's world, wireless mobile communication devices are creating new dimensions of interconnection among people, places, and urban infrastructure. Aggregate records collected from communication networks allow us to visualize the dynamics of these coalescing systems in the contemporary city: traces of information and communication networks, movement patterns of people and transportation systems, even the spatial and social usage of streets and neighborhoods. Observing the real-time city becomes a means of understanding the present and anticipating the future of urban environments.

The SCL's research in this area also aimed to show how technology can help individuals make more informed decisions about their environment, beginning with a small-scale experiment mapping cell phone activity in Graz, Austria (1A). It then expanded to Rome, where aggregated data from cell phones, buses, and taxis were plotted to better understand urban dynamics during a unique period of high activity: the day of Italy's victory in the final match of the 2006 World Cup. National triumph shook the city, creating a euphoria that could be measured in the activity patterns of mobile phone networks. In this project's maps (1B–1C), the researchers visualized mobile phone usage and synchronous flows of pedestrians, public transit, and other vehicular traffic. Overlaying this mobility information on Rome's geographic references unveils the relationships between fixed and fluid urban elements. These real-time maps help us understand how neighborhoods are used in the course of a day, how the distribution of buses and taxis correlates with densities of people, how goods and services are distributed, and how different social groups, such as tourists and residents, inhabit the city.

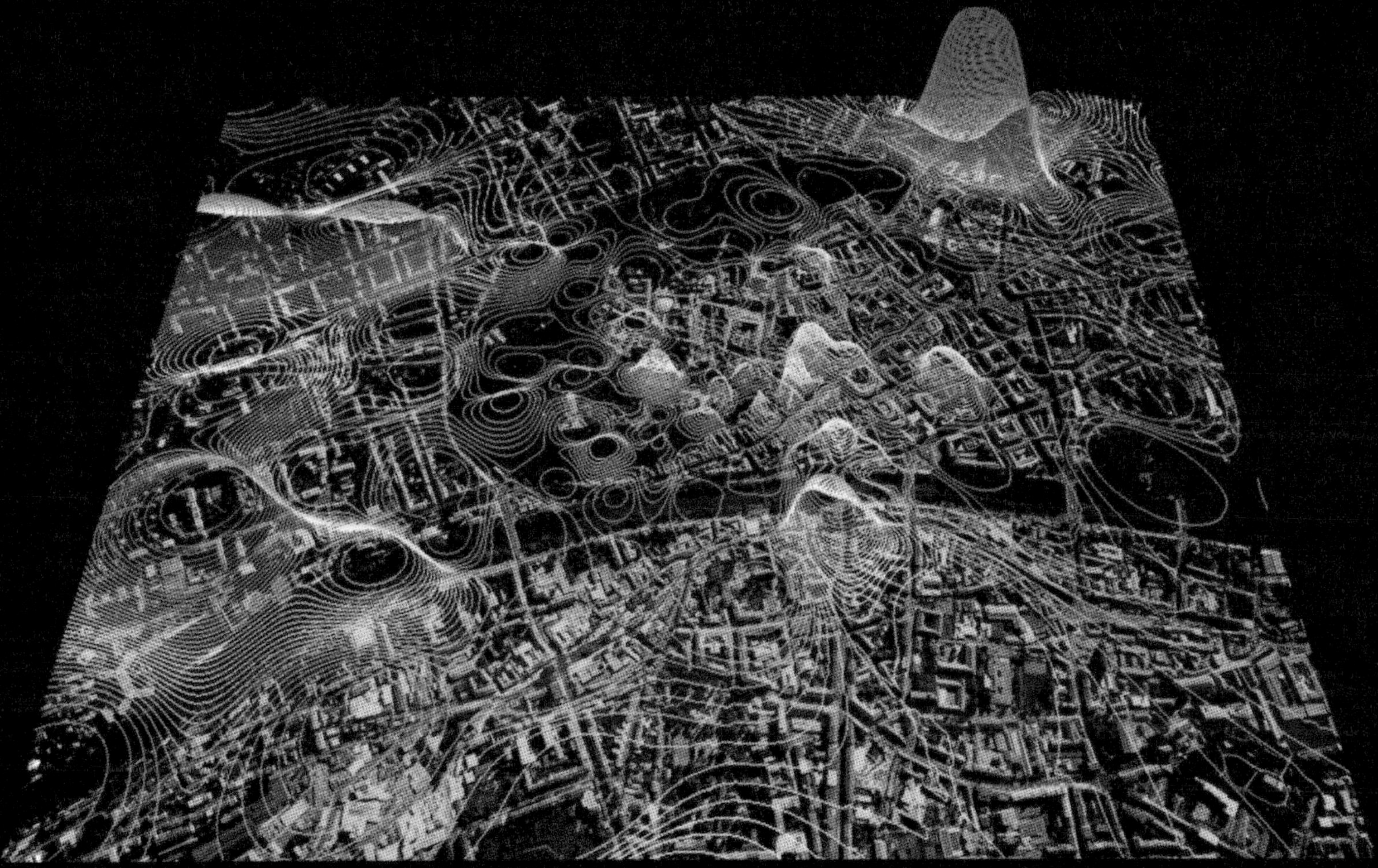

1A

1B
1B

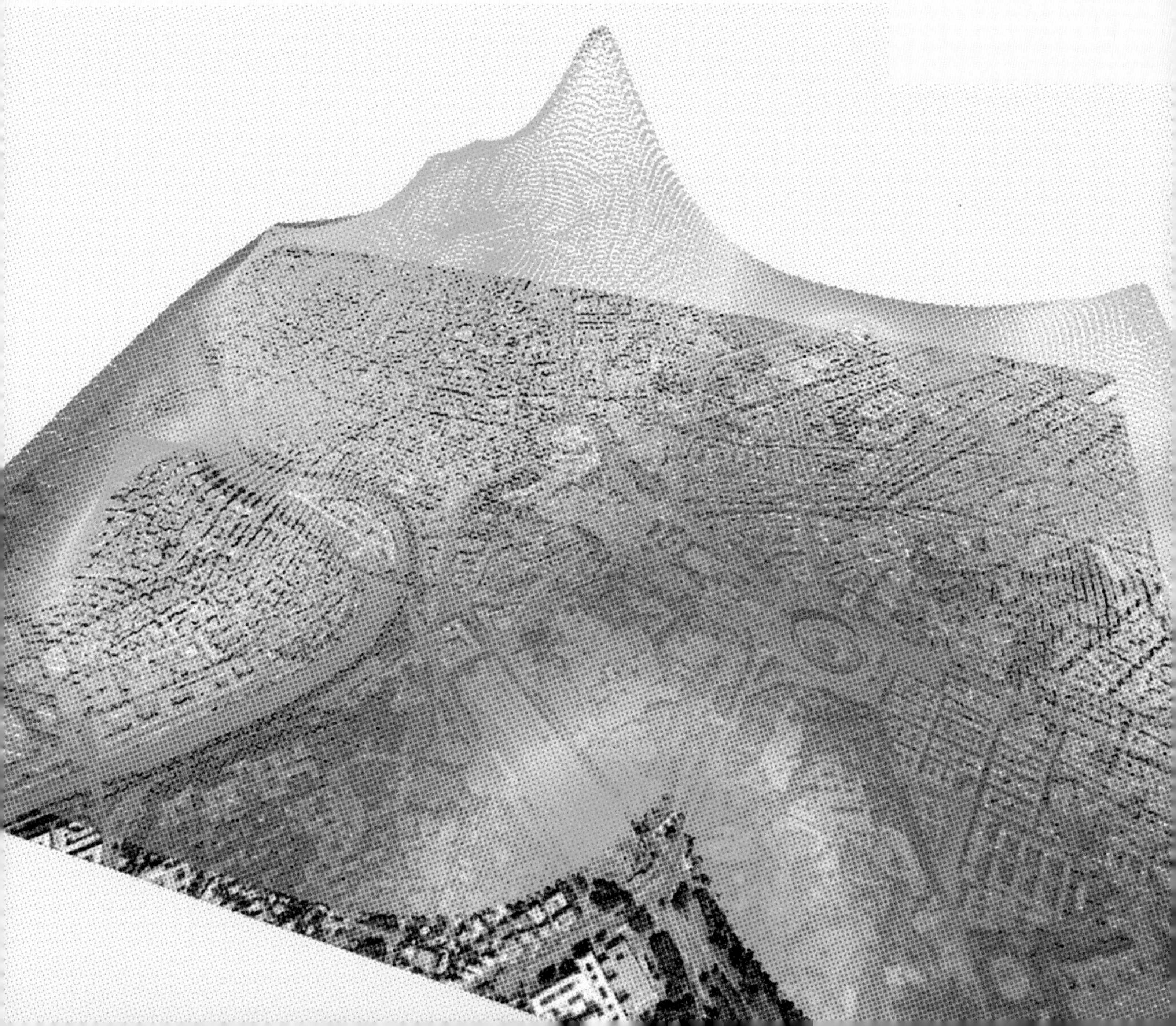

02.
LIVE Singapore! — 2010

LIVE Singapore! reveals the complexity that can be achieved when multiple kinds of datasets are combined. The project is an open platform for the collection, elaboration, and distribution of real-time data on various facets of urban activity in Singapore, which are provided to city dwellers in the form of large-scale visualizations.

Usually, people moving within a city base their decisions on static information that does not represent the space's current state—reading printed transportation timetables that do not reflect delays, for instance, or driving to a store only to find a product out of stock. Companies, local authorities, and individuals are increasingly managing their networks in real time—but the data each of them generates are not always shared. LIVE Singapore! changes this dynamic by collecting and combining a variety of data—mobile phone usage, taxi requests, weather patterns, energy usage, and more—closing the feedback loop between real-time data and those who generate them.

These combined datasets can generate many useful maps. *Isochronic Singapore* captures traffic density across the city in an isochronic map—which visualizes the estimated travel time, not the distance, between points—and reflects changing traffic patterns over the course of a day (2A). *Raining Taxis* explores how the use of taxis, a very popular form of transportation in Singapore, changes when rainfall throws supply and demand out of sync (2B). *Urban Heat Islands* pairs estimated temperature changes with data on energy consumption in different parts of Singapore to reveal the vicious cycle of urban air-conditioning: temperatures in cities are several degrees higher than in the surrounding countryside, leading to the use of more air-conditioning, which, in turn, causes temperatures to rise further. *Formula One City* is a map of Singapore during the Formula One Grand Prix (a parallel to Real Time Rome), in which the color and size of the glows vary depending on the amount of text messaging during the race (2C). *Real-Time Talk* uses height and color intensity to map the level of mobile phone penetration across Singapore. Last but not least, *Hub of the World* shows the global reach of Singapore's busy airport and bustling seaport, the largest trans-shipment container port on Earth (2D).

2A

20 min
10 min
5 min
5 min
10 min
20 min
chronic
parts of
ore can be reached in the
hortest time, using road transporation? employing
axi travel time data between different locations, the
ity distorts to reflect this perspective of temporal
roximity of the continuously changing condition of
rban mobility
lick on the map to choose the trip origin
ata source ComfortDelGro
reset map
01 August 2010 | 10:00
senseable city lab

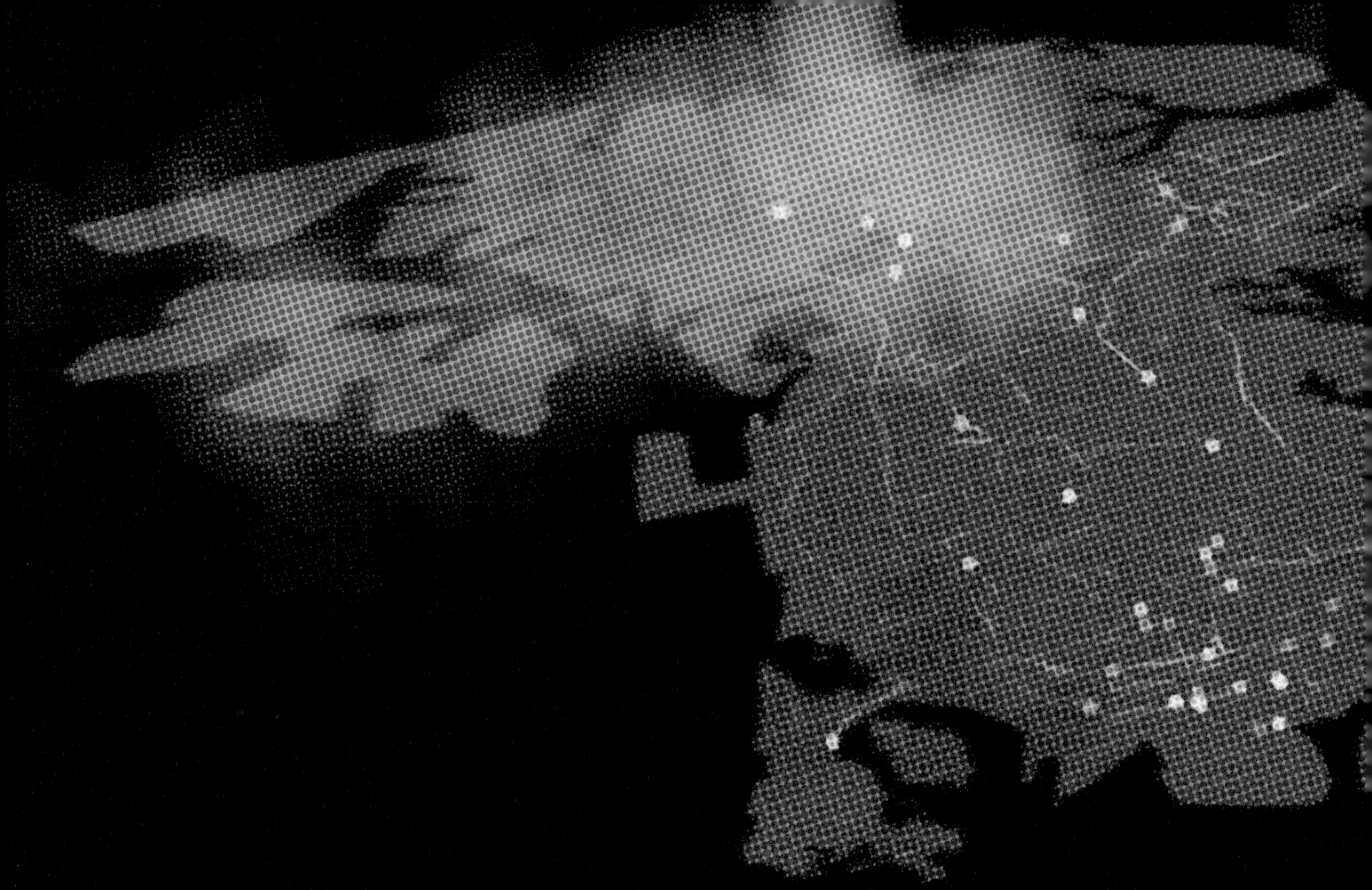

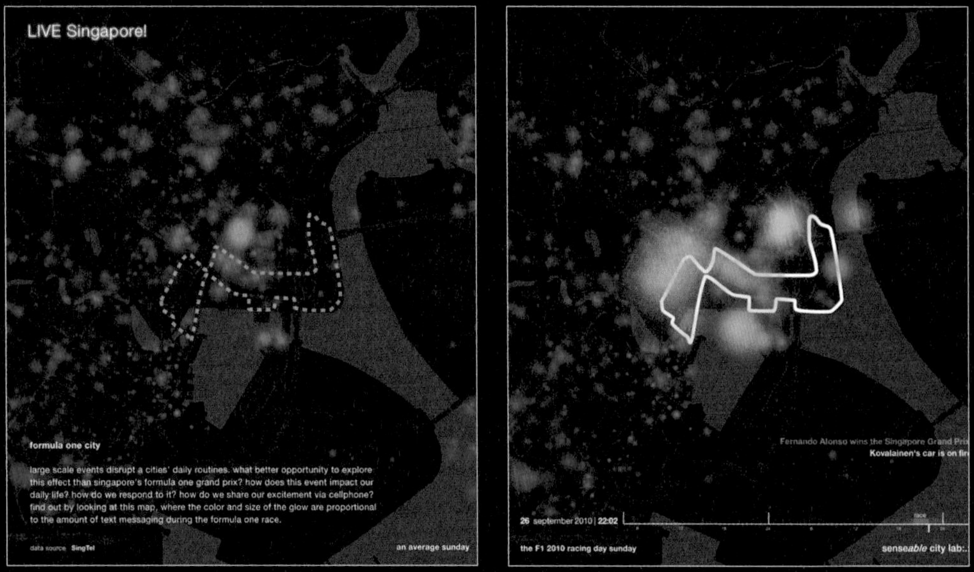
LIVE Singapore!
formula one city
large scale events disrupt a cities' daily routines. what better opportunity to explore this effect than singapore's formula one grand prix? how does this event impact our daily life? how do we respond to it? how do we share our excitement via cellphone? find out by looking at this map, where the color and size of the glow are proportional to the amount of text messaging during the formula one race.
data source SingTel
an average sunday
Fernando Alonso wins the Singapore Grand
Kovalainen's car is on
26 september 2010 | 22:02
the F1 2010 racing day sunday
senseable city lab

2C

2B

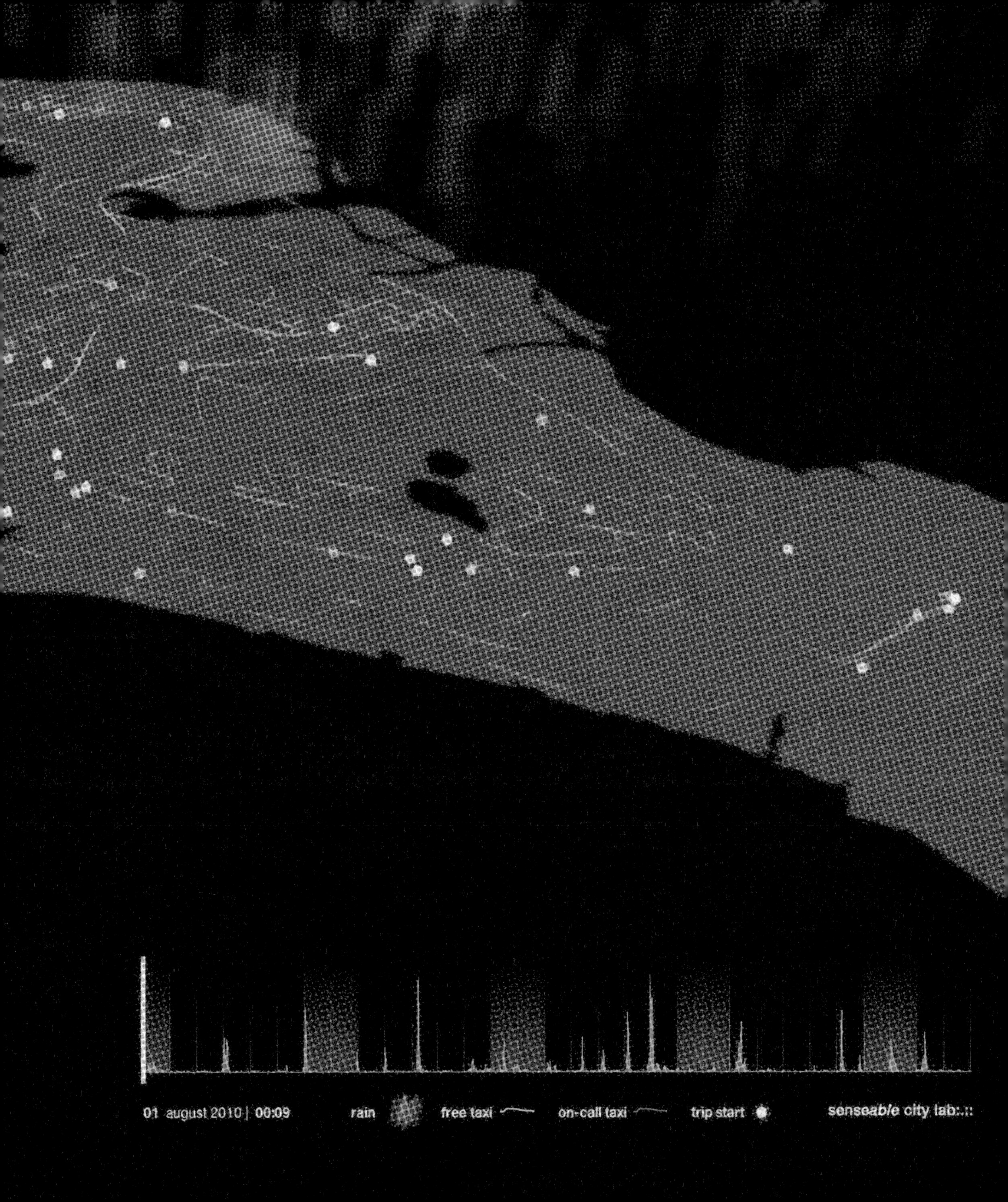
01 august 2010 | 00:09
rain
free taxi
on-call taxi
trip start
senseable city lab:.::

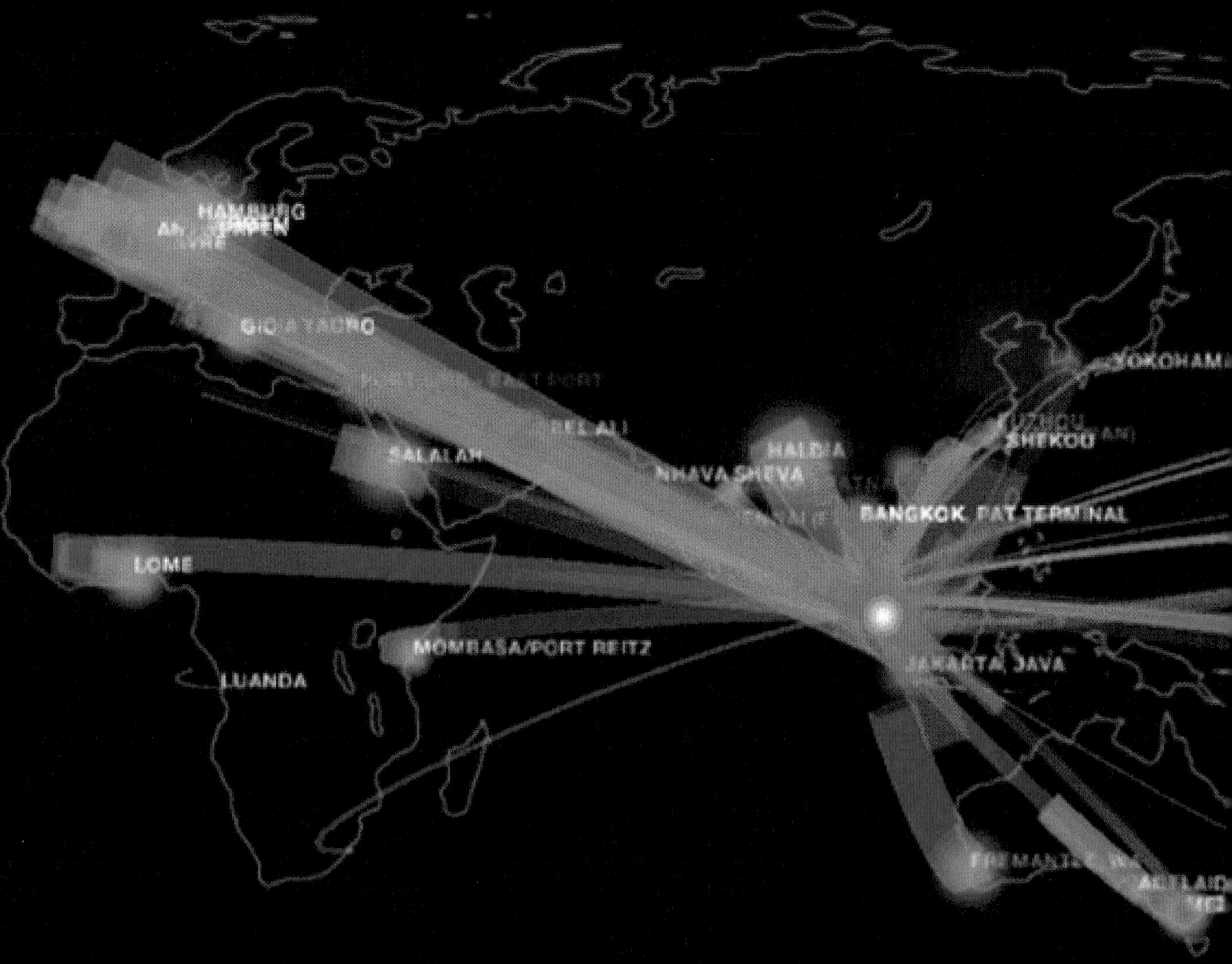
HAMBURG
SALALAH
NHAVA SHEVA
HALDIA
SHEKOU
BANGKOK
PAT TERMINAL
LOME
MOMBASA/PORT REITZ
LUANDA

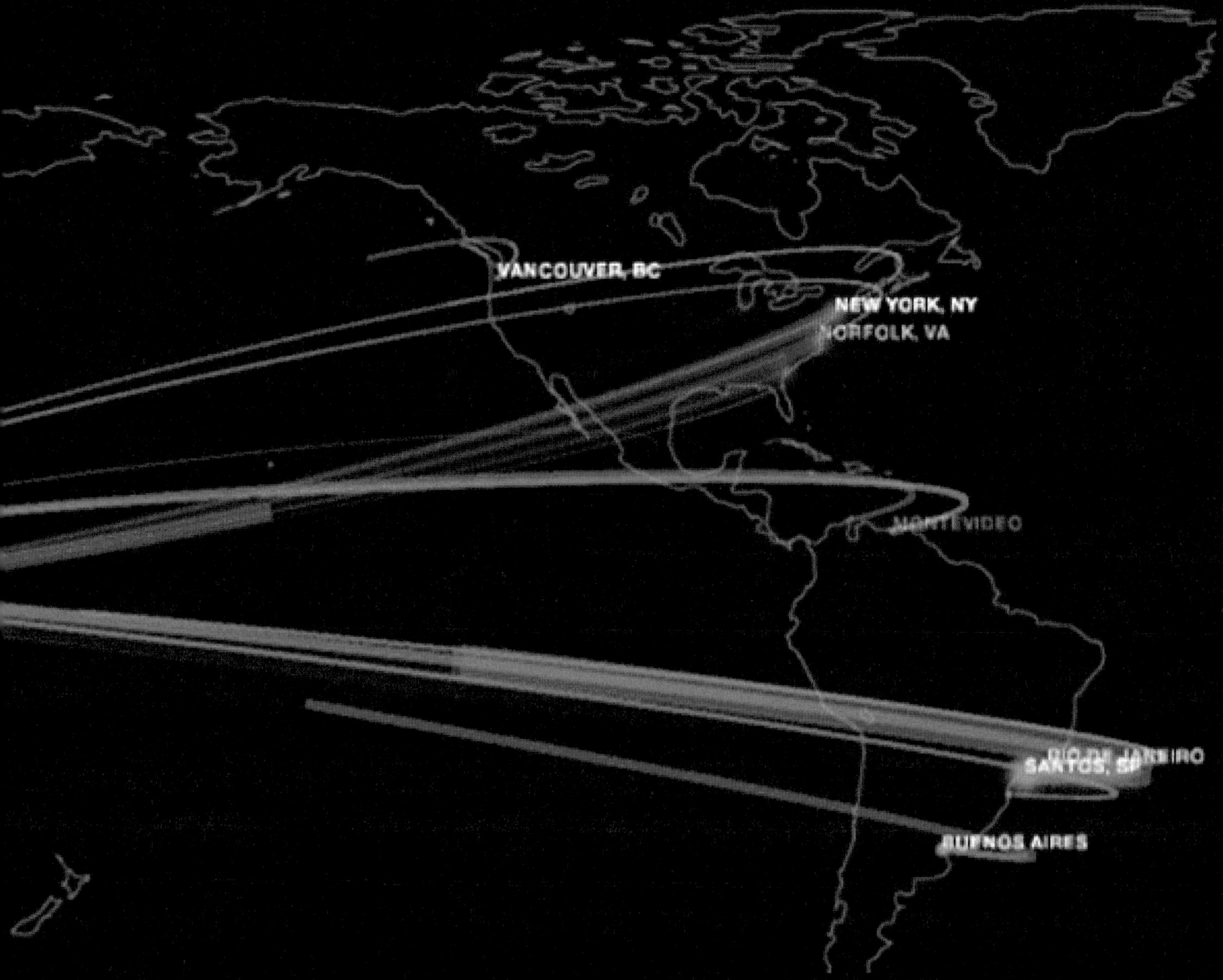
VANCOUVER, BC
NEW YORK, NY
NORFOLK, VA
MONTEVIDEO
SANTOS, SP
BUENOS AIRES

03.
Touching Bus Rides — 2012

Touching Bus Rides is a development of LIVE Singapore! that goes deeper into Singapore's public transport system. Because this system requires passengers to tap their smart-card passes when entering and exiting subways and buses, to generate distance-based prices, it also offers insights about who is using public transportation at any given time and what kinds of journeys they are undertaking. Using this data, the SCL created an interactive, multitouch interface that enables examination of Singapore's bus network—to see where most passengers get on and off, understand the routes people take between the island's stations, and track how these patterns change throughout the day.

Users can switch among various visualization modes for different perspectives on the same dataset, always with teal representing passengers boarding and orange representing passengers alighting. For instance, one visualization shows the number of people getting on and off a bus at different stops during a certain period, with arches connecting each passenger's entry and exit. A second map displays multiple bus service charts, with circles of different sizes representing the activity at different bus stations and stops over time. A third visualization focuses on single selected bus routes on the map of Singapore; people can explore the various routes and maps interactively (3A-3C).

All of these visualization modes include histograms representing passenger load on the buses at different times. This temporal dimension is critical for understanding a system that is always on the move: Singapore's public transportation is an entirely different animal from one hour to another. For instance, it was found that the morning peak of bus usage is short, while the evening peak is longer. This might be due to the wider time range in which people are active at night—whether to leave the office, run errands, or go out to dinner—before retiring for the day.

3A

Public transit ridership
05:30–06:30
legend
bus lines
line direction
information display
time
passengers
05:30 - 06:30
data source: LTA
SMART
SENSEable City Lab
Public transit ridership
18:00–19:30
VivoCity (14141)
legend
bus lines
line direction
information display
time
passengers
18:00 - 19:30

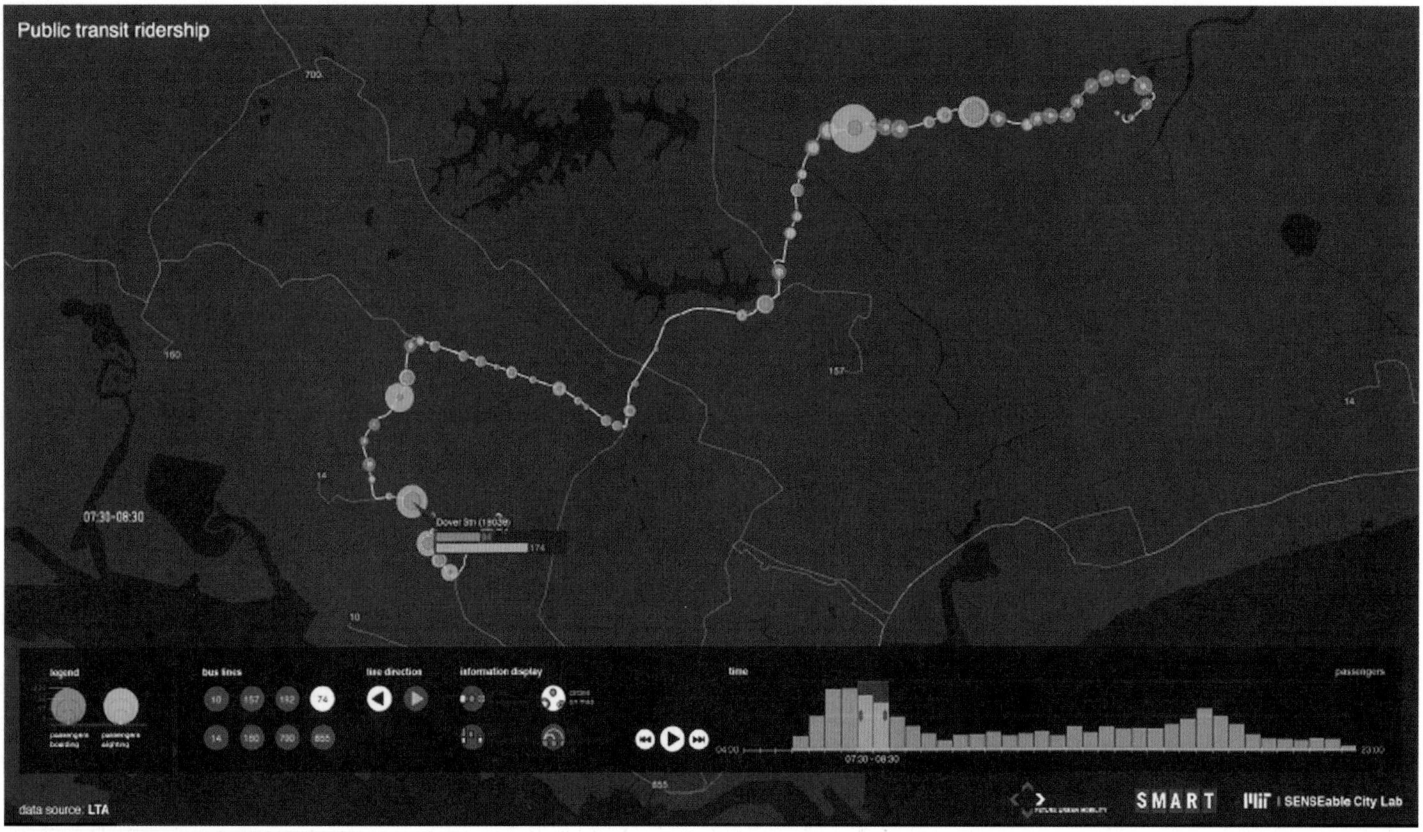
Public transit ridership
07:30–08:30
legend
bus lines
line direction
information display
time
passengers
10
157
74
14
04:00
07:30 - 08:30
23:00
data source: LTA
SMART
SENSEable City Lab

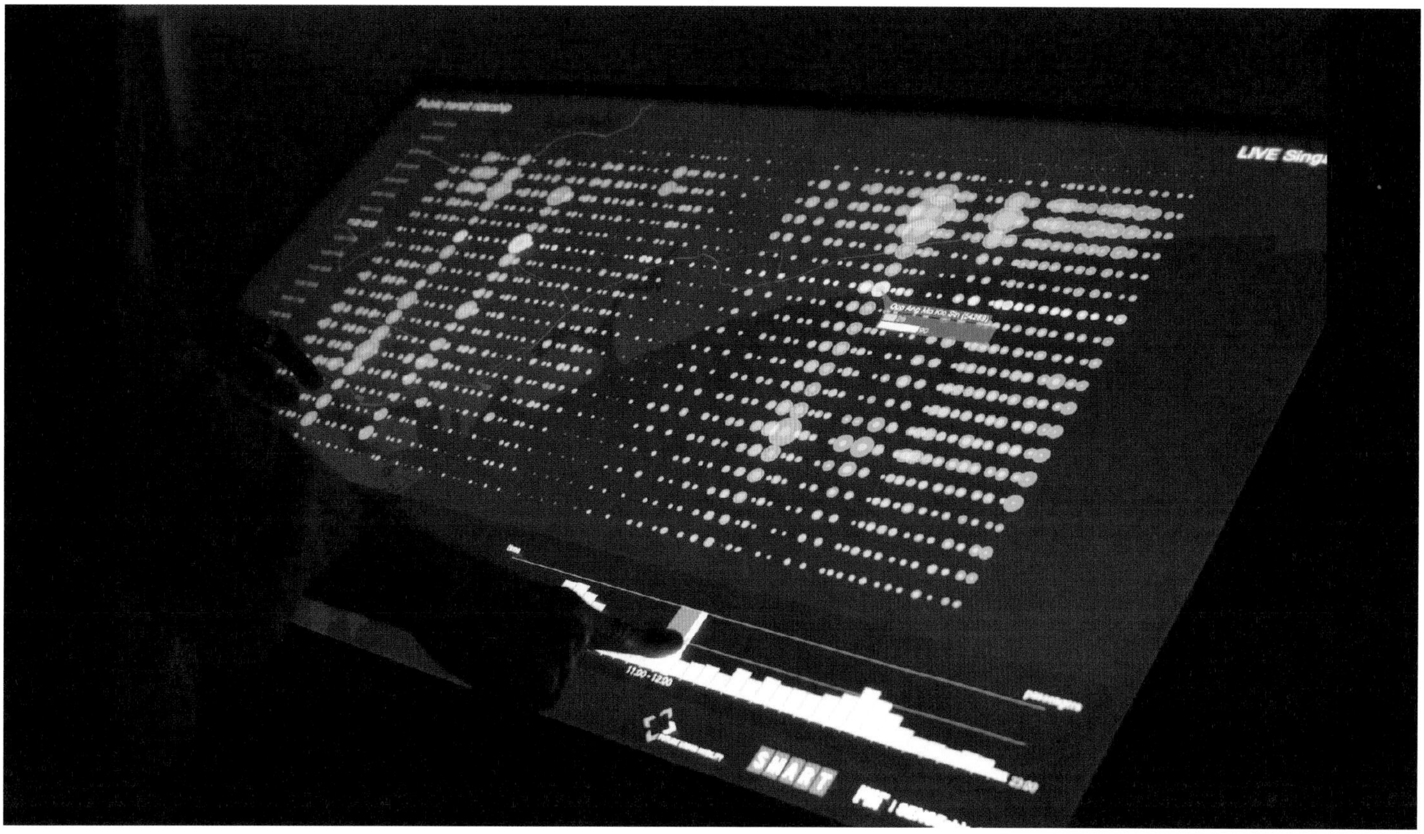
SMART

04.
SNCF Trains of Data — 2011

Developed in partnership with SNCF (Société nationale des chemins de fer français), France's national railway company, Trains of Data investigates new ways of analyzing how people move around France on the country's high-speed railway system. Its focus is on tracing large-scale flows.

The first visualization, *Isochronic France*, deforms the existing train network (4A) by making distances between stations proportional to the travel time from one to another, revealing how this changes—due to wait times and delays—over the course of a week (4B). The maps below use Paris as the center of the country, but on the platform users can select any location as the origin. From the perspective of Nice or Marseille, *Isochronic France* contorts very differently. In these visualizations, the France of traditional maps is still somewhat visible, but the practical realities of terrain, technology, and time take precedence over actual physical distances, which mean comparatively less to most travelers.

The second type of visualization aims to help minimize the inconvenience caused by train delays. While rail network operators want to reduce all delays, it is important for them to consider the number of passengers affected by each slowdown. Here, data on one variable—amount of time behind schedule—are combined with data on another—number of passengers—and represented at the location of each delayed train (4C). Every minute of delay makes the dot representing a train redder, and a higher number of passengers make it larger. With these data dimensions simultaneously visible, rail operators can quickly see where the most passengers are affected by the most severe delays. They can then take appropriate action with well-informed priorities, limiting delay per passenger and increasing overall passenger satisfaction.

4A

Day
Hour
ISOCHRONIC FRANCE, Monday 0AM
Play
Reset
Zoom Out
Zoom In
LILLE
AEROPORT CDG2 TGV ROISSY
PARIS
MARNE LA VALLEE CHESSY
STRASBOURG
RENNES
LE MANS
ANGERS ST LAUD
ST PIERRE DES CORPS
DIJON VILLE
POITIERS
LYON
VALENCE
BORDEAUX ST JEAN
AVIGNON
MONTPELLIER SAINT-ROCH
AIX EN PROVENCE TGV
MARSEILLE
TOULON

ISOCHRONIC FRANCE, Monday 0AM
Play
Reset
Zoom Out
Zoom In
Day
Hour
LILLE
AEROPORT CDG2 TGV ROISSY
STRASBOURG
RENNES
PARIS
MARNE LA VALLEE CHESSY
LE MANS
16 hrs
8 hrs
4 hrs
2 hrs
ANGERS ST LAUD
ST PIERRE DES CORPS
POITIERS
DIJON VILLE
BORDEAUX ST JEAN

Le Havre
Rouen
Bruxelles
Luxembourg
Strasbourg
Rennes
Le Mans
Tours
Nantes
Poitiers
Dijon
Besançon
Zurich
Berne
Genève
Lyon Part-Dieu
Annecy
St-Etienne
Chambéry
Valence-TGV
Grenoble
Bordeaux
Toulouse
Nimes
Avignon-TGV
Aix-en-Provence-TGV
Montpellier
Marseille
Toulon
Perpignan
On Time
5min Late
10
800 Passengers
senseable city lab:.::
SNCF

05.
HubCab — 2014

HubCab takes the SCL's interest in tracing large-scale flows of people in cities and applies it to a specific transportation option: individual taxicabs. Taxicab trips are but one example of an urban data stream that has been flowing for a long time—"hackney carriages" prowled the streets of London as early as the seventeenth century—but became visible to us only through new technology.[9] There is much debate as to whether social media and the Internet of Things can connect people to one another, but one of big data's greatest potentials is to reveal connections we already share. Programs like Google Maps allow individuals to dodge traffic jams; HubCab can help us collectively improve the flow of traffic and thus reduce transportation's social and environmental costs. With aggregate data, we can work for the aggregate good.

HubCab's interactive visualization invites users to explore the more than 170 million yearly taxi trips in the city of New York (5B). By tracking the times and locations of pickups and drop-offs, we can identify hotbeds across the city and throughout the day. By following individual trips, we can discover how many people are taking identical or similar journeys. Analyzing the HubCab dataset, researchers at the SCL developed a mathematical tool to identify "shareability networks," enabling the efficient modeling and optimization of ridesharing opportunities.

Only a data-driven, community-oriented model can unleash the true potential of twenty-first-century transportation: less congestion, fewer minutes spent idling, and a less polluted environment. Indeed, the research shows that taxi sharing could reduce the number of trips by 40 percent, with only minimal inconvenience to passengers. This study led to a major collaboration between MIT and Uber, whose results have been popularized through Uber Pool (now UberX Share) and similar ridesharing services.

HubCab's data visualizations use different colors to show pickups (yellow) and drop-offs (blue) in specific areas at specific times: for instance, all taxi pickups and drop-offs at JFK airport daily between 3 and 6 a.m. (5A), or all taxi drop-off points in New York City of passengers who were picked up in Times Square regularly between noon and 3 p.m. (5C).

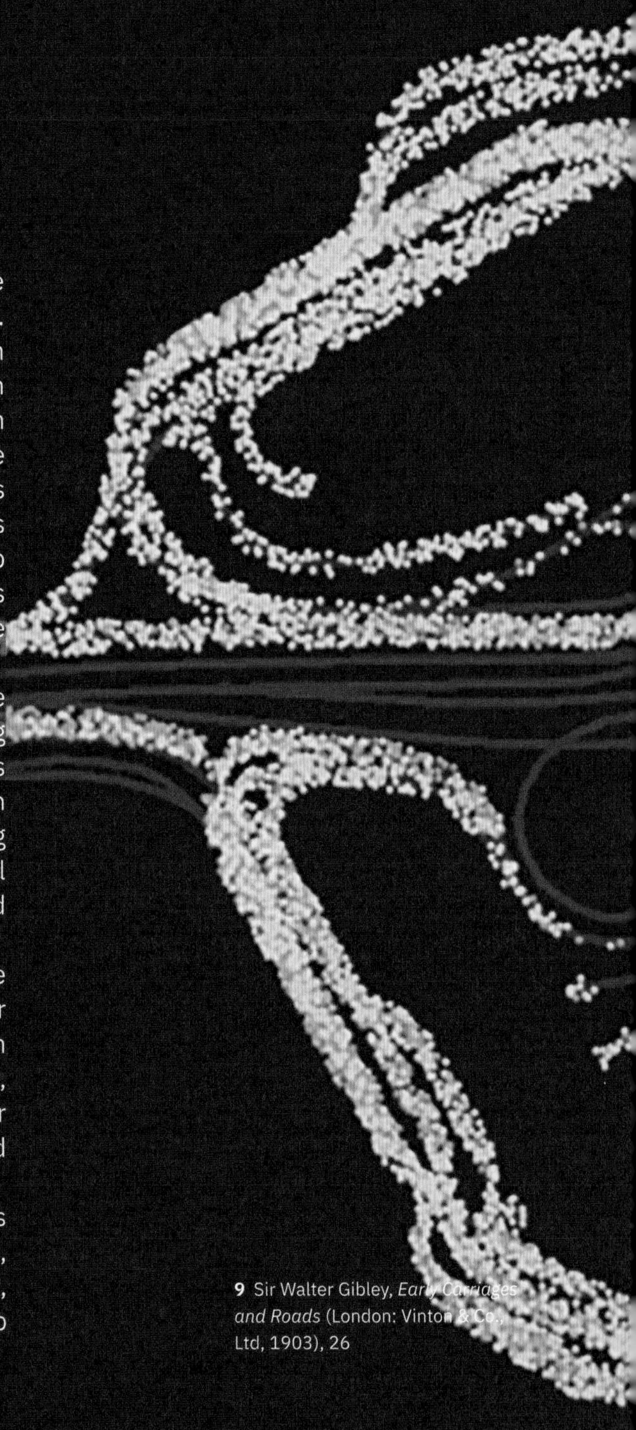

9 Sir Walter Gibley, *Early Carriages and Roads* (London: Vinton & Co., Ltd, 1903), 26

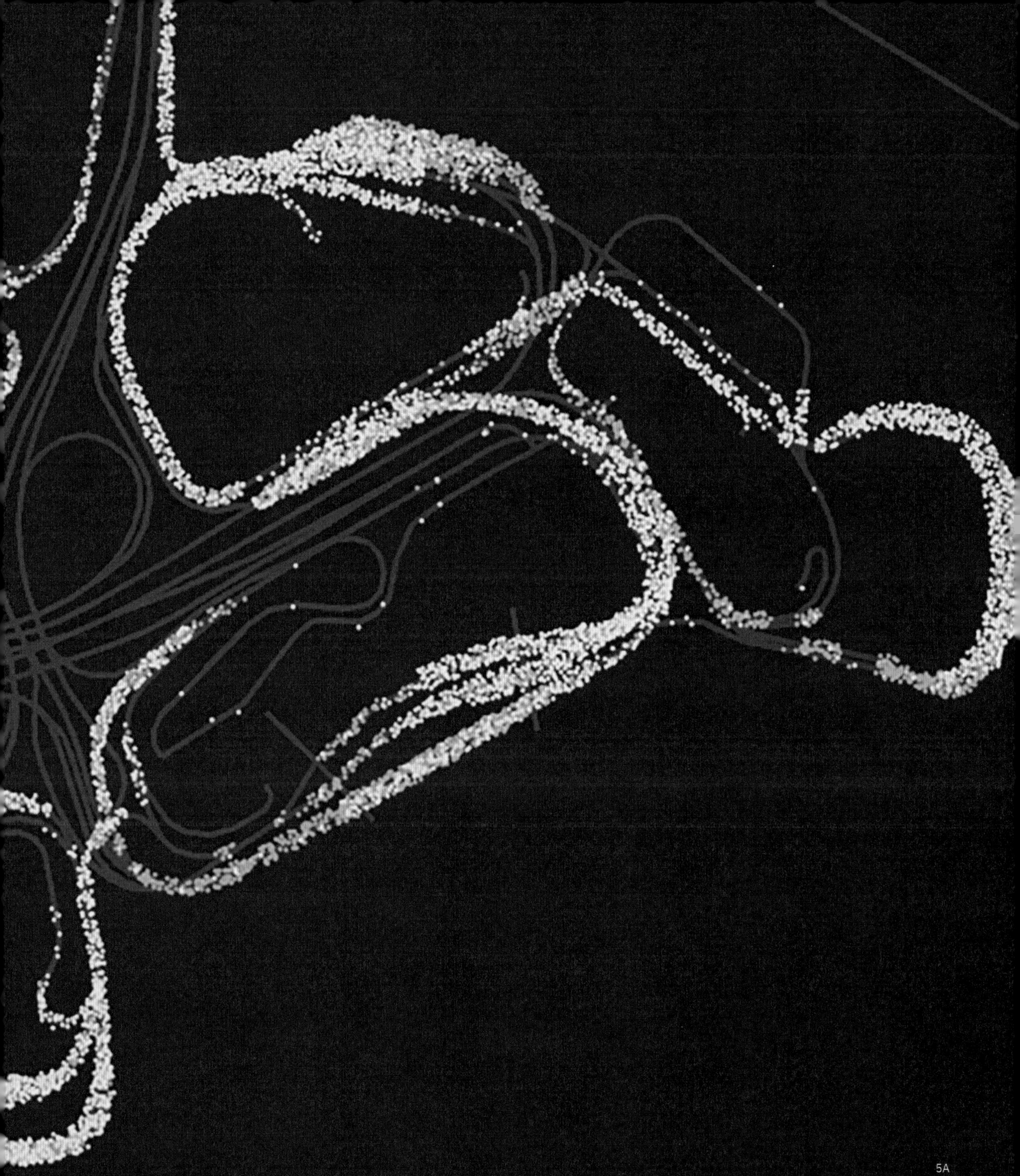

5A

5B

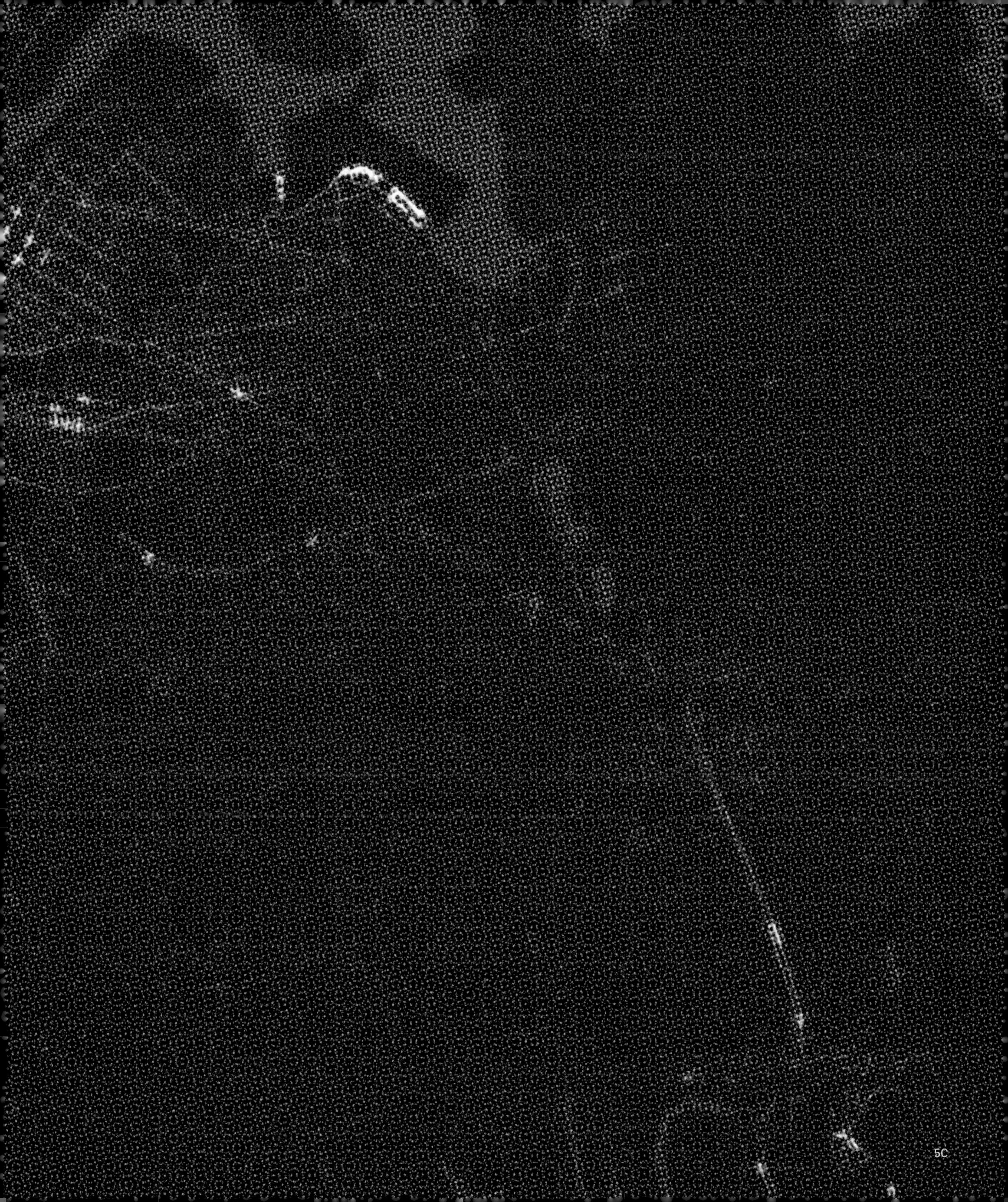

5C

06.
Minimum Fleet — 2018

The SCL's Minimum Fleet project calculates how a coordinated dispatching model could increase the efficiency of New York's taxis, reducing the number on the road without changing wait times. Today, New York's thirteen thousand cabs are empty more than half the time, "deadheading" between fares. Individual drivers navigate haphazardly from passenger to passenger, circling the city and jostling with one another to answer hails. Using a dataset of 150 million taxi rides taken over the course of a year, the SCL estimated how much this system could be improved. If drivers followed the instructions of a mobile app, informed by data on overall demand that predicted where the next passenger would appear, they could minimize the time between trips. In the map below, a driver makes three trips on opposite sides of Manhattan (6C). With an optimized app, she could transport far more people—and earn more fares—in the exact same period.

Without necessitating ridesharing (as described in HubCab), new regulations, or new passenger habits, this method could reduce the overall volume of New York's taxicab fleet by 30 percent. The advent of networked, self-driving cars could allow for even more fine-tuning of this coordination. Personal vehicles spend most of their time waiting to be used, so sharing them has even more potential for optimization than sharing taxis. The SCL calculates that if all of New York's automobiles worked together, the city would be able to stay on the move with only 50 percent of their current number. It goes without saying that the improvements to affordability, traffic congestion, and pollution that would arise from such a change would be immense. In the visualizations below, current fleets are represented in yellow, while the new model—in which many fewer cabs make the same number of trips—is in blue (6A–6C).

6A

1 hour
3 taxi trips
1 hour
8 fleet optimization trips
MONDAY
Total fleet on the road
Current taxi situation
Minimum Fleet Network model
12,000
8,000
4,000
0
0 2 4 6 8 10 12 14 16 18 20 22 24
Activity of the fleet in the model
With passenger
Driving to pick up
Waiting to pick up
4,000
2,000
0
0 2 4 6 8 10 12 14 16 18 20 22 24
mapbox
mapbox

1 hour
3 taxi trips
1 hour
8 fleet optimization trips
mapbox
mapbox

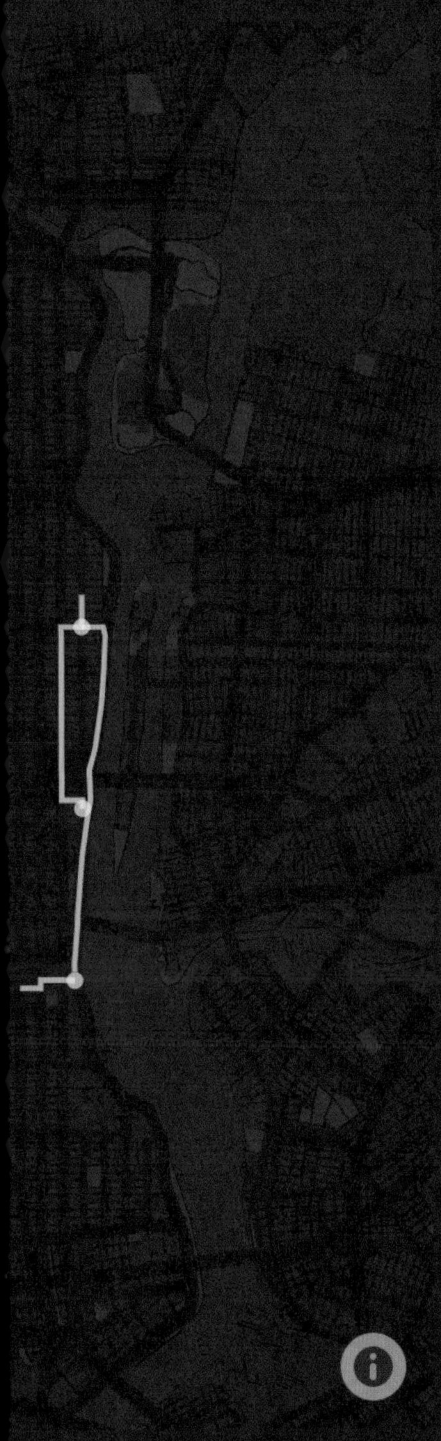

MONDAY

Total fleet on the road

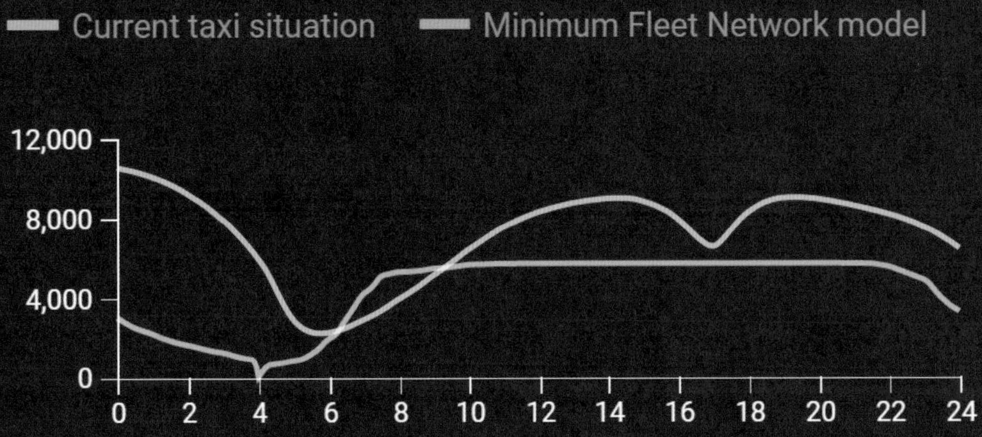

Activity of the fleet in the model

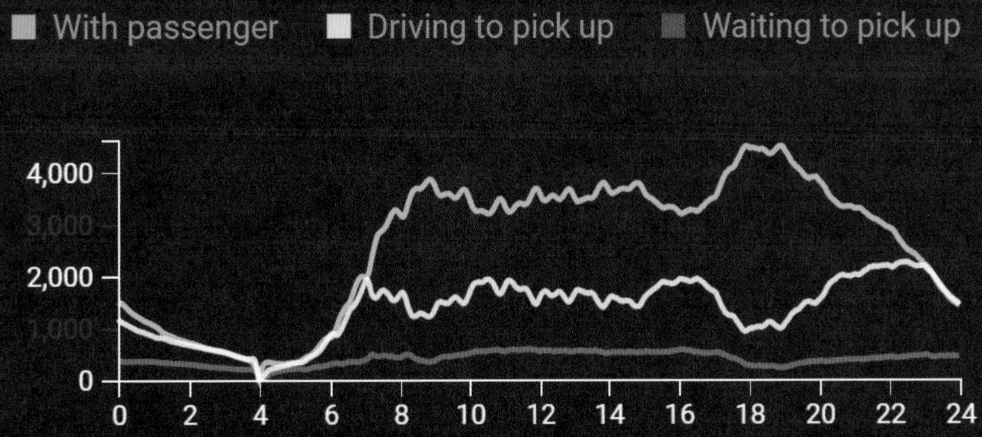

07.
Light Traffic — 2014

Light Traffic continues the SCL's research into urban movement, imagining a future in which real-time data play a central role in real-time traffic measurement and analysis. The project envisions the replacement of traffic lights by slot-based intersections for controlling urban traffic in the city of tomorrow, seamlessly knitting together flows of self-driving cars, pedestrians, and cyclists. Its visualizations explore the ways in which this "digital traffic controller" might soon become a reality.

In this scenario, sensor-laden vehicles pass through intersections while communicating with and remaining at safe distances from one another, rather than grinding to a halt at traffic lights. The model describes a performance breakthrough: all safety requirements being equal, traffic efficiency would double that allowed by current state-of-the-art traffic lights. Even maintaining today's volume of vehicles, which clogs the arteries of the current system, long lines would vanish and travel delays due to intersections would be cut almost to zero.

To understand slot-based intersections, consider the similar management system used for air-traffic control. Upon approaching such an intersection, a vehicle would automatically contact a virtual traffic management system to request access. The system—analogous to an air traffic controller—would assign each self-driving vehicle a time, or "slot," to enter. Unlike air traffic control, which in the US still involves verbal communication between pilots and people on the ground, the intersection's slot-based system would take advantage of self-driving cars to operate at lightning-fast speeds. With this level of coordination, very few cars would need to stop and start, reducing the pollution caused by acceleration and deceleration cycles and simultaneously making traffic run faster. Furthermore, slot-based intersections can easily and safely accommodate pedestrian and bicycle crossings as well. Traffic lights are places where people, technology, and the environment intersect, and this innovation could help us to achieve efficiency and harmony among all of them.

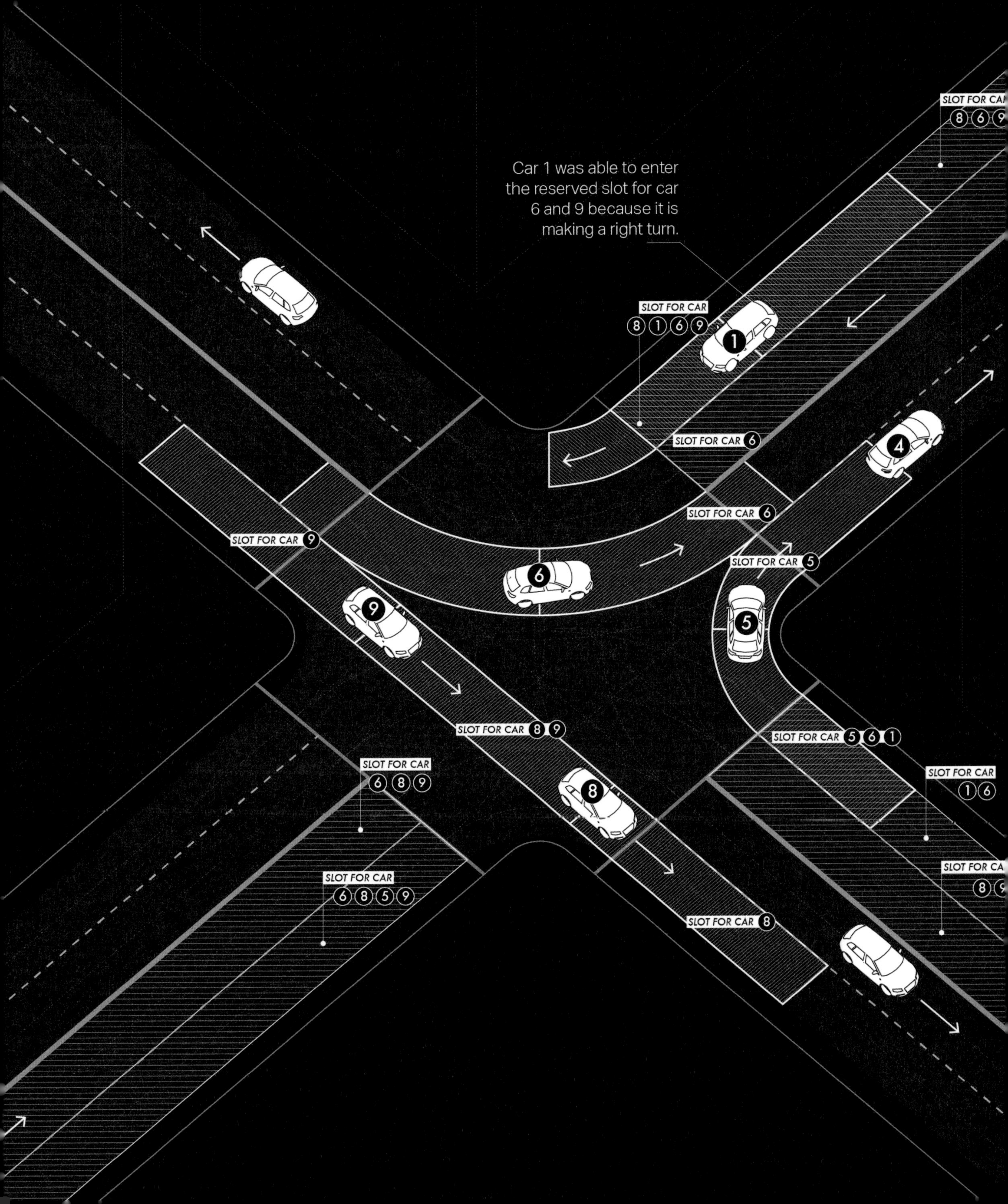

Car 1 was able to enter the reserved slot for car 6 and 9 because it is making a right turn.
SLOT FOR CAR 8 6 9
SLOT FOR CAR 8 1 6 9
SLOT FOR CAR 6
SLOT FOR CAR 6
SLOT FOR CAR 9
SLOT FOR CAR 5
SLOT FOR CAR 8 9
SLOT FOR CAR 5 6 1
SLOT FOR CAR 6 8 9
SLOT FOR CAR 1 6
SLOT FOR CAR 6 8 5 9
SLOT FOR CAR 8
1
4
5
6
8
9

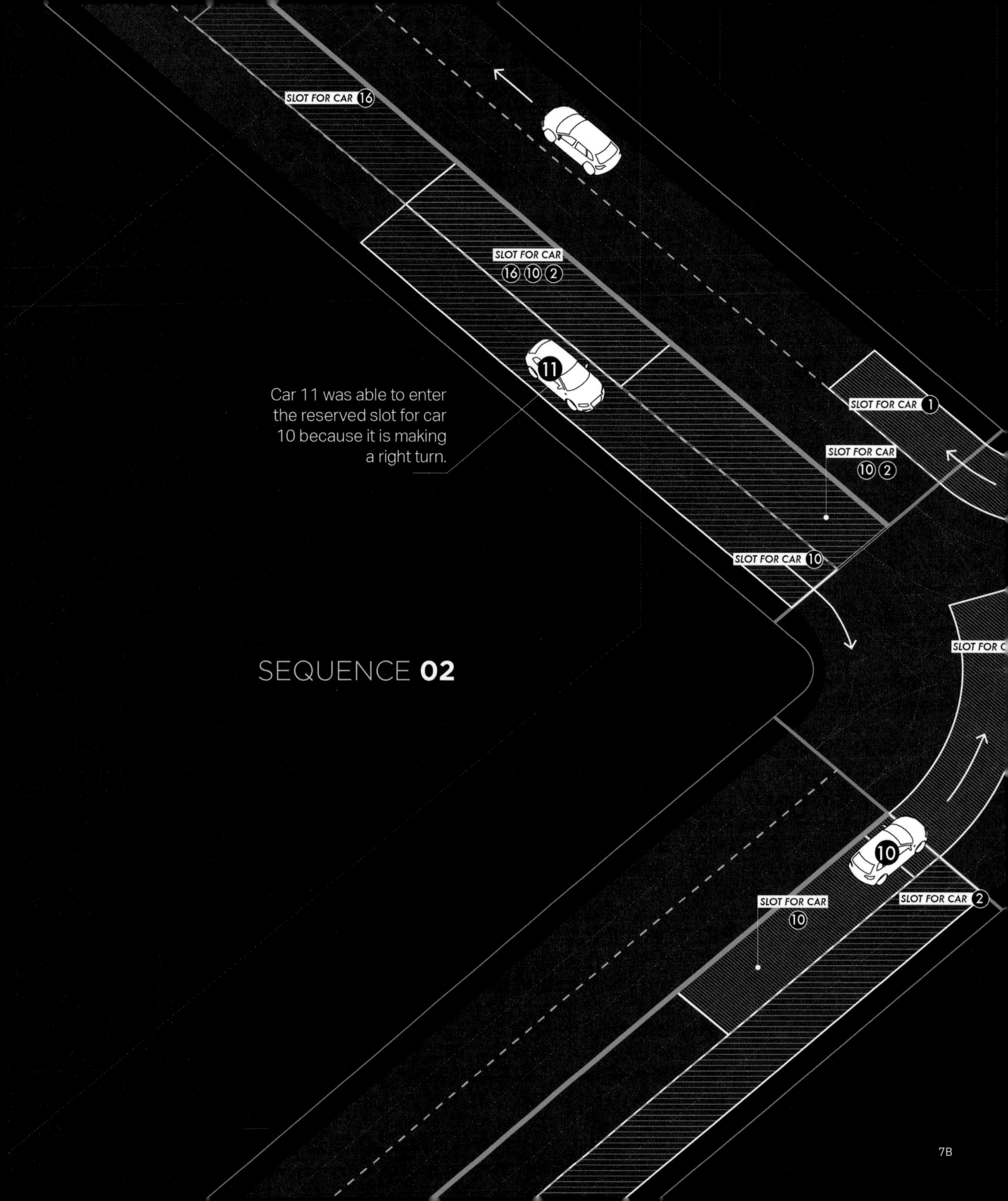
SLOT FOR CAR 16
SLOT FOR CAR
16 10 2
11
Car 11 was able to enter the reserved slot for car 10 because it is making a right turn.
SLOT FOR CAR 1
SLOT FOR CAR
10 2
SLOT FOR CAR 10
SEQUENCE 02
SLOT FOR C
10
SLOT FOR CAR
10
SLOT FOR CAR 2

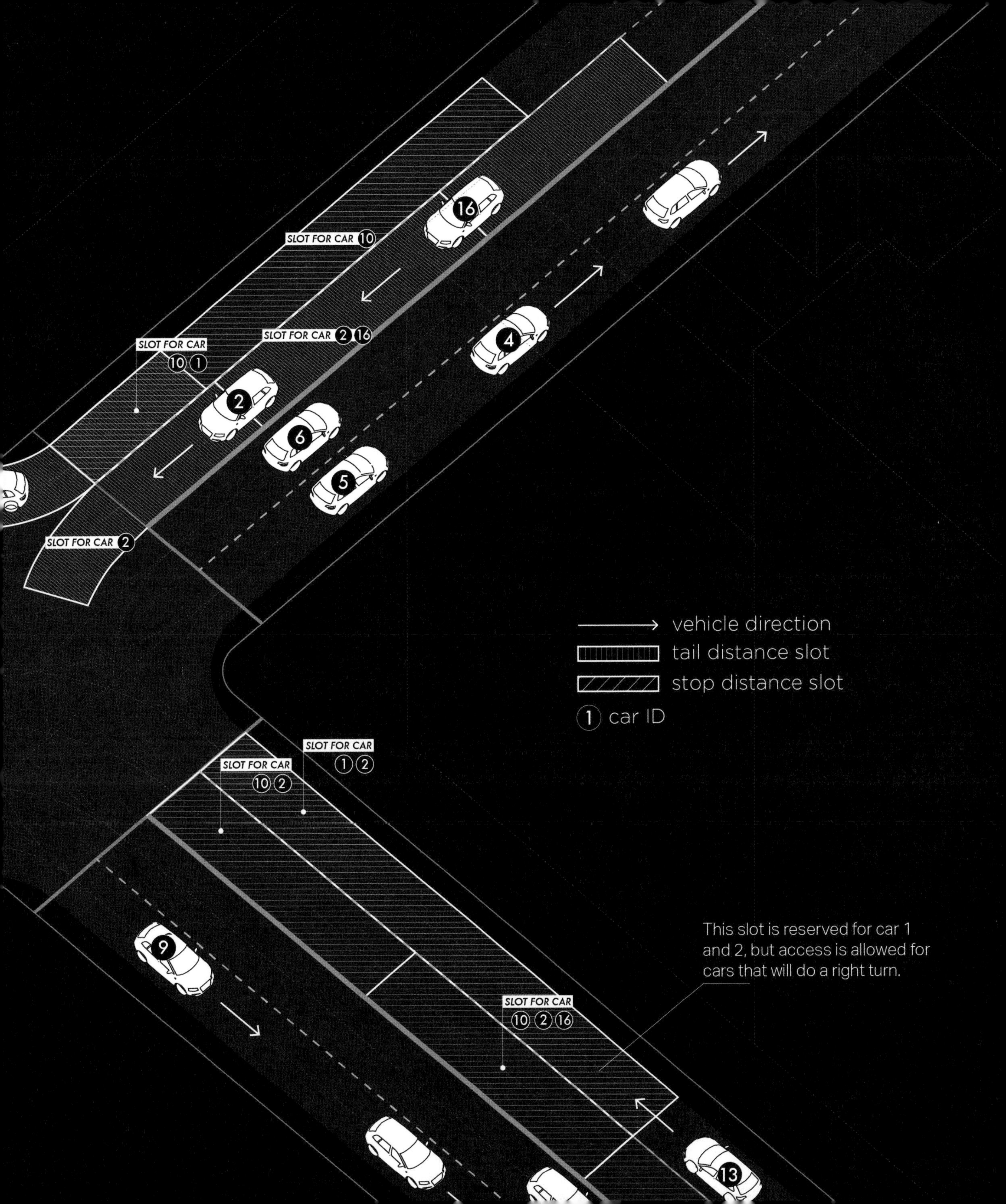
SLOT FOR CAR 10
SLOT FOR CAR 2 16
SLOT FOR CAR 10 1
SLOT FOR CAR 2
vehicle direction
tail distance slot
stop distance slot
1 car ID
SLOT FOR CAR 1 2
SLOT FOR CAR 10 2
This slot is reserved for car 1 and 2, but access is allowed for cars that will do a right turn.
SLOT FOR CAR 10 2 16

SEQUENCE 03

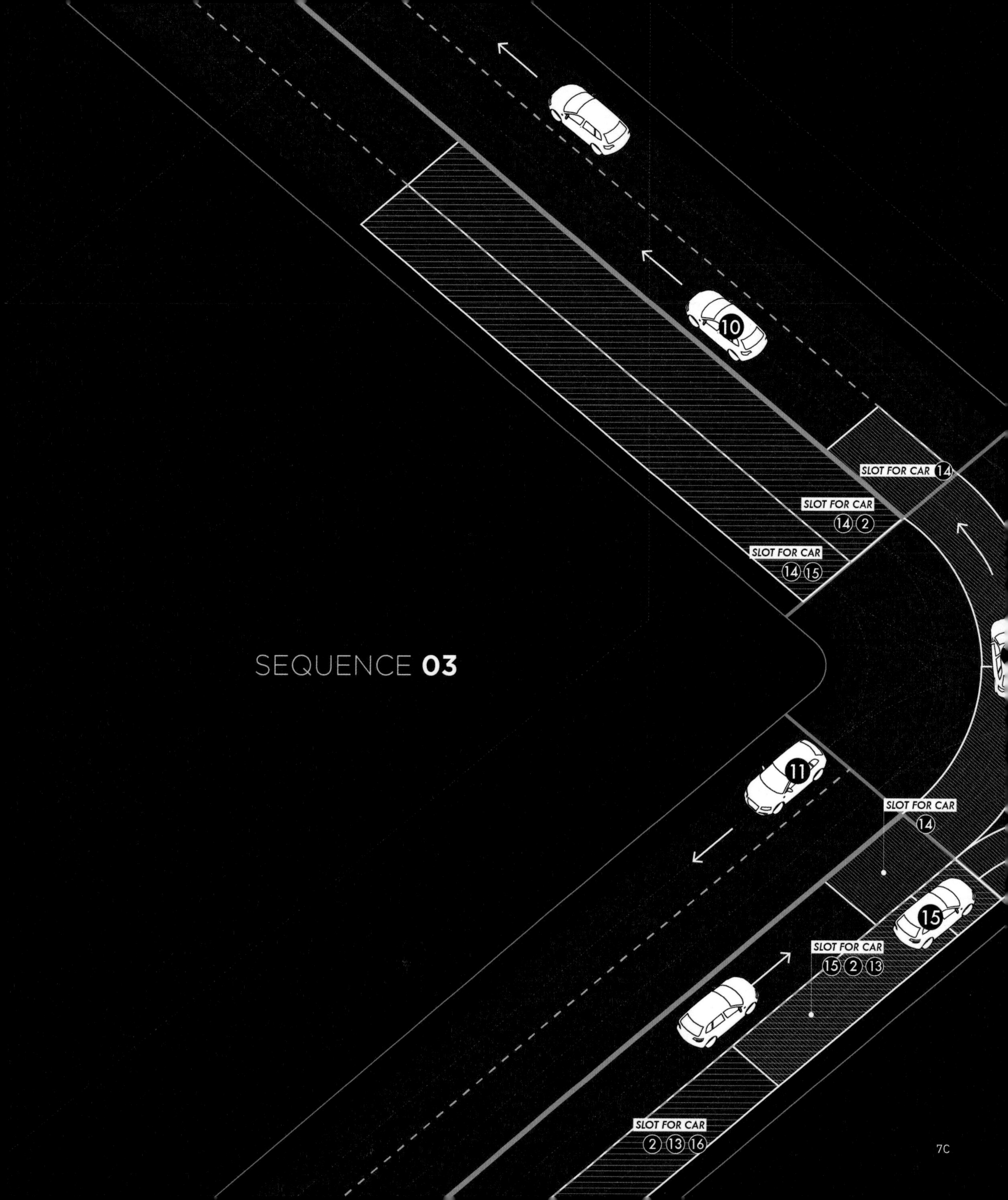
10
SLOT FOR CAR 14
SLOT FOR CAR
14 2
SLOT FOR CAR
14 15
11
SLOT FOR CAR
14
15
SLOT FOR CAR
15 2 13
SLOT FOR CAR
2 13 16

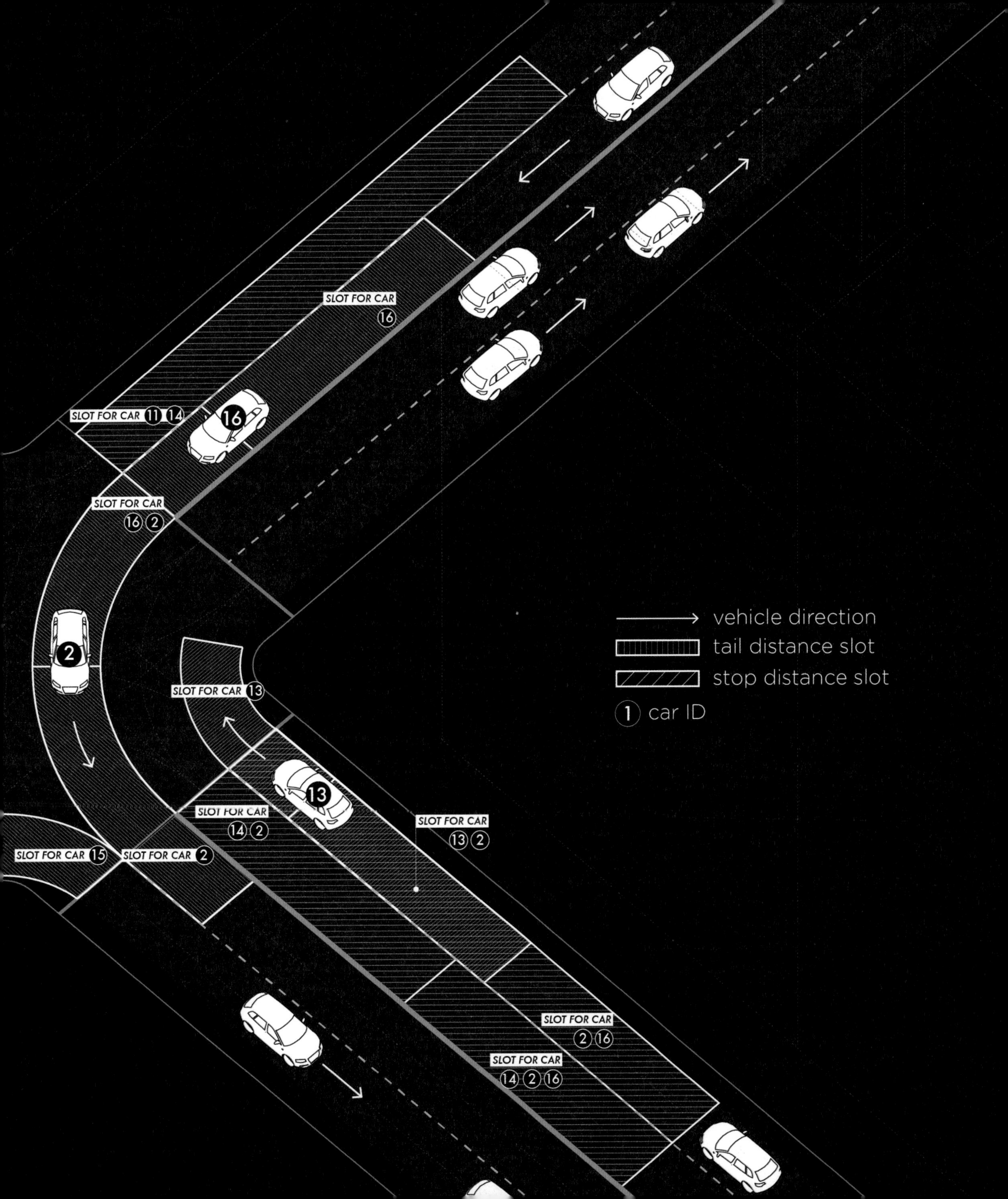
SLOT FOR CAR 16
SLOT FOR CAR 11 14
SLOT FOR CAR 16 2
SLOT FOR CAR 13
SLOT FOR CAR 14 2
SLOT FOR CAR 13 2
SLOT FOR CAR 15
SLOT FOR CAR 2
SLOT FOR CAR 2 16
SLOT FOR CAR 14 2 16
vehicle direction
tail distance slot
stop distance slot
1 car ID

How often do you travel to any particular place? You might presume that you decide your daily destinations based on distance, but never before in the history of the social sciences has sufficiently large-scale evidence been available to support this assumption. Now, however, big data can verify and expand upon this intuition with unprecedented precision—and reveal extraordinary similarities in human behavior.

Drawing on cell phone location data from numerous cities (Abidjan, Ivory Coast; Boston, United States; Braga, Lisbon, and Porto, Portugal; Dakar, Senegal; and Singapore), researchers at the SCL discovered a trend that holds across cultures and continents, which we named the universal visitation law of human mobility. According to this law, the number of visitors to a given location decreases, in a predictable pattern, as the frequency of visitation (how often each individual stops by) and the distance traveled increase. For example, most people that visit Boston's Beacon Hill neighborhood do so just a few times rather than many times. Moreover, many more visitors (to any place) come from nearby rather than from far away, and the farther away a place is, the less often we travel there. Remarkably, the same pattern appeared in every city studied. With an awareness of this precise mathematical relationship, we could reshape urban life for the better. For example, this law supports the French-Colombian urban theorist Carlo Moreno's "fifteen-minute city" notion that neighborhoods can be designed to include 90 percent of residents' basic needs—food, work, childcare, schools, health services, public spaces—within a short walking distance of their homes. We can save our longer trips for when they count—to stadiums, museums, and specialty restaurants—making the most of urban specialization while keeping the necessities close at hand.

The first two maps below visualize the flow of individuals across the greater Boston area as lines (visiting frequency as color, number of unique visitors as width) that cluster around attractive places, with height representing location-specific attractiveness (8A–8B). The last map shows universal mobility patterns in countries across the planet, from Senegal to Singapore and Portugal (8C).

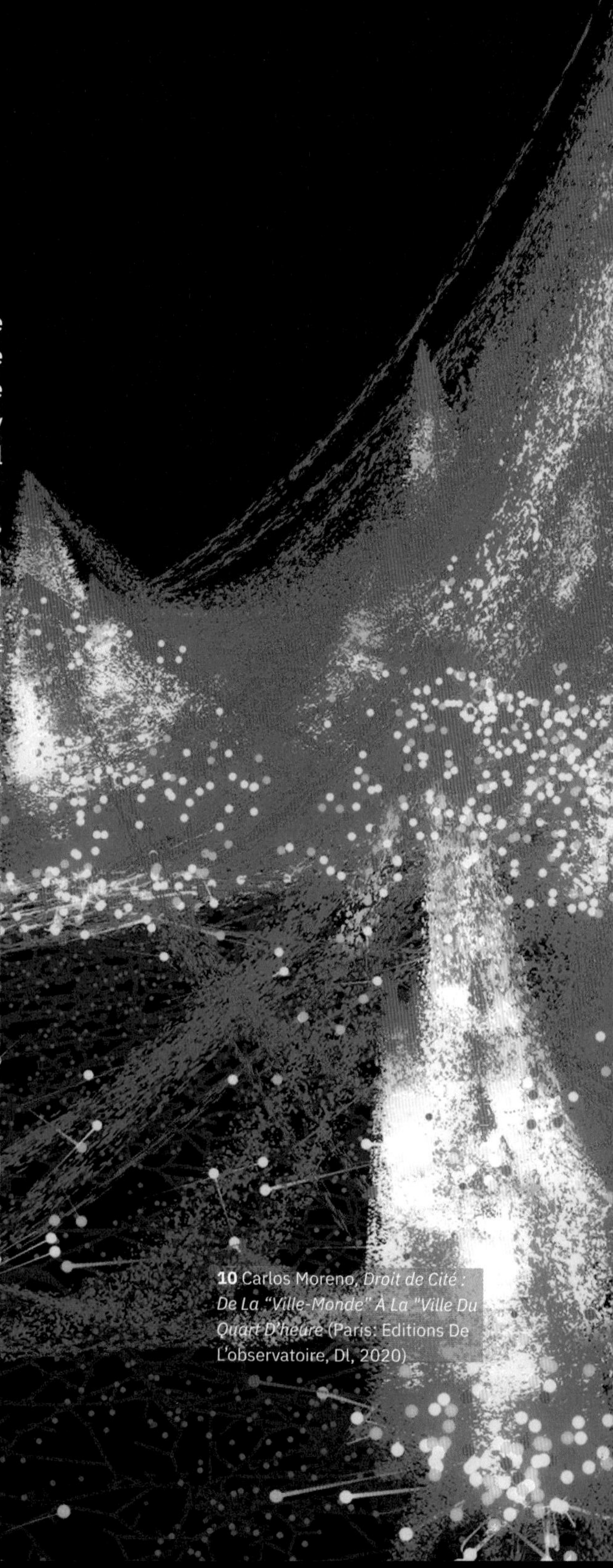

10 Carlos Moreno, *Droit de Cité : De La "Ville-Monde" À La "Ville Du Quart D'heure* (Paris: Editions De L'observatoire, Dl, 2020)

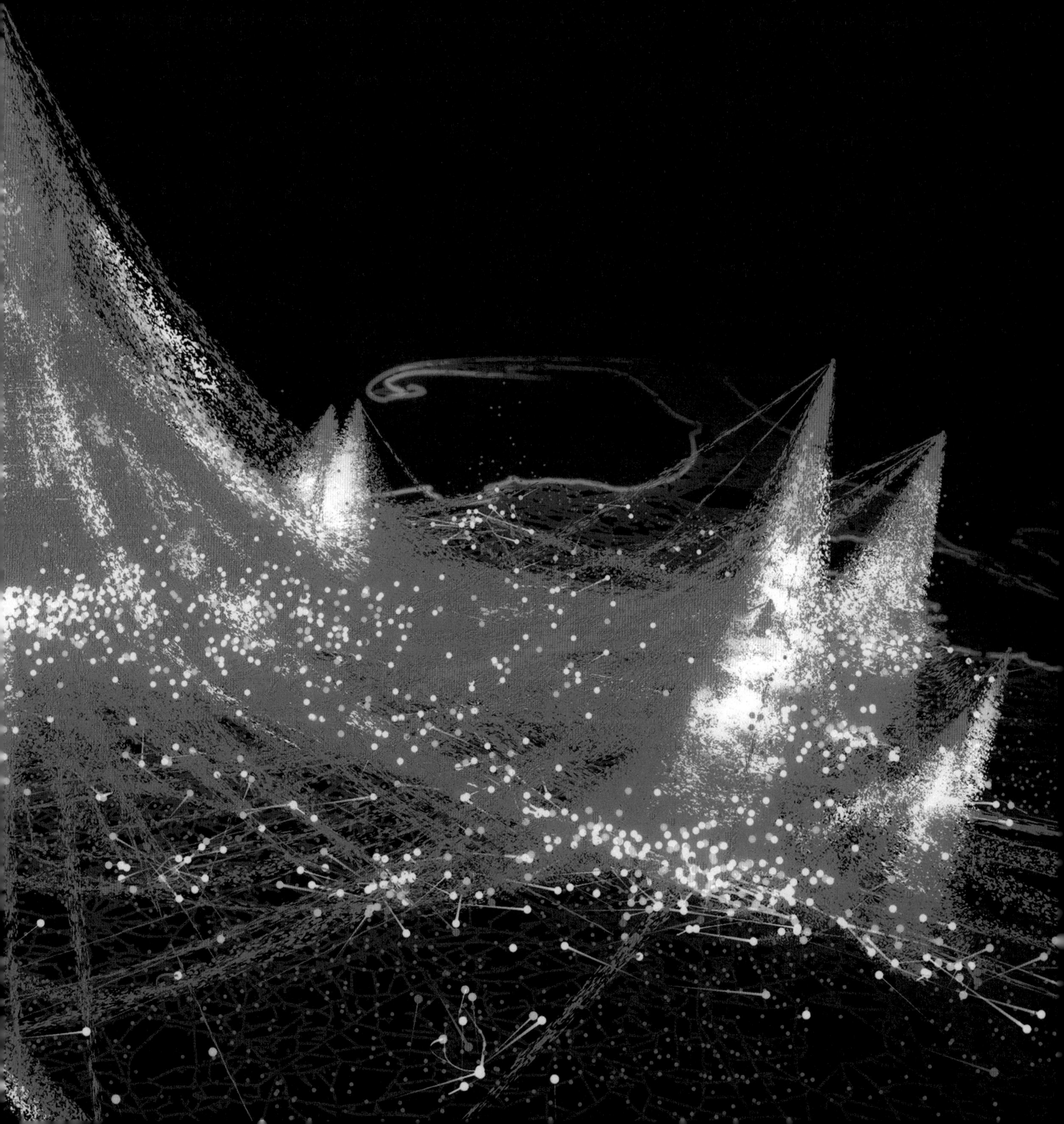

8B

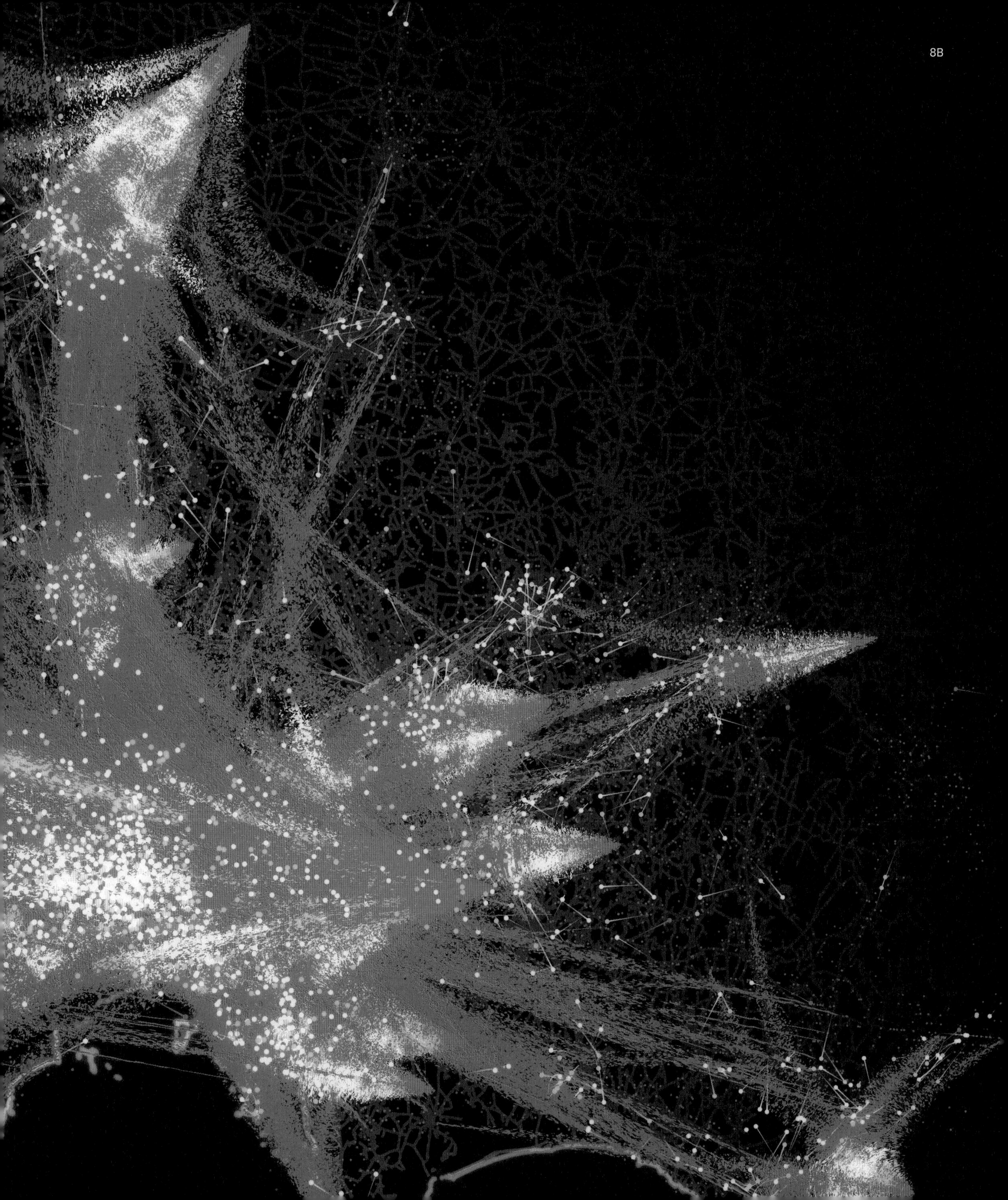

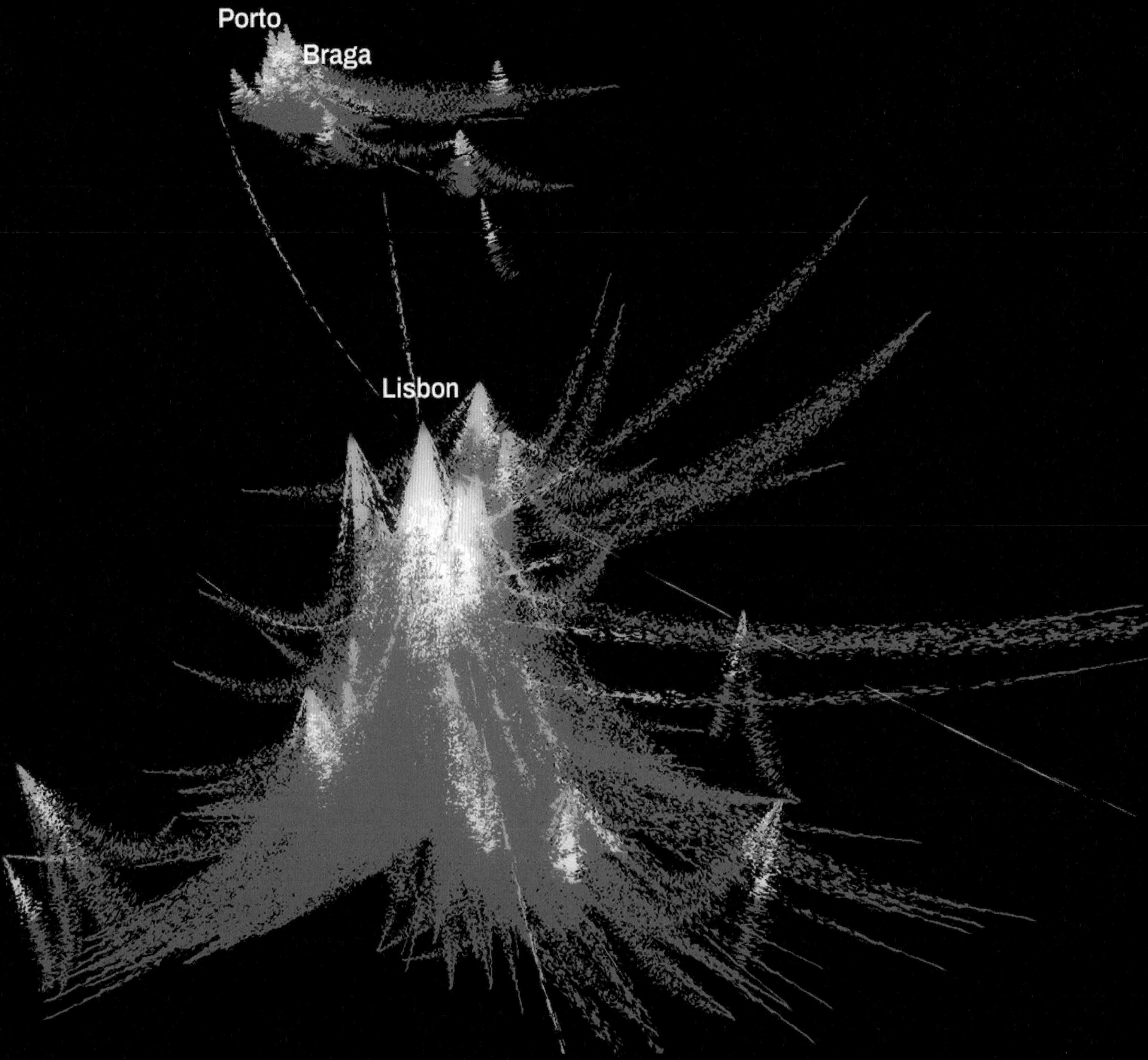
Porto
Braga
Lisbon

Singapore

Dakar

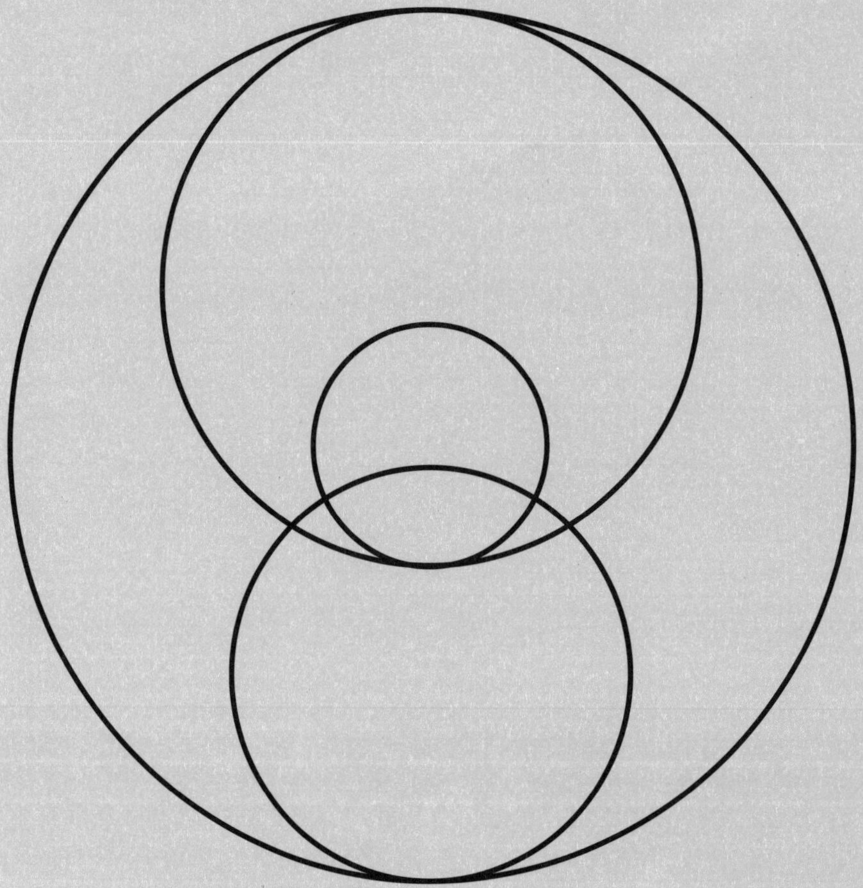

CONNECTION

CHAPTER — 2

Connection

"Mr. Watson, come here, I want to see you" became the first words spoken through a telephone when they were uttered on 10 March 1876. The pioneering phone call between the inventor Alexander Graham Bell and his colleague Thomas Watson made history, marking the birth of telecommunications—although it hardly revolutionized information transmission in that moment. When Watson put down the mouthpiece and joined Bell, he only had to walk to the adjacent room.[1]

Telecommunication technology had ample opportunities to demonstrate its potential: as the incipient network grew, it gained in both numbers and public notice. One of the first telephones was installed in the White House in 1877 by the techno-enthusiast President Rutherford B. Hayes (the presidential telephone number was 1), and by 1911, AT&T's network stretched from New York to Denver.[2] Businesspeople in New York could talk to Detroit-based factory managers as if they were side by side. Telecommunications brought about a new era in human production, favoring the creation of knowledge over the creation of commercial objects. Communication networks were the engine of the Second Industrial Revolution as much as factories and mass production were that of the first. As telecommunications spread at the turn of the twentieth century, there was a wholesale shift toward a more information-based society. "When wireless is perfectly applied, the whole earth will be converted into a huge brain," Nikola Tesla quipped in 1926.[3] It was the beginning of what Manuel Castells later termed "the space of flows"—a virtual landscape that would become the subject of cartographic enquiry.[4] If we measure phone calls and emails instead of only miles, we can see how New York and London may be more connected to each other than to geographically nearby villages.

1 "Notebook by Alexander Graham Bell, from 1875 to 1876," 41, *Alexander Graham Bell Family Papers, 1834–1974*, Manuscript / Mixed Material, Library of Congress, Washington, DC, https://www.loc.gov/resource/magbell.25300201/.

2 Richard T. Loomis, "The Telephone Comes to Washington: George C. Maynard, 1839–1919," *Washington History* 12, no. 2 (2000): 22–40.

3 Nikola Tesla, "When Woman Is Boss," interview by John B. Kennedy, *Collier's Magazine* 77 (30 January 1926): 17.

4 Manuel Castells, *The Informational City: Information Technology, Economic Restructuring, and the Urban-Regional Process* (Oxford: Blackwell, 1989).

While rulers, scales, and timers can describe physical flows, the data transfers of telecommunication systems are much more difficult to measure. Jacques Bertillon tried his hand at it in the late nineteenth century, mapping the volume of telegraphs and letters to and from Paris over a decade. The challenge of understanding and mapping information flows gave rise to the telecommunications-based field of data analytics, pioneered by mathematicians such as George Zipf.[5] Instantaneous data-driven cartographies became a holy grail as technologies and network infrastructures grew increasingly central to economics, governance, business, and life in the 1960s and 1970s. The American designer and inventor Richard Buckminster Fuller enthusiastically rose to the challenge with a visionary plan for mapping flows in real time. The simple question "How does the world work?" guided his proposal for the 1967 Montreal World Expo: the Geoscope, a geodesic globe with a diameter of two hundred feet (sixty-one meters) for visualizing flows of real-time data, information, and patterns from across the world, including those "too slow for the human eye and mind to comprehend, such as the multimillions-of-years-to-transpire changes in the geology of our Planet."[6] This animated map would have shown all the resources on earth, as well as human and natural activity from troop deployment to ocean currents. The Expo's chief of design and operations dismissed the project as a "kooky thought," but today it may be not too far outside the realm of possibility.

With exponential advances in computing, the capacity to represent large amounts of information paved the way for data visualization as a discipline in its own right. At the beginning of the twenty-first century, the possibility of truly mapping telecommunications was demonstrated by the first map of the Internet, while its pulse—the rhythms and global patterns of use—was taken soon after, by the SCL's Signature of Humanity and other studies. Other experiments by the Lab, such as Borderline and the Connected States of America, demonstrate how telecommunications can reveal truths about humanity's spatial organization that official geopolitical boundaries would never suggest. This research has gone hand in hand with the growth in complexity of networks and their systems of nodes, connections, and interactions. Telecommunications rapidly connects atoms to distant atoms, creating a hybrid space at the intersection of the digital and the physical—

5 See, e.g., George Kingsley Zipf, *The Psycho-biology of Language: An Introduction to Dynamic Philology,* Human Relations Collection (Boston: Houghton Mifflin, 1935).

6 R. Buckminster Fuller, *Critical Path,* with Kiyoshi Kuromiya (New York: St. Martin's, 1981), 418.

again, Castells's space of flows.

Beyond just virtual platforms, the space of flows marries geographic position with technological infrastructure and information systems, all driven by human sociability. Their emergent awareness of this has prompted researchers to map the space of flows onto physical space. NYTE: New York Talk Exchange, for instance, shows links between that city and the rest of the world; iSPOTS zooms in to the scale of a single campus, revealing characteristic patterns of work and play at MIT with online data traffic—and surprising us by illuminating how some spaces were not necessarily being used for their intended purposes. With Spring Spree, the SCL mapped how consumer activity in Spain spikes every year during a pre-Easter shopping binge. Telecommunications have quickly entered daily life: human beings are generating much more than simple audio and text communication data, as they now track and share their patterns of movement, eating, sleeping, and working—and even their heartbeats. Indeed, mapping current human connections allows us to chart a path toward stronger ones: the SCL's investigations of social segregation in Singapore Calling and Stockholm Flows highlight the places where we must intervene to promote encounters and diversity.

As time has passed and digital devices have proliferated, the space of flows has swelled and grown into a flood. A new hybrid reality, between virtual systems (maps of information) and physical geographies (maps of space), demands a new practice of cartography: the map of maps. With recent developments, every human and material flow can potentially be charted. This points toward far-reaching ramifications: the birth of society's digital twin in a virtual space, moving in sync with our own lives and changing them in the process.

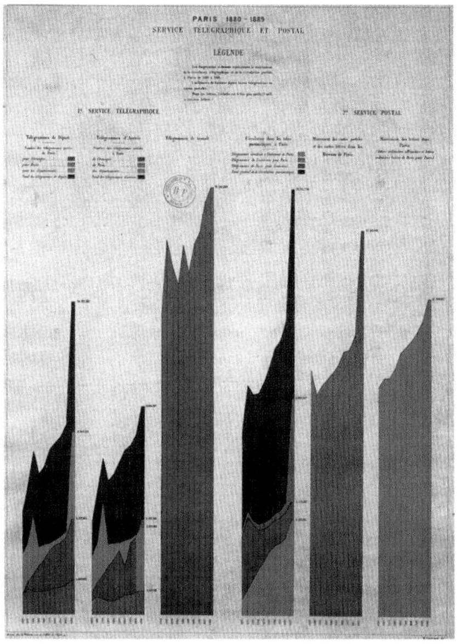

01

01. JACQUES BERTILLON, PARIS, 1880-1889: TELEGRAPH AND POSTAL SERVICE, 1891.

Before the dominance of the telephone and the email, information flowed through Paris by way of telegrams and letters. These forms of communication leave clear traces, records that Jacques Bertillon transformed into a chart of human connection over time. His infographic represents telegrams and letters that were sent and received, according to their trajectory: within Paris, between Paris and the other departments of France, and between Paris and foreign countries. The relative prevalence of each correspondence type changes significantly over the ten-year span that Bertillon measures here, illustrating with only a few colors and bars how the people of the City of Lights connected with one another, their nation, and the entire globe. In the age of imperialism and global commerce, understanding these far-flung connections was critical to understanding the life of a city like Paris.

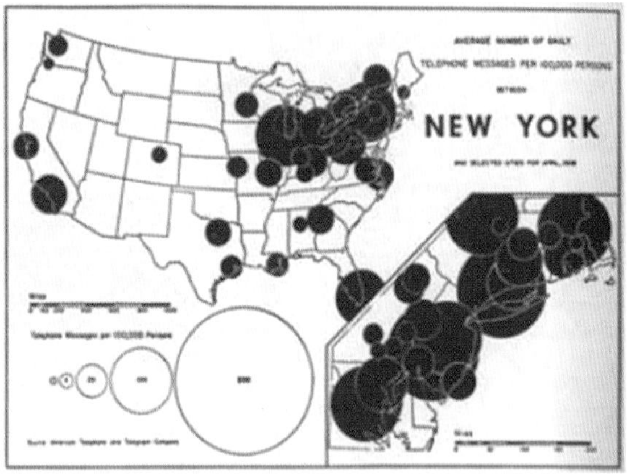

02

02. NEIL C. GUSTAFSON, MAP OF AT&T PHONE CALLS TO AND FROM NEW YORK, 1961.

In the 1950s and 1960s, Neil C. Gustafson created maps of AT&T phone calls across the United States. These were early examples of using datasets from a telecommunication network to identify patterns and relationships between specific cities and other parts of the country: a living, network-based cartography. In Gustafson's maps, certain trends emerge among the bigger cities, through which a large proportion of the country's communications passed. The French geographer Jean Gottmann used these maps to study the Northeast Corridor, the most heavily urbanized agglomeration in the United States, spanning from Boston's northern suburbs to the southernmost tip of Washington, DC. In Gustafson's map, this is clearly the place of highest activity in the network, a hub of connectivity that transcends administrative and political geographies. Gottmann characterized this region as a single Megalopolis—"the cradle of a new order in the organization of inhabited space."[7] Telecommunication data, among other pieces of information, can be essential in defining areas according to their levels of exchange and activity.

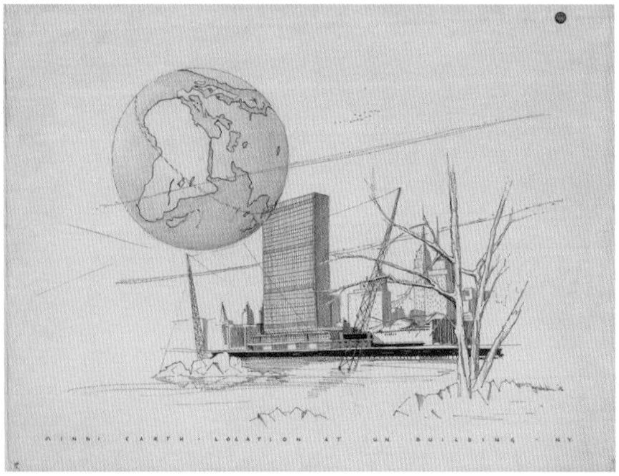

03

03. BUCKMINSTER FULLER, GEOSCOPE ILLUSTRATION, 1962.

In 1962, Buckminster Fuller proposed the creation of a Geoscope: a globe, two hundred feet (sixty-one meters) in diameter and fitted with colored lights, that could provide viewers with detailed information about the world's economy, environmental resources, and other properties. Fuller envisioned the Geoscope as connected to computers so that it could display both historical and real-time data—one of the first suggestions for such a visualization; it was meant to be open to the public and to inform all interested viewers about the Earth's current state. Although this proposal was not realized at the time, modern virtual globes have repurposed its ideas. Google Earth and other 3-D software models allow viewers to easily interact with the planet from different angles and, in line with Fuller's conception, overlay visualizations of various abstract or invisible datasets onto its geography. The resulting maps hybridize physical and virtual space and, unlike the Geoscope, can be transmitted to anyone with an Internet connection. We've come a long way since the early 1960s, but it was then that Fuller's project already recognized the importance of visualizing converging data streams and making the results accessible to everyone.

7 Jean Gottmann, *Megalopolis: The Urbanized Northeastern Seaboard of the United States* (New York: Twentieth Century Fund, 1961), 9.

04

04.BARRETT LYON, OPTE.ORG, MAP OF THE INTERNET, 2003.

The challenge of visualizing the Internet, a network whose size defies the limits of human cognition, has driven explorers of the virtual world to imagine it as a physical space. This map is an early capture by Barrett Lyon, an artist and computer scientist, who created the open-source Opte Project in 2003. Capturing tens of millions of nodes, Opte Project visualizations apply a spatial logic to the Internet, which gives a sense of its scale, its complexity, and even its beauty. Lines on the map represent connections between IP addresses, with the color signifying area of origin: North America is blue, Latin America and the Caribbean are yellow, Africa and western Eurasia are green, and the Asia-Pacific region is red. Private networks, whose physical locations are masked to observers, are in cyan. The colorful image that results from these simple rules shows how the discrete continents of the physical globe are in fact inextricably entangled. The dominant, North American web extends its technological tendrils across the entire picture. Connectivity in East Asia, which exploded as the twentieth century ended, was only beginning to emerge on the edges at this early date.

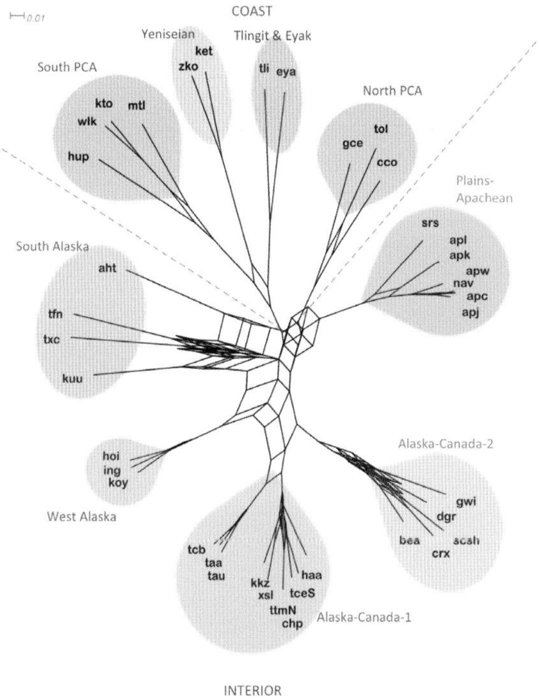

05

05. MARK A. SICOLI, MAP OF NORTH AMERICAN AND SIBERIAN LANGUAGES, 2014.

This network map uses datasets from linguistic studies to analyze movements of ancient humans, enhancing our knowledge of our ancestors. It is known that languages evolve slowly, and researchers are now using the markers of this process—the similarities or lack thereof between neighboring languages—to understand human migratory patterns. This map was created by Dr. Mark A. Sicoli, a linguistic anthropologist at the University of Virginia who studies indigenous languages from the Pacific Northwest, Alaska, and Central Siberia. He used techniques of big data analysis—cataloging dialects from three regions and combining maps and language networks—to investigate how these languages might have developed over time, based on certain similarities among them. The results suggest that people crossed into the American continent from Asia via the Bering land bridge, with subsequent migrations back and forth between central Asia and North America. This is a more complex picture than the original theory about the first human settlers of the Americas, which posited a single wave of colonization over the bridge, which was created during the last ice age. The analysis that is now possible, incorporating linguistic data into models that once used fossils alone, can create better maps and visualizations of the history of our species on this planet.

CHAPTER • 2

Connection ↓
MIT Senseable City Lab Projects

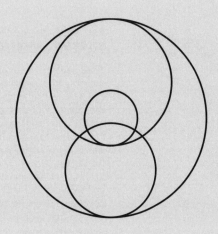

09.
iSPOTS — 2005

10.
NYTE: New York Talk Exchange — 2007

11.
Borderline — 2010

12.
The Connected States of America — 2011

13.
Spring Spree — 2012

14.
Signature of Humanity — 2013

15.
Friendly Cities — 2017 and Singapore Calling — 2019

16.
MIT Email Collaboration — 2021

09.
iSPOTS — 2005

The iSPOTS project was an early investigation of the ideas behind other projects, like NYTE: New York Talk Exchange (project 10, below), applied to a much smaller environment: the MIT campus in Cambridge, Massachusetts. In 2005, this was one of the places where it was most evident that new wireless communication technologies were changing the ways we live and work, creating virtual networks of information exchange on top of the old physical ones. The aim of iSPOTS was to reveal the complex and dispersed individual movement patterns that made up daily life on campus, and the hybrid (virtual-physical) connections that could be observed between people. One of the most pervasive wireless Internet networks on earth and a very high percentage of laptop ownership made MIT uniquely well positioned for this research.

The resulting data visualizations answer a variety of questions about the MIT community: Which physical spaces were preferred for work and socialization? Which location-based services, from benches to charging pads, were most useful for students and staff? How could future physical campus planning suit the community's changing needs? In one image, a colored, elevated digital topography of space usage illustrates patterns of individual movement (9A). The digital peaks identify preferred spaces for working and living. Another map shows how Wi-Fi was used at MIT over a twenty-four-hour period: log files with the number of connections to each access point were collected at fifteen-minute intervals and then plotted as a color field overlaid on a map of campus, providing a quick visual comparison of different areas (9B). Red indicates a large number of users per access point, black a small number. Finally, a third figure uses log information from Internet service providers (ISPs) to represent spatial patterns of traffic on large Wi-Fi networks (9C).

The iSPOTS project was among the first to show the new possibilities for mapping the flows of communication technologies in order to better understand a space—be it a campus, a city, or the world.

9A

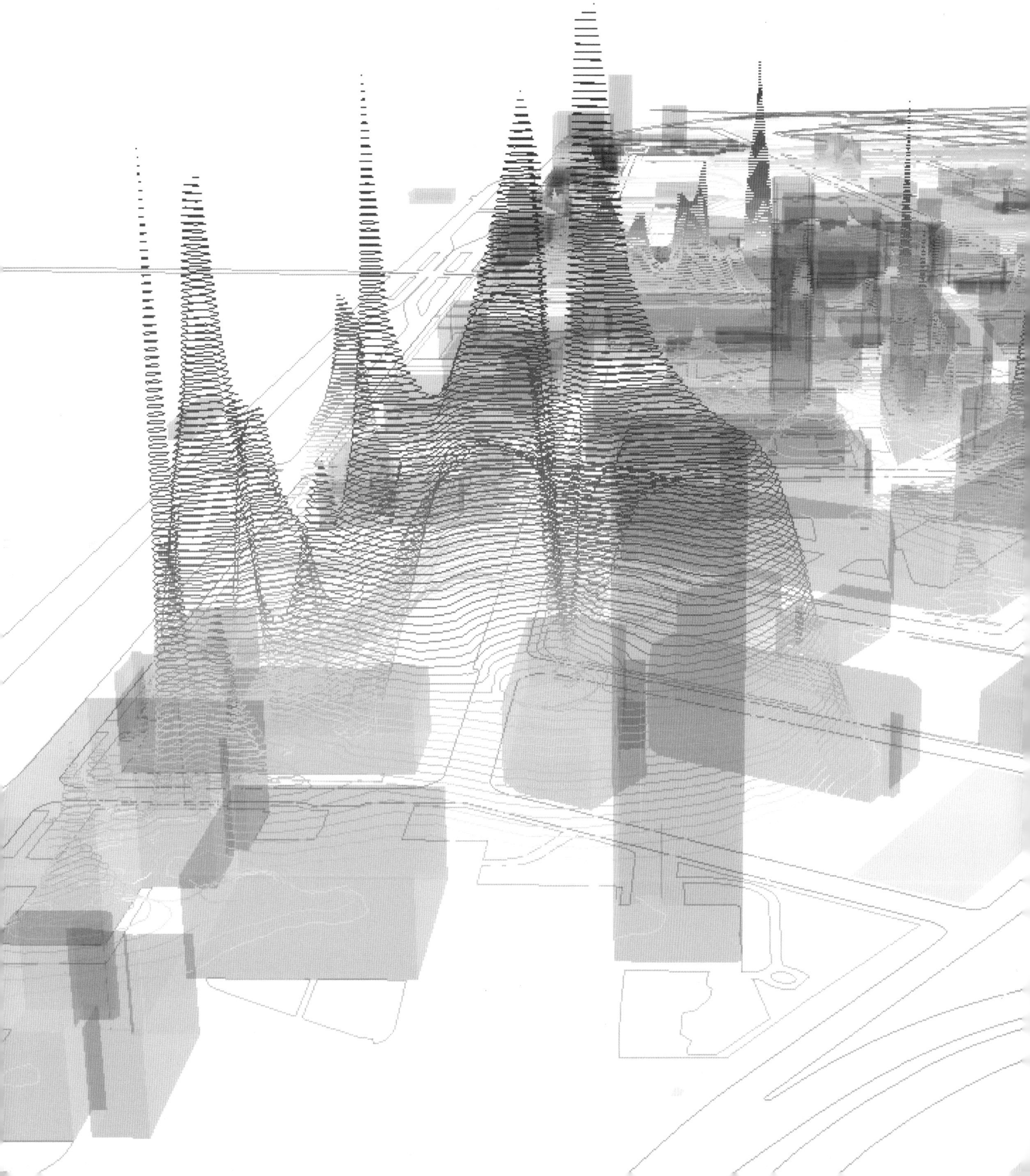

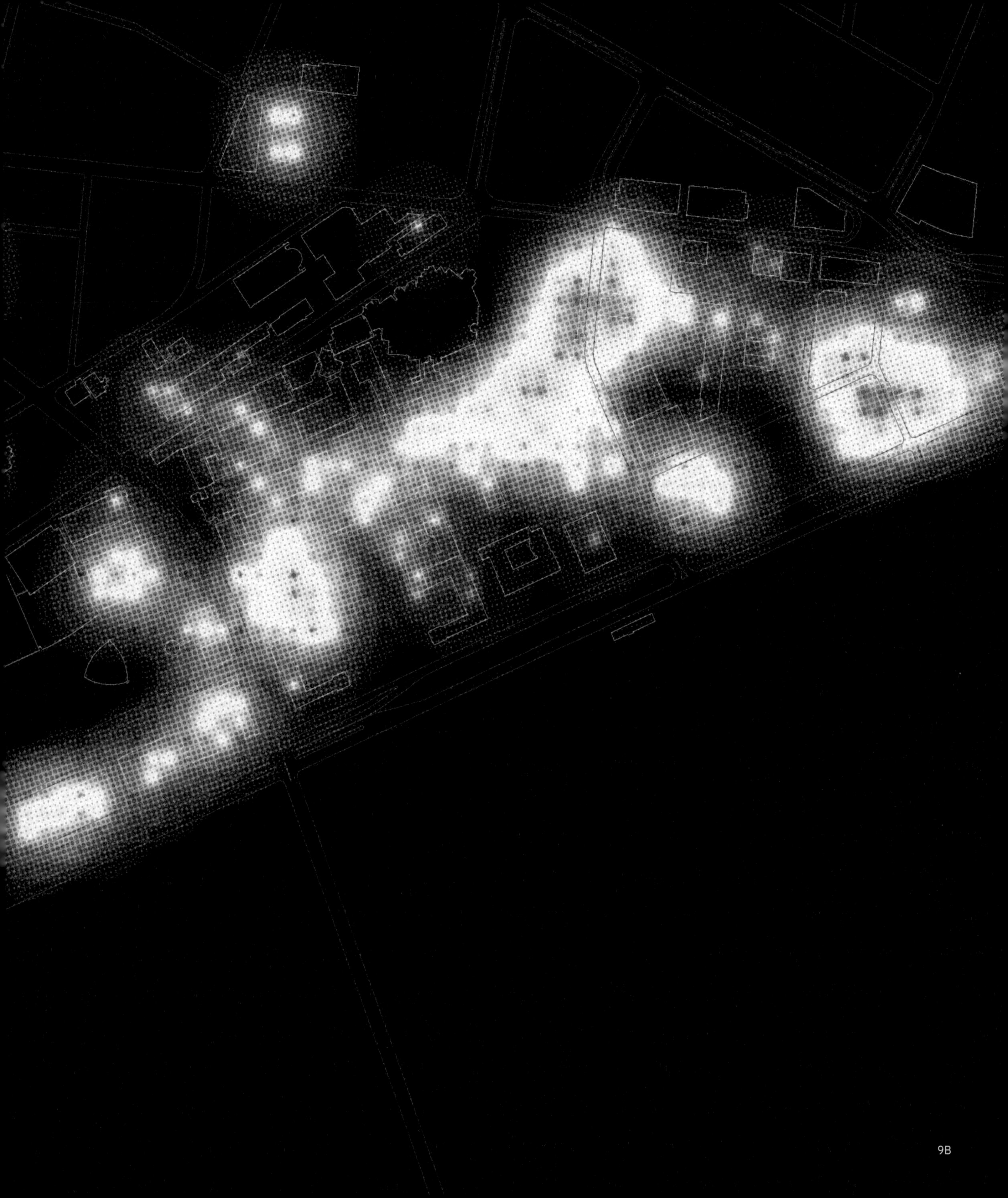

9B

10.
NYTE: New York Talk Exchange — 2007

NYTE: New York Talk Exchange, which debuted as part of the Museum of Modern Art's exhibition *Design and the Elastic Mind*, shows how telecommunication exchanges reveal and alter existing geographic and administrative realities. In the information age, telecommunications bind people across space. This project uses the data that such connections produce to explore the relationships that New Yorkers have with the rest of the world: How does New York City connect to other cities? How do these connections shift from neighborhood to neighborhood, and from hour to hour?

Several visualizations were created to answer these questions. The first, *Globe Encounters*, uses real-time 3-D animations to show New York's connections to other world cities—a kind of "globalization in real time" (10A). The size of the glow on each city corresponds to the amount of IP traffic flowing between it and New York. The second map, *Pulse of the Planet*, shows how the connections change as night and day sweep across the earth (10B). It also reveals that New York follows a twenty-four-hour schedule, a true city that never sleeps. The third visualization, *World within New York*, shows how the city's neighborhoods reach out to the rest of the world via the AT&T telephone network (10C). Each pixel represents two square kilometers and is colored according to the global regions with which its residents communicate the most (more contact means a taller bar). Also encoded within each pixel is a list of the world cities that together account for 70 percent of all international communication with New York.

10A

NYTE
new york talk exchange
IP traffic | total
outgoing from new york
12:00
new york time
night
morning
afternoon
evening

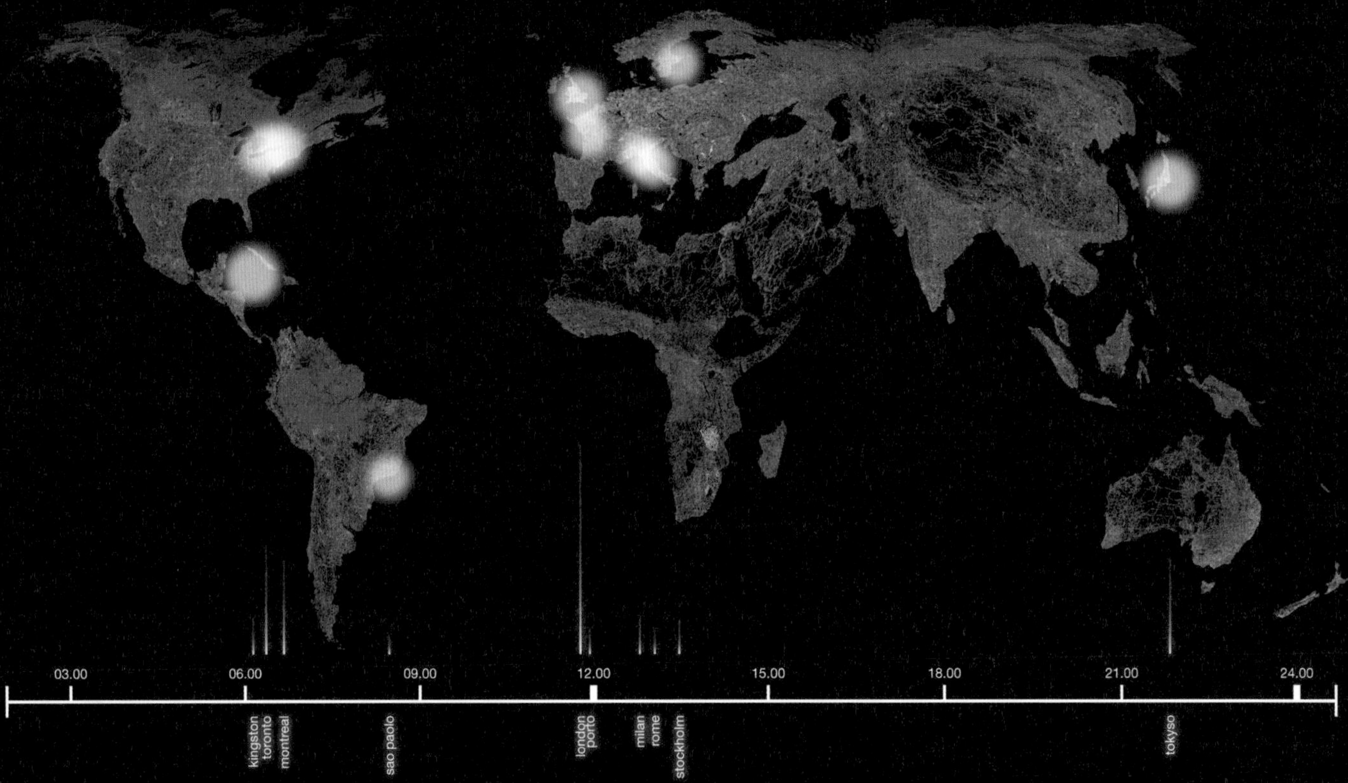
03.00
06.00
09.00
12.00
15.00
18.00
21.00
24.00
kingston
toronto
montreal
sao paolo
london
porto
milan
rome
stockholm
tokyso

World Within New York

World Within New York shows how different neighborhoods reach out to the rest of the world via the AT&T telephone network. The city is divided into a grid of square pixels where each pixel is colored according to the regions of the world wherein the top connecting cities are located. The heights of the color bars represent the proportion of world regions in contact with each neighborhood. Encoded within each pixel is also a list of the top ranking world cities that account for the communications with that particular area of New York.

11.
Borderline — 2010

Borderline redraws Great Britain based on a network of human interactions—moving our understanding of the island beyond its administrative and political borders. The project offers a novel, fine-grained approach to regional delineation by analyzing billions of individual telephone calls, part of the largest non-Internet human network.

The first map displays the strongest 80 percent of links, as measured by total talk time, between areas within Britain (11A). The opacity of each link is proportional to the call time, while the colors represent different regions. An algorithm used network modularity optimization analysis to determine the regions: connections *within* are stronger than connections *between* regions. In the next figure, Great Britain gets more and more finely partitioned, with ever higher modularity, to identify regions of different dimensions (11B). Finally, the last image combines several modularity optimization methods and compares the results with Great Britain's official political boundaries, which are indicated with thick black lines (11C).

As it turns out, the algorithmic partitioning agrees with existing administrative, geographic, and historical boundaries to a large extent. But there are a few notable exceptions: some parts of Wales, for instance, have much stronger connections to cities in western England than to the rest of Wales, suggesting that in some ways the historical distinction between England and Wales may be obsolete. The value of this work is that it shows how analyzing information flows in telecommunication data could be a useful tool in drawing political boundaries. Although the border between England and Wales might not be redrawn, this algorithm is being applied to telephone data from countries where the redrawing of political maps is a very real possibility—even a legal necessity. In such cases, analysis of communication patterns could help define boundaries that reflect actual lived experiences and human connections.

11A

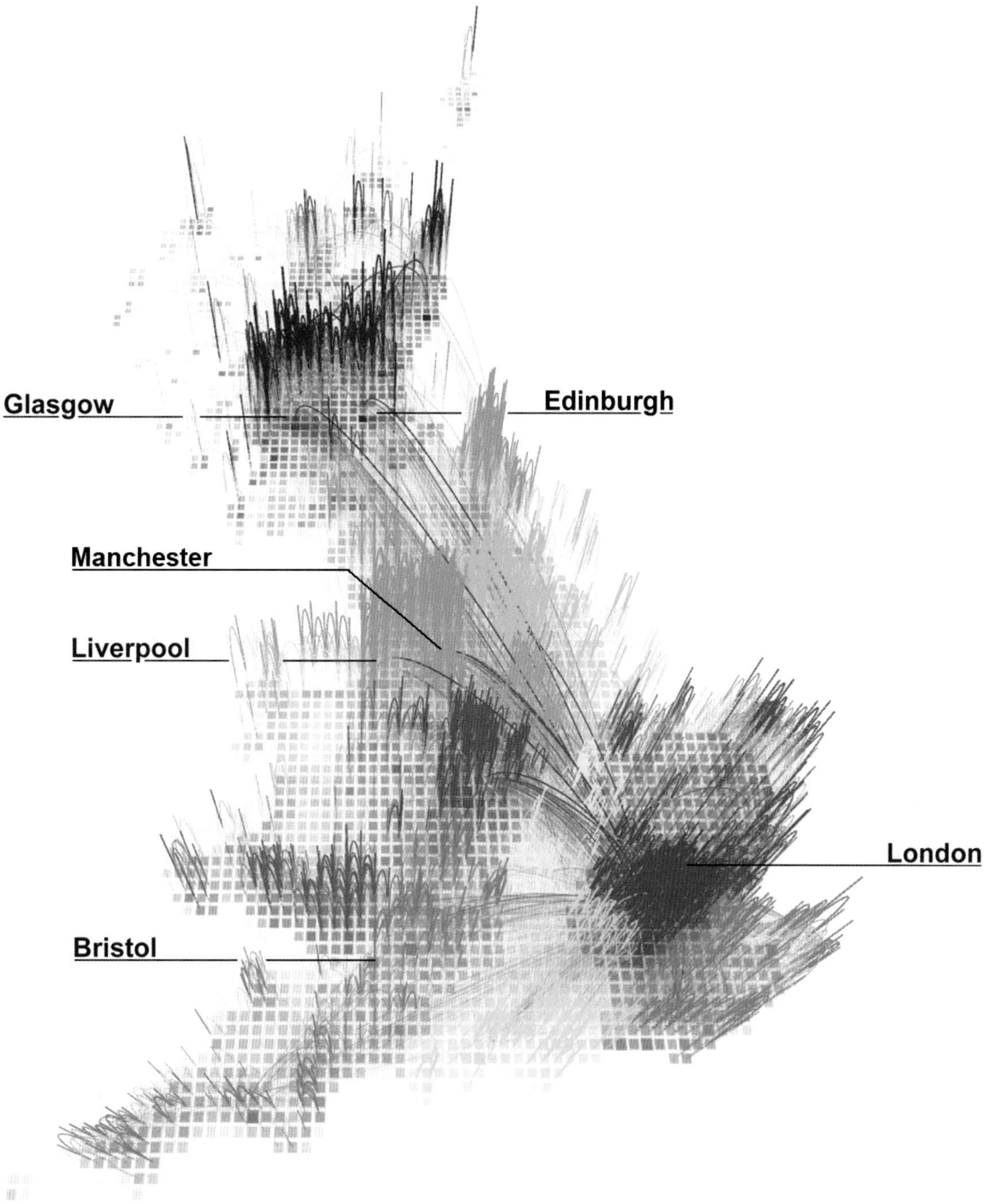
Glasgow
Edinburgh
Manchester
Liverpool
London
Bristol

a

b

c

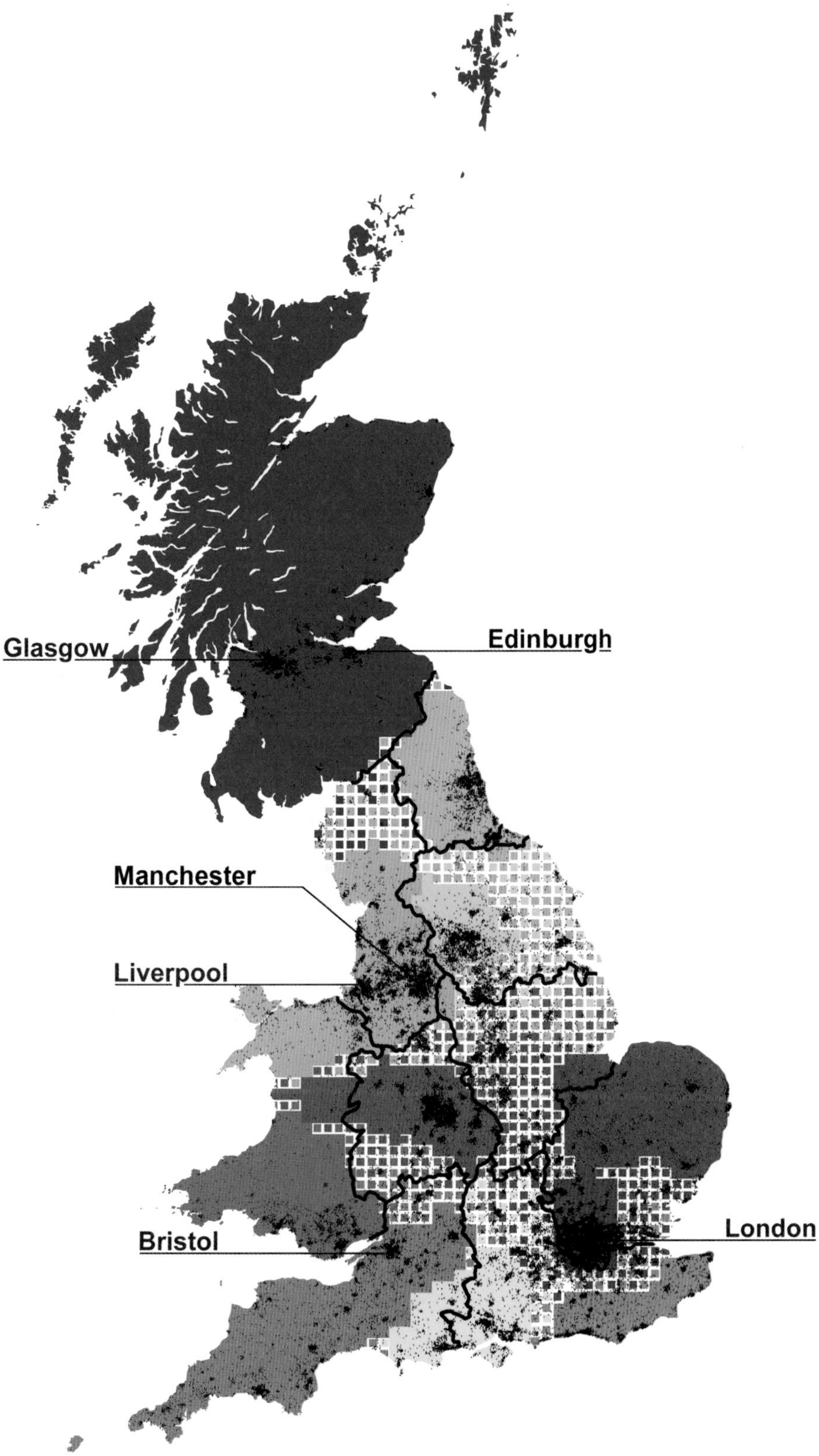
Glasgow
Edinburgh
Manchester
Liverpool
Bristol
London

12.
The Connected States of America — 2011

The Connected States of America uses telecommunication data to show communicative realities that transcend existing borders in the US, just as Neil Gustafson did in the 1960s. Relative to those in the UK, the regions created by these information flows in the US align far less neatly to political and administrative borders. Anonymized mobile phone data show a constant flux of people commuting, migrating, and traveling across the country, without consideration for state boundaries, and concentrating around large cities. Even with all that movement, the ubiquity of mobile phones has allowed people to maintain friendships, family connections, and business relationships across distance with ease. SCL researchers used phone call data to define geographic communities that correspond to such virtual relationships. The striking result is completely at odds with administrative boundaries: some states seamlessly merge, while others split in two (12A). Investigating human interaction networks reveals interesting realities of how we use or ignore space.

The second map shows the three layers of cartography involved: the bottom one is population density per square mile; the middle one depicts the mobile connections between people across the country, with each link representing reciprocal phone calls and grouped, by color, into the relevant data-derived community; and the top one uses the same colors to map these communities over physical space (12B). The project also includes an interactive map that shows the county-to-county social interactions (in total call minutes or total number of SMS messages sent—interestingly, these represent noticeably different communities) through anonymous, aggregated AT&T mobile phone data. By selecting their county, users can see the relationship between it and the rest of the country (12C).

12A

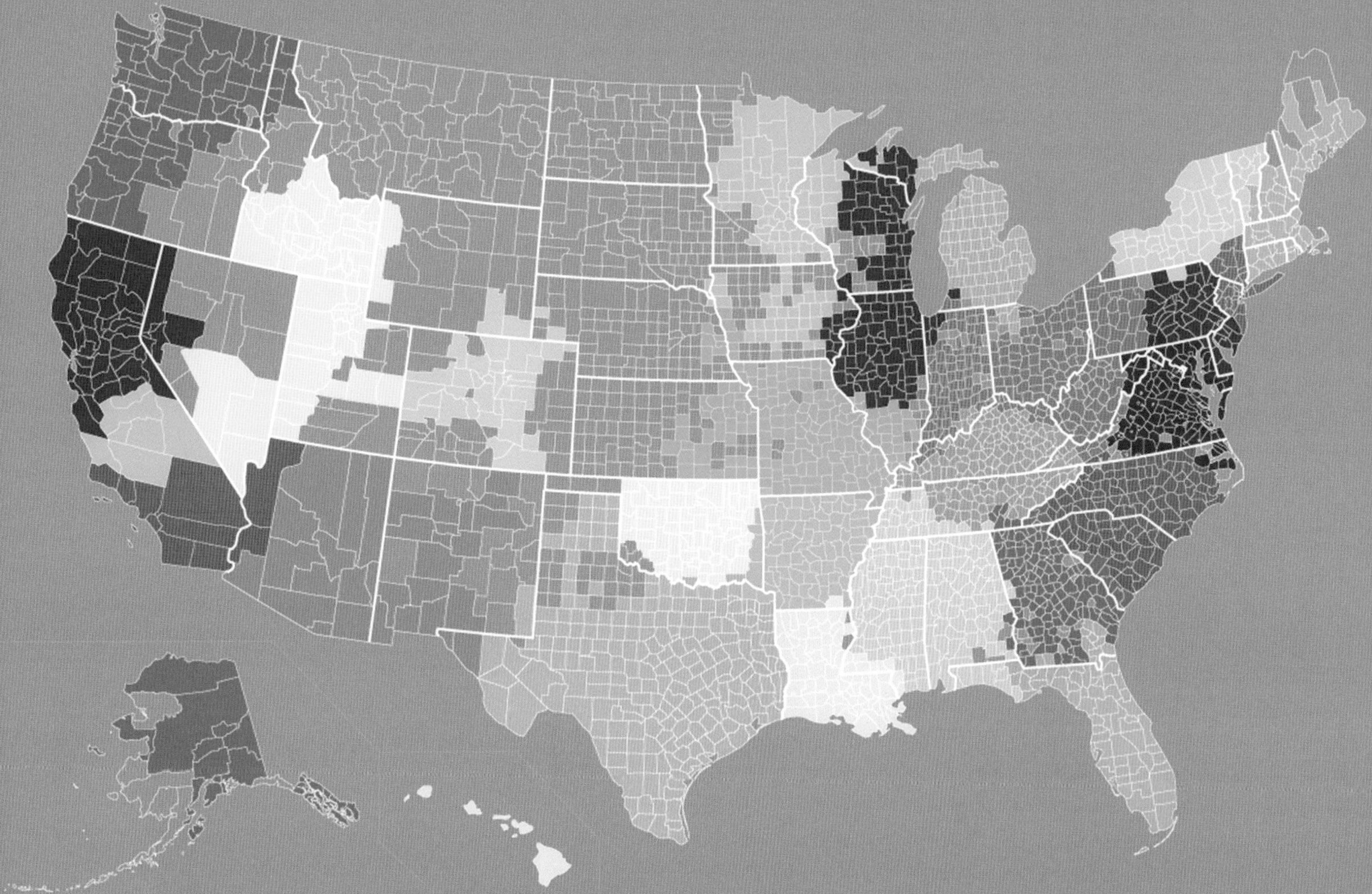

senseable city lab:.:: MIT at&t IBM Research

insufficient data
ppl/sqm
.1 1 10 10^2 10^3 10^4

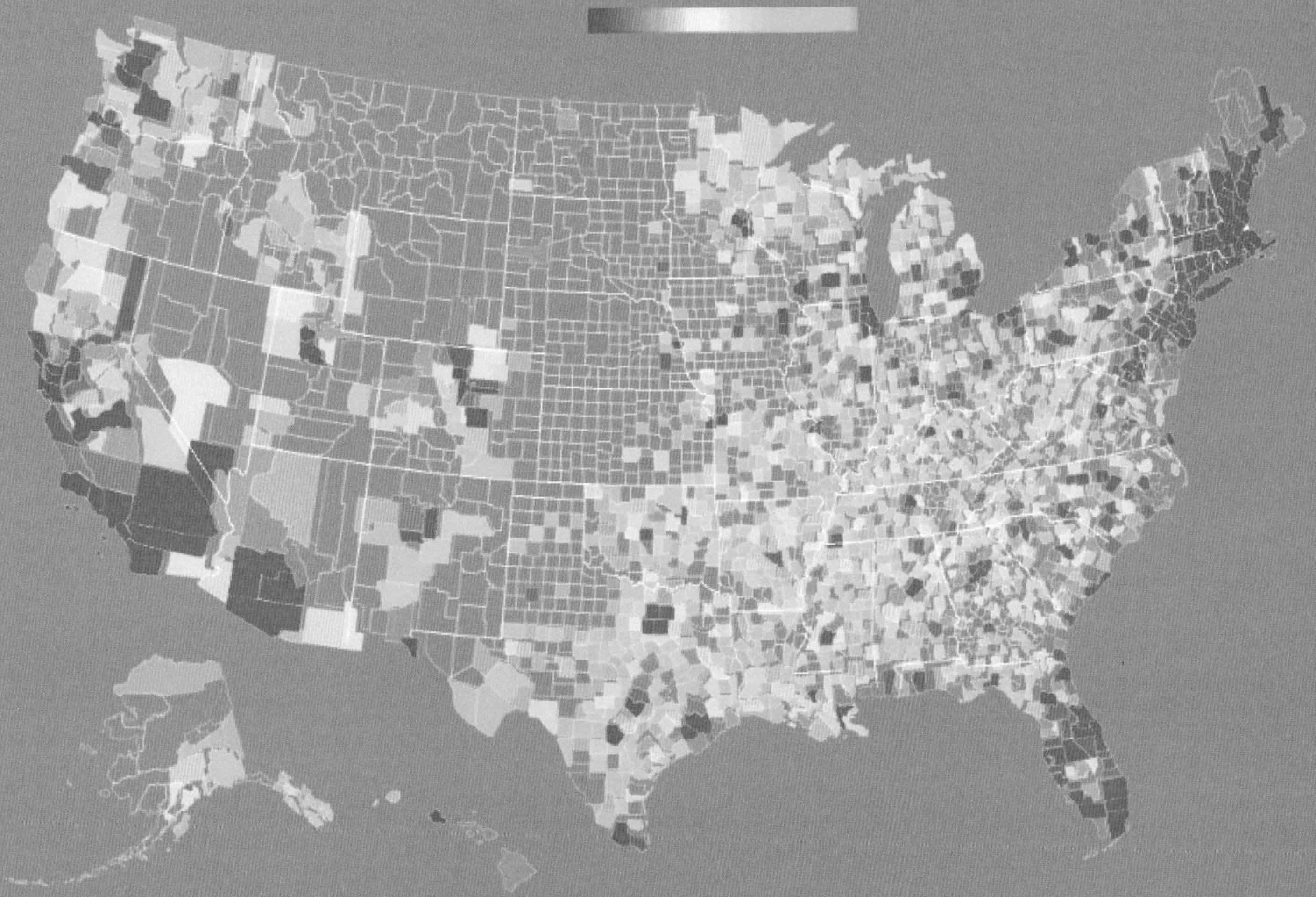

12C

13.
Spring Spree — 2012

Spring Spree maps a different form of information flow than that offered by telecommunication networks. To create these maps, the SCL partnered with the leading Spanish bank BBVA to examine expenditure patterns and Spain at large by using an unprecedented dataset of financial transactions made during la Semana Santa, the week leading up to Easter, in 2011. In this period, 1.4 million individuals and 375,000 businesses performed more than 4 million transactions, totaling over 200 million euros. The Spring Spree maps categorize and color these transactions by type (groceries, gas stations, fashion, bars, and restaurants). Larger dots represent larger expenditures. As these data are plotted, distinctive patterns emerge, such as spikes in the purchase of food in the days preceding the Easter holiday and its much-anticipated, expensive feasts. The map can be animated, tracing Spain's spending as it happened from 16 to 27 April, with graphs on the left summarizing each day's overall pattern (13A–13C). On Easter Sunday itself, and even more so the next day, consumption cratered as Spaniards attended church services, enjoyed the fruits of the previous week's shopping alongside friends and family, and finally returned to their normal lives.

As future Easters come and go, will these spending patterns be replicated? If so, can we use this predictability to improve urban services and better serve city dwellers? The project's next steps aim to delve into the underlying drivers of economic activities, from the risk analysis frameworks of individuals and businesses to the ever-present cultural tides that disrupt them. We can better understand cities by noting the digital footprints left behind by their inhabitants, and we can aspire to help future footprints land in more user-friendly urban environments.

13A

1000€ 500€ 100€
APRIL 2011 TRANSACTIONS IN
GROCERIES GAS STATIONS FASHION BARS AND RESTAURANTS

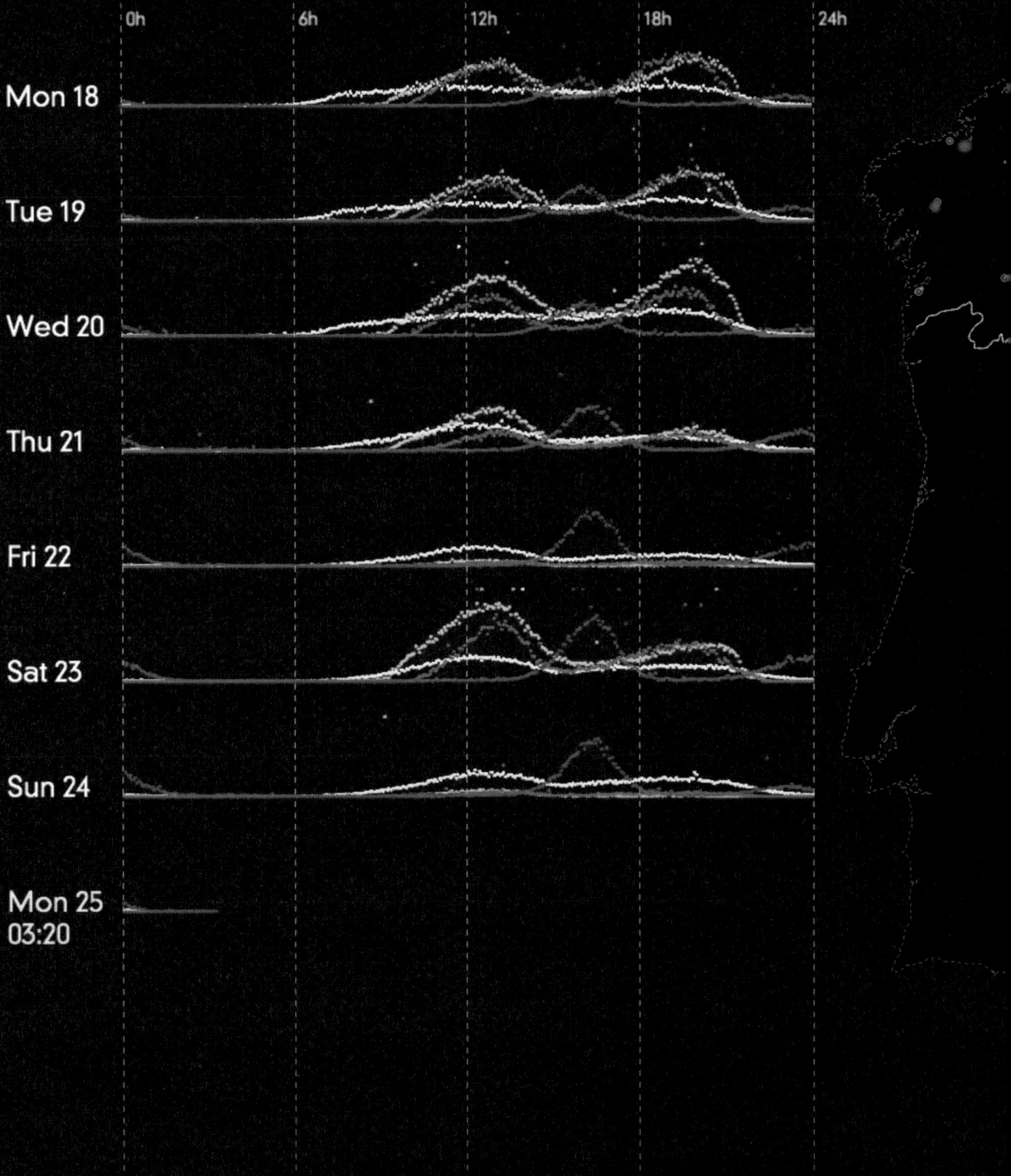
0h
6h
12h
18h
24h
Mon 18
Tue 19
Wed 20
Thu 21
Fri 22
Sat 23
Sun 24
Mon 25
03:20

1000€ 500€ 100€
APRIL 2011 TRANSACTIONS IN
GROCERIES GAS STATIONS FASHION BARS AND RESTAURANTS

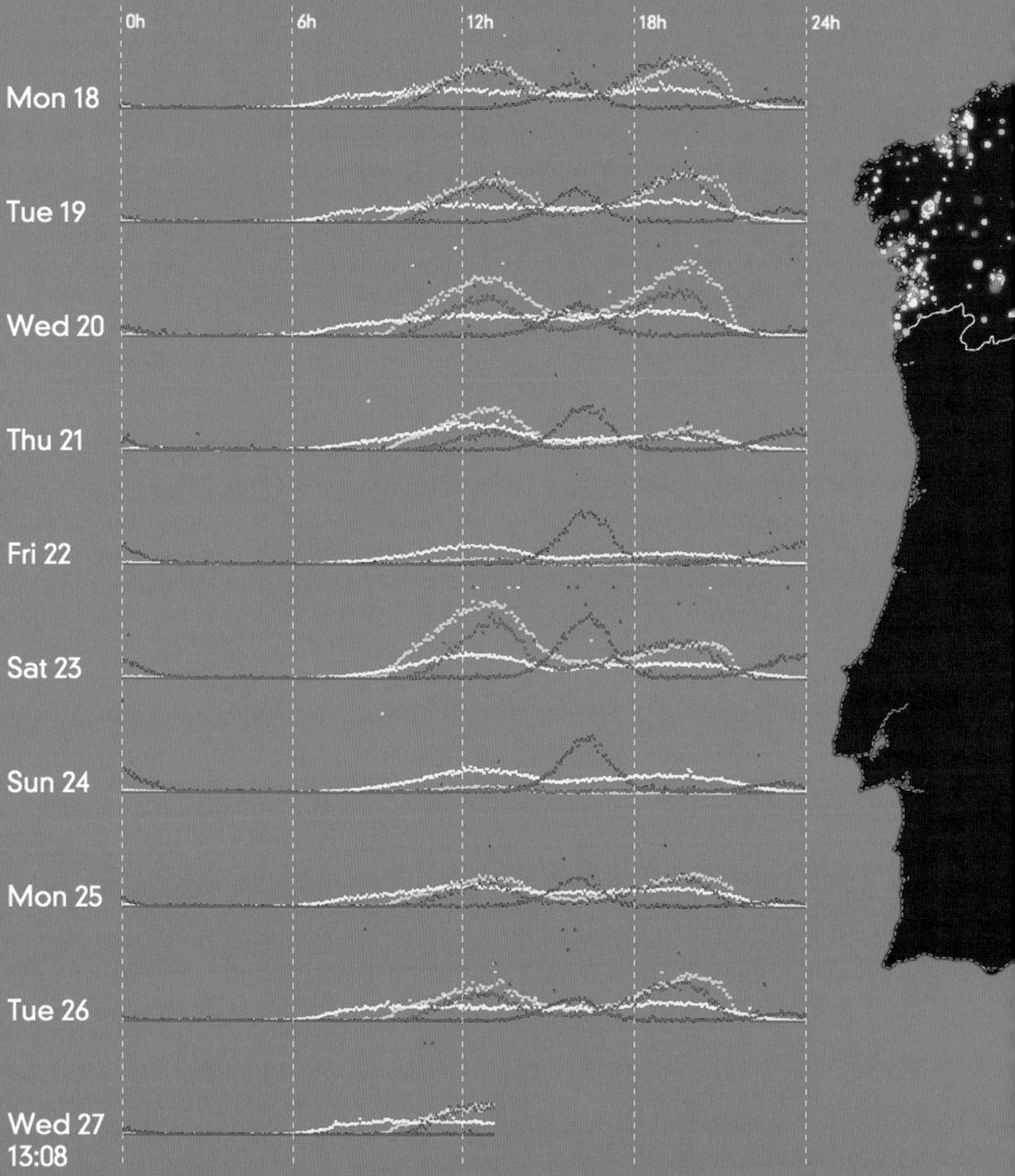
0h
6h
12h
18h
24h
Mon 18
Tue 19
Wed 20
Thu 21
Fri 22
Sat 23
Sun 24
Mon 25
Tue 26
Wed 27
13:08

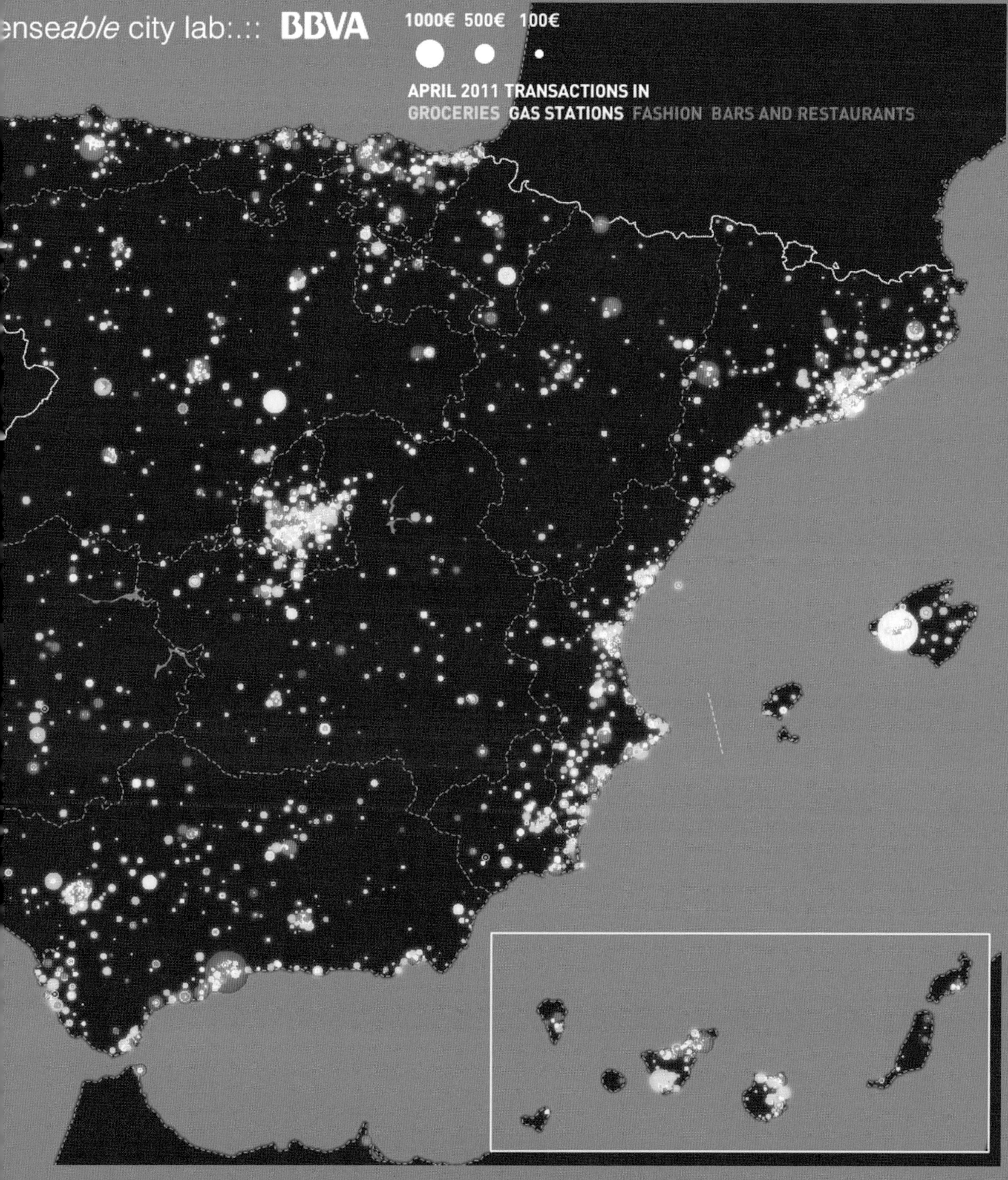

enseable city lab:.::
BBVA
1000€ 500€ 100€
APRIL 2011 TRANSACTIONS IN
GROCERIES GAS STATIONS FASHION BARS AND RESTAURANTS

14.
Signature of Humanity — 2013

For Signature of Humanity, the SCL and the Swedish telecommunications company Ericsson embarked on an unprecedented journey inside the latter's mobile network. This project aimed to identify dynamic patterns, similarities, and differences among major cities around the world by exploring their calls, SMS messages, data requests (initiated by either users or background applications), and data traffic.

Preliminary results suggested that while a city's signature—the amount and typology of its data traffic—is influenced by its cultural background (cities from the same country have similar signatures), all major cities exhibit a similar partitioning into areas with internally consistent patterns of data use. The pulses of cities around the world interact to shape a single signal, the signature of humanity. The SCL's researchers have made a visual approximation of this signature, which aggregates activities done by people around the world at different times (14A). The dots represent the number of people doing each activity, including social networking (white), web browsing (turquoise), and video streaming (blue).

This project led to the creation of a tool, *Many Cities*, that continues to map the virtual flows of mobile phone traffic onto specific urban spaces—collecting information on the number of calls, SMS messages, and data requests and the amount of data uploaded and downloaded by subscribers in, for instance, London (14B), New York (14C), Hong Kong, and Los Angeles during a ten-month period. The application allows mobile operators to check the completeness of their records and define new development strategies and also a more general audience to visualize its (collective) behaviors—and perhaps to change them.

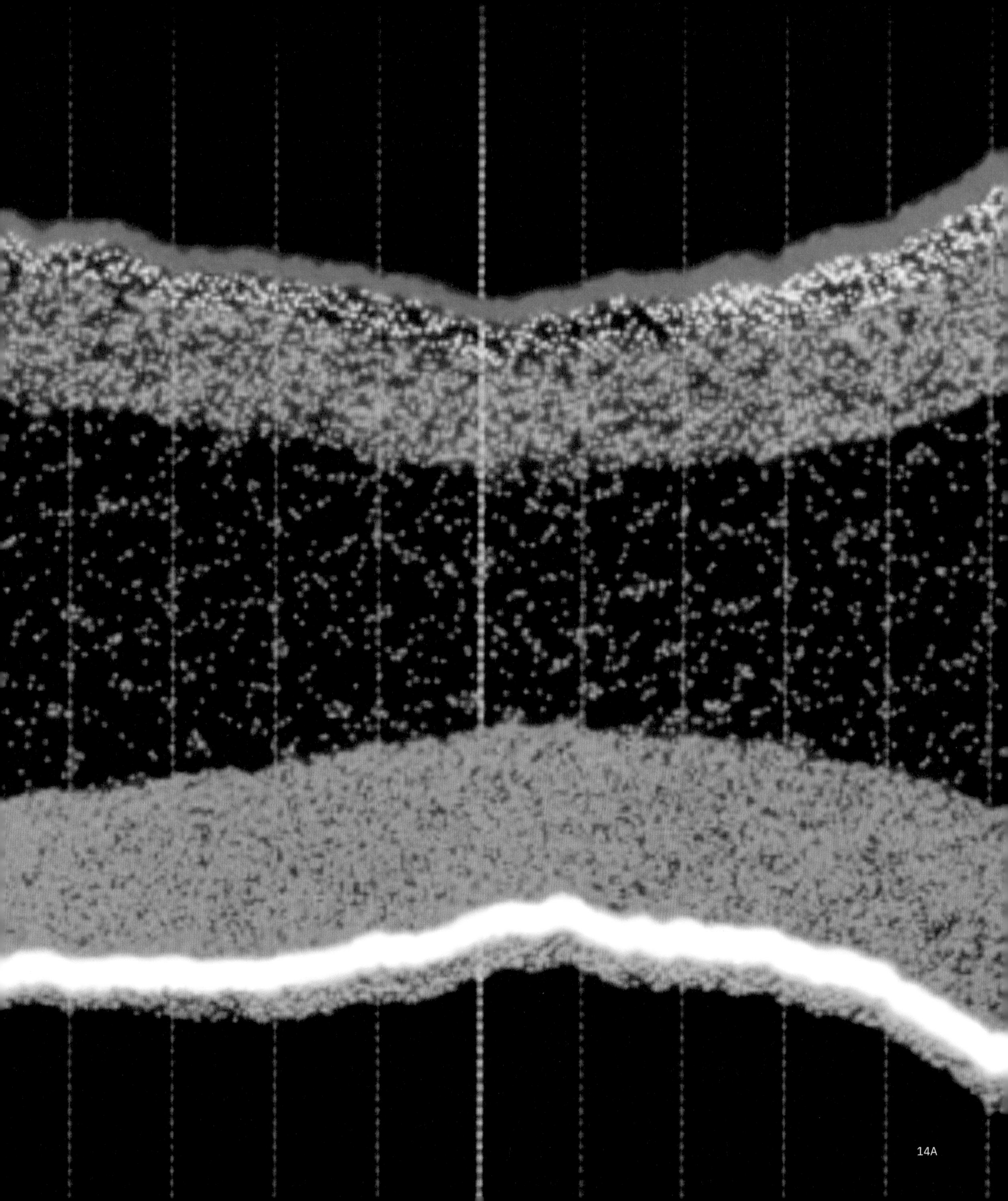

14A

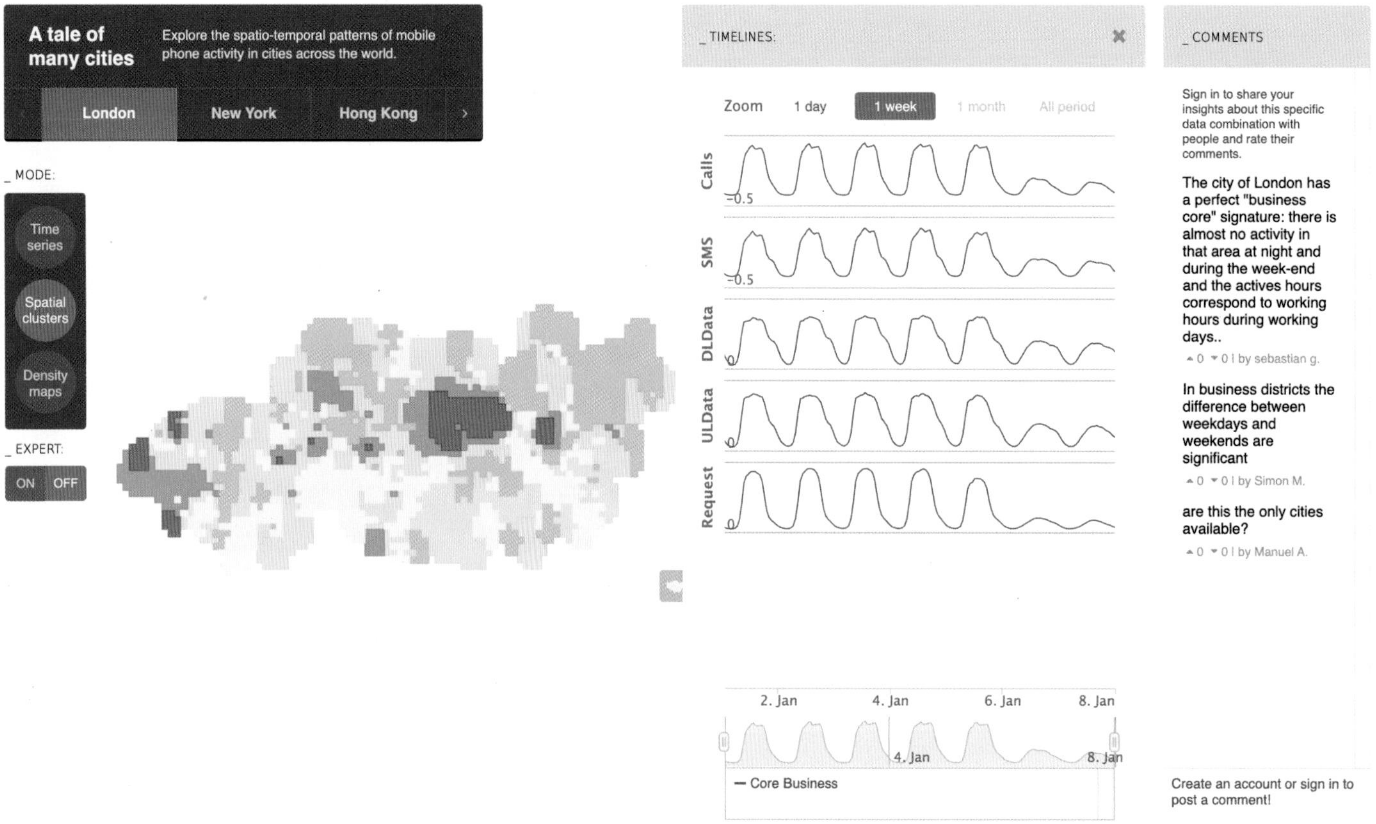
A tale of many cities
Explore the spatio-temporal patterns of mobile phone activity in cities across the world.
London
New York
Hong Kong
_ MODE:
Time series
Spatial clusters
Density maps
_ EXPERT:
ON
OFF
_ TIMELINES:
Zoom
1 day
1 week
1 month
All period
Calls
SMS
DLData
ULData
Request
2. Jan
4. Jan
6. Jan
8. Jan
Core Business
_ COMMENTS
Sign in to share your insights about this specific data combination with people and rate their comments.
The city of London has a perfect "business core" signature: there is almost no activity in that area at night and during the week-end and the actives hours correspond to working hours during working days..
0 0 | by sebastian g.
In business districts the difference between weekdays and weekends are significant
0 0 | by Simon M.
are this the only cities available?
0 0 | by Manuel A.
Create an account or sign in to post a comment!

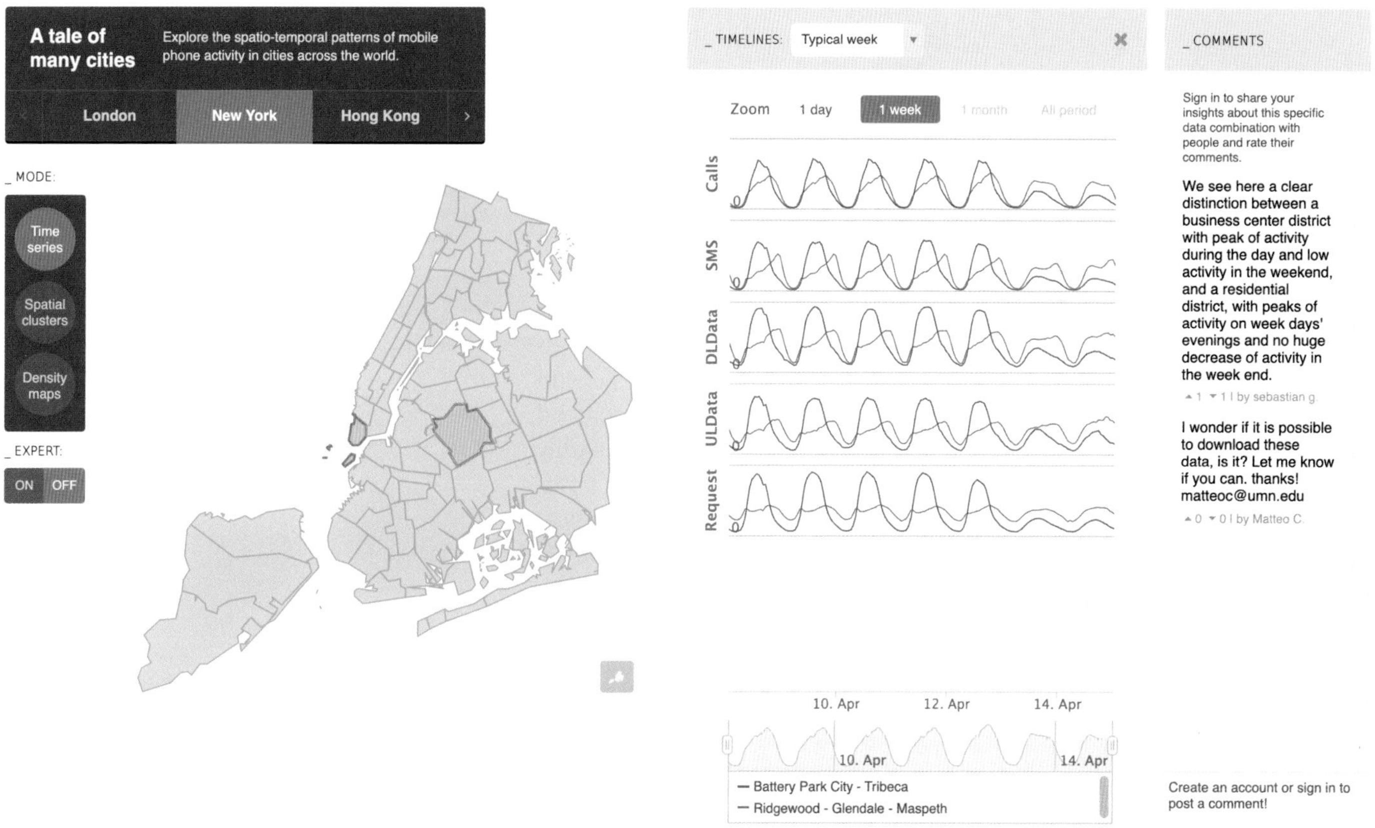
A tale of many cities
Explore the spatio-temporal patterns of mobile phone activity in cities across the world.
London
New York
Hong Kong
_ MODE:
Time series
Spatial clusters
Density maps
_ EXPERT:
ON
OFF
_ TIMELINES:
Typical week
Zoom
1 day
1 week
1 month
All period
Calls
SMS
DLData
ULData
Request
10. Apr
12. Apr
14. Apr
10. Apr
14. Apr
— Battery Park City - Tribeca
— Ridgewood - Glendale - Maspeth
_ COMMENTS
Sign in to share your insights about this specific data combination with people and rate their comments.
We see here a clear distinction between a business center district with peak of activity during the day and low activity in the weekend, and a residential district, with peaks of activity on week days' evenings and no huge decrease of activity in the week end.
1 1 | by sebastian g.
I wonder if it is possible to download these data, is it? Let me know if you can. thanks! matteoc@umn.edu
0 0 | by Matteo C.
Create an account or sign in to post a comment!

15.
Friendly Cities — 2017 and Singapore Calling — 2019

Over the course of two projects, Friendly Cities (2017) and Singapore Calling (2019), the SCL studied cell phone data to measure social and physical segregation in Singapore—and how urban space can overcome these divides. In Friendly Cities, the research team analyzed the calls and location traces of 2.1 million cell phone users, establishing a city-wide social network capable of identifying any pair of phone users as social contacts (i.e., "friends") or strangers. With these metrics, the researchers learned more about the city's physical spaces. Places where friends came together 15A
were said to have *bonding* capability, and places where strangers could encounter one another had social *bridging* capability. At different times and on different days, these values change significantly. For example, weekday bridging is highly concentrated in the Singapore's core (15A). Bonding sites, such as the National University of Singapore and Nanyang Technological University, are more spread out (15B). Friends and acquaintances meet in different places during the week, but bonding and bridging sites overlap significantly on weekends. Among the most important weekend hot spots for both metrics is Orchard Road, Singapore's retail and entertainment hub.

The Singapore Calling project continued this analysis, with the additional data dimension of socioeconomic status. Researchers calculated a communication segregation index (CSI) value for each subject, reflecting how often they texted or called someone outside their socioeconomic cohort. A similar indicator, the physical separation index (PSI), measures how often a physical space facilitates socioeconomic diversity. Mapping CSI, researchers found that while poor and middle-class residents had a diverse range of interactions with other groups, the wealthiest people interacted mostly with a "rich club" of one another (15C). Moreover, segregation levels rise in the city when people are sleeping and eating breakfast in stratified residential areas. When the workday begins, Singapore's shared physical spaces force people to encounter one another—on the bus, in the streets, and in their workplaces (15D). Going to work may not solve social inequities, but it does bring people together.

15B

Bridging Capability
Daytime, Weekdays

11:00-14:00

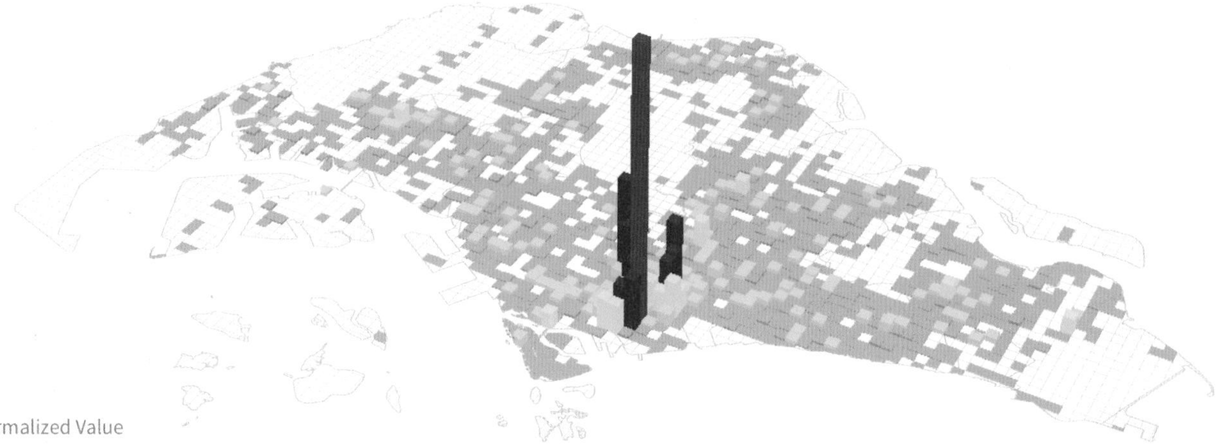

Normalized Value

- 0.31-0.87
- 0.12-0.31
- 0.04-0.12
- 0.01-0.04
- 0.00-0.01

Similarly, the normalized value (i.e., **relative bridging capability**) of a place here refers to its bridging capability normalized by the maximum value across all the places during the sixteen time windows.

Bonding Capability
Daytime, Weekdays

11:00-14:00

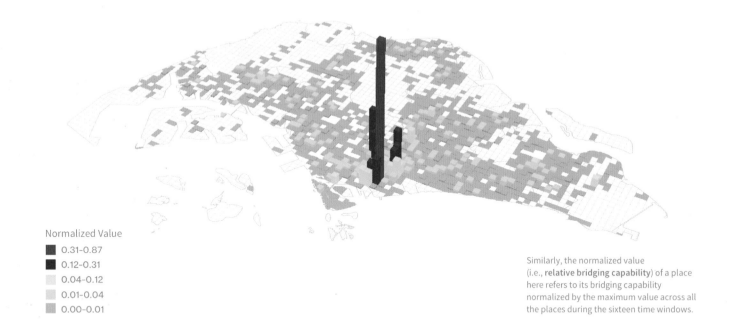

Normalized Value

- 0.35-1.00
- 0.16-0.35
- 0.07-0.16
- 0.02-0.07
- 0.00-0.02

When measuring bonding and bridging capabilities, we separate weekdays and weekends, and each type of day is divided into eight 3-hour time windows. In this figure, the normalized value (i.e., **relative bonding capability**) at each place is calculated as its bonding capability normalized by the maximum value across all the places in the city during the sixteen time windows.

Socio-economic Status
Lower 90-100%
Poorer
Richer
Communication Segregation Index (CSI)
0.706
0.71
0.0 Less Seg.
0.5 Baseline
1.0 More Seg.

As morning commutes begin, segregation levels fall across the city.

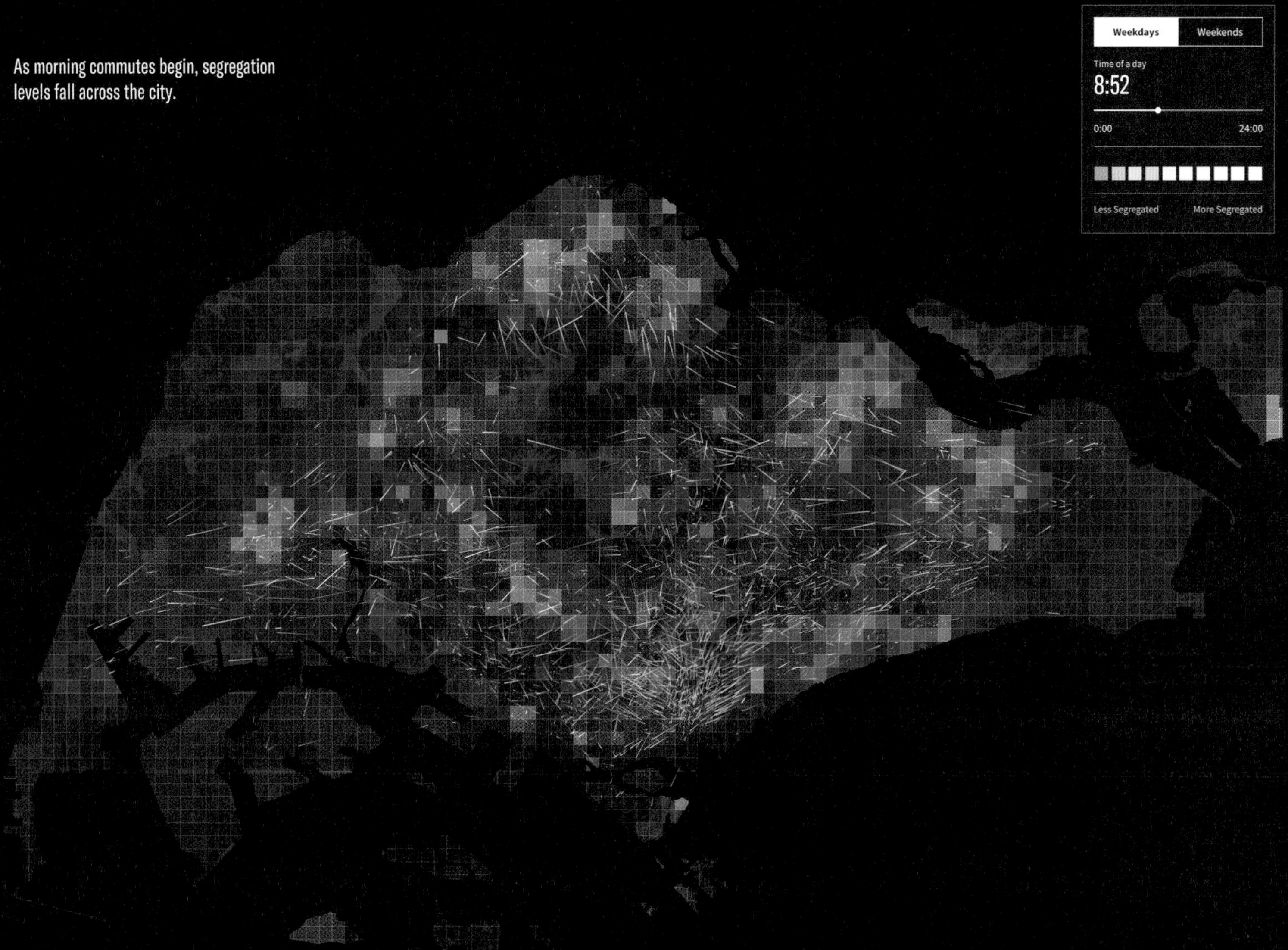

16.
MIT Email Collaboration — 2021

The COVID-19 lockdowns of early 2020, beyond being desperate measures to save lives from a deadly threat, inadvertently became the world's most ambitious experiment on the effects of removing human society from physical space. Those with the means to do so entered a purely digital world, living, working, and socializing remotely—and transforming the makeup of their collective social fabric.

When the world shifts online in a matter of weeks, what changes? To assess the impact of the digital transformation, the SCL mapped MIT's email networks before and after the campus was abruptly closed on 23 March 2020 (16A–16B). Researchers discovered that after the closing, different groups of students, scholars, and faculty members—engineers and humanists, architects and computer scientists—became more insular, communicating more with a smaller number of contacts and eschewing the diversity of the full campus. Digital life allows us to maintain what the sociologist Mark Granovetter calls "strong ties" with close friends and family, but only the serendipity of physical space allows us to form weak ties with casual acquaintances.[8] A society relies on the "strength of weak ties": it is these relationships that connect us to the diversity beyond our immediate circles, exposing us to new ideas and points of view.

The digital world, with its algorithmic filtering, is depriving us of these weak ties. The images below reveal the profound and lasting changes within the MIT email network ever since the 2020 lockdown. The number of weak ties and the rate of weak tie formation fell sharply, and even a year later—when this measure was taken—they were struggling to flicker back to life. The vitality of MIT's social networks depends on the power of physical proximity.

8 Mark S. Granovetter, "The Strength of Weak Ties," *American Journal of Sociology* 78, no. 6 (1973): 1360–1380.

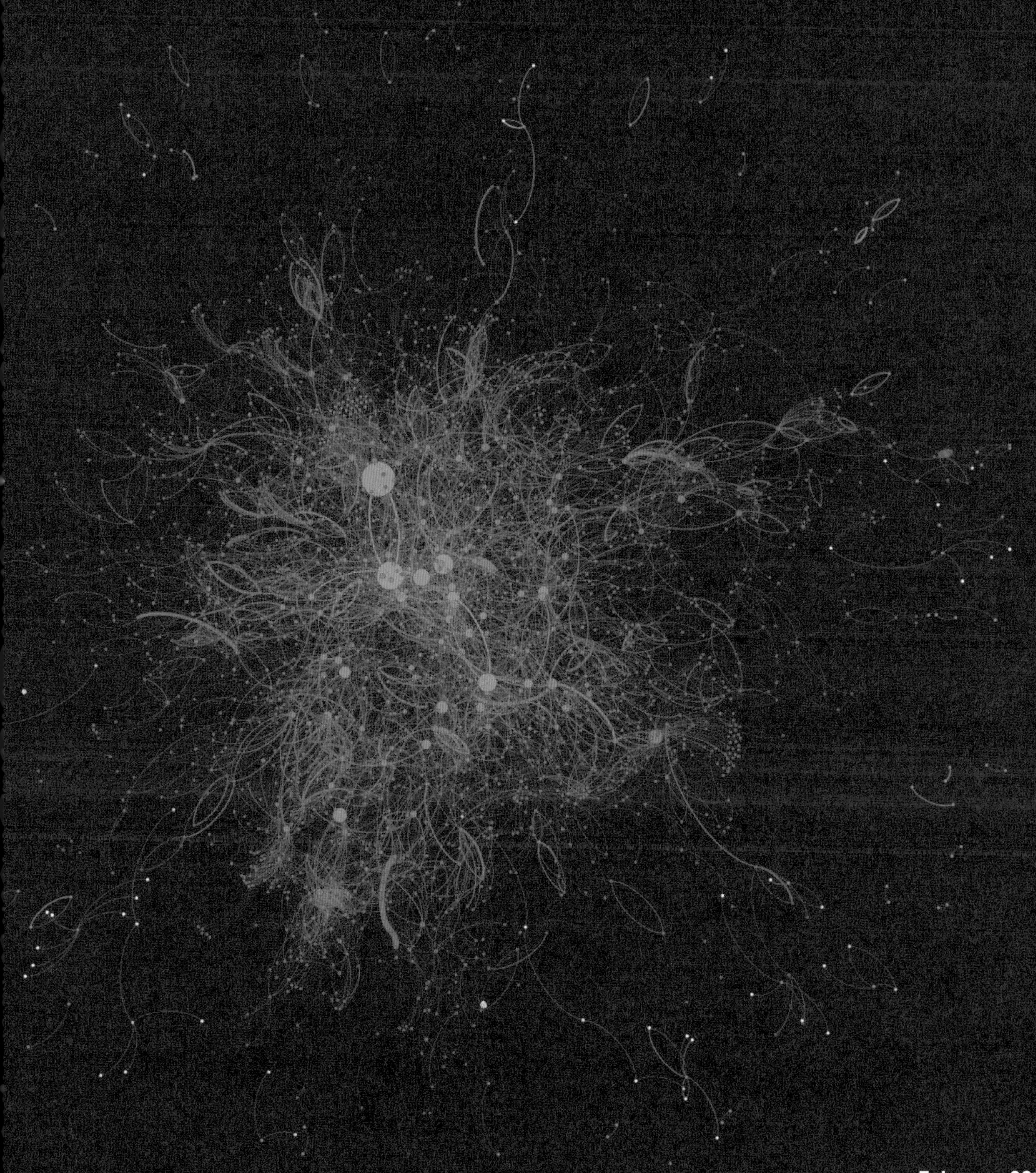

February 20th, 2020

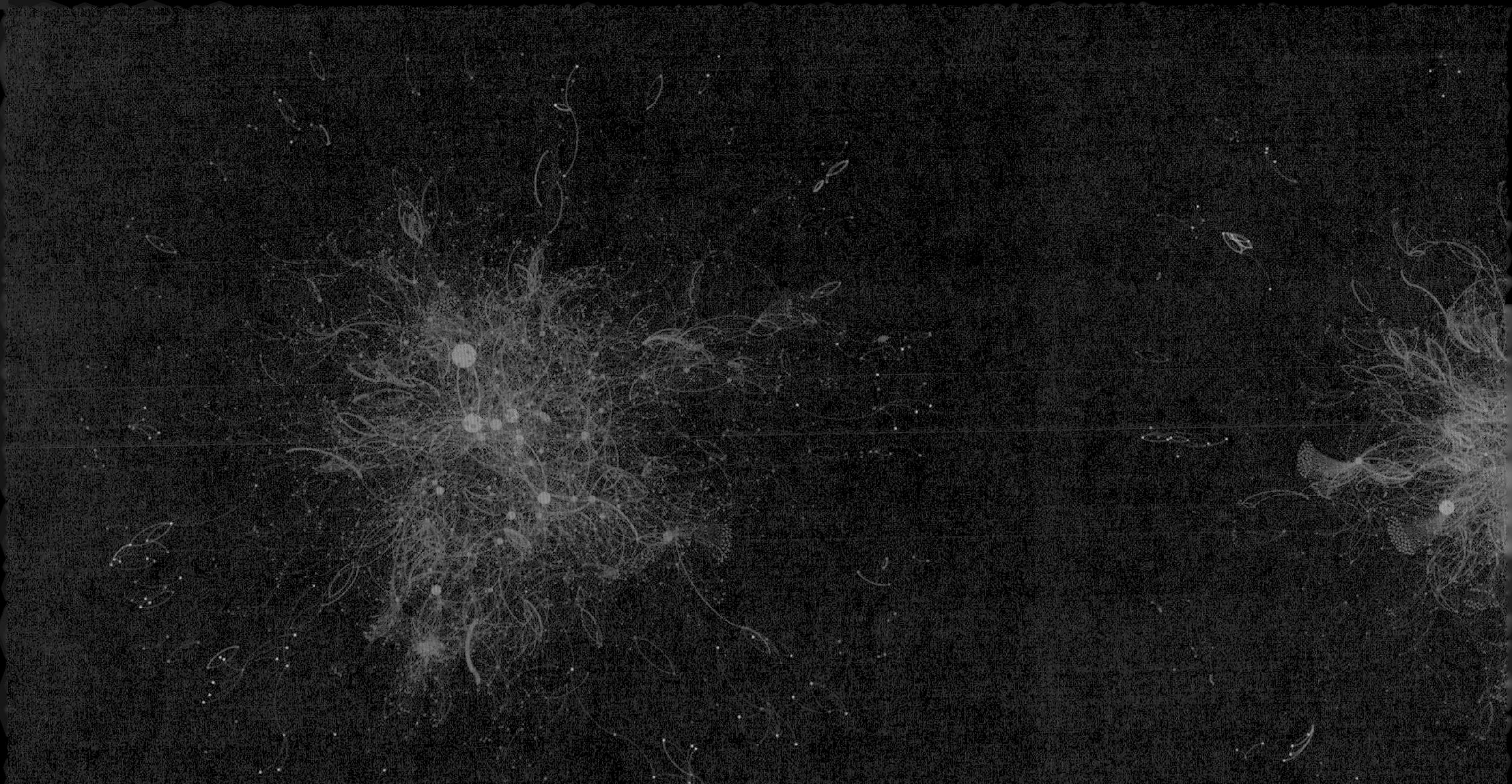

February 20th, 2020

September 24th, 2020

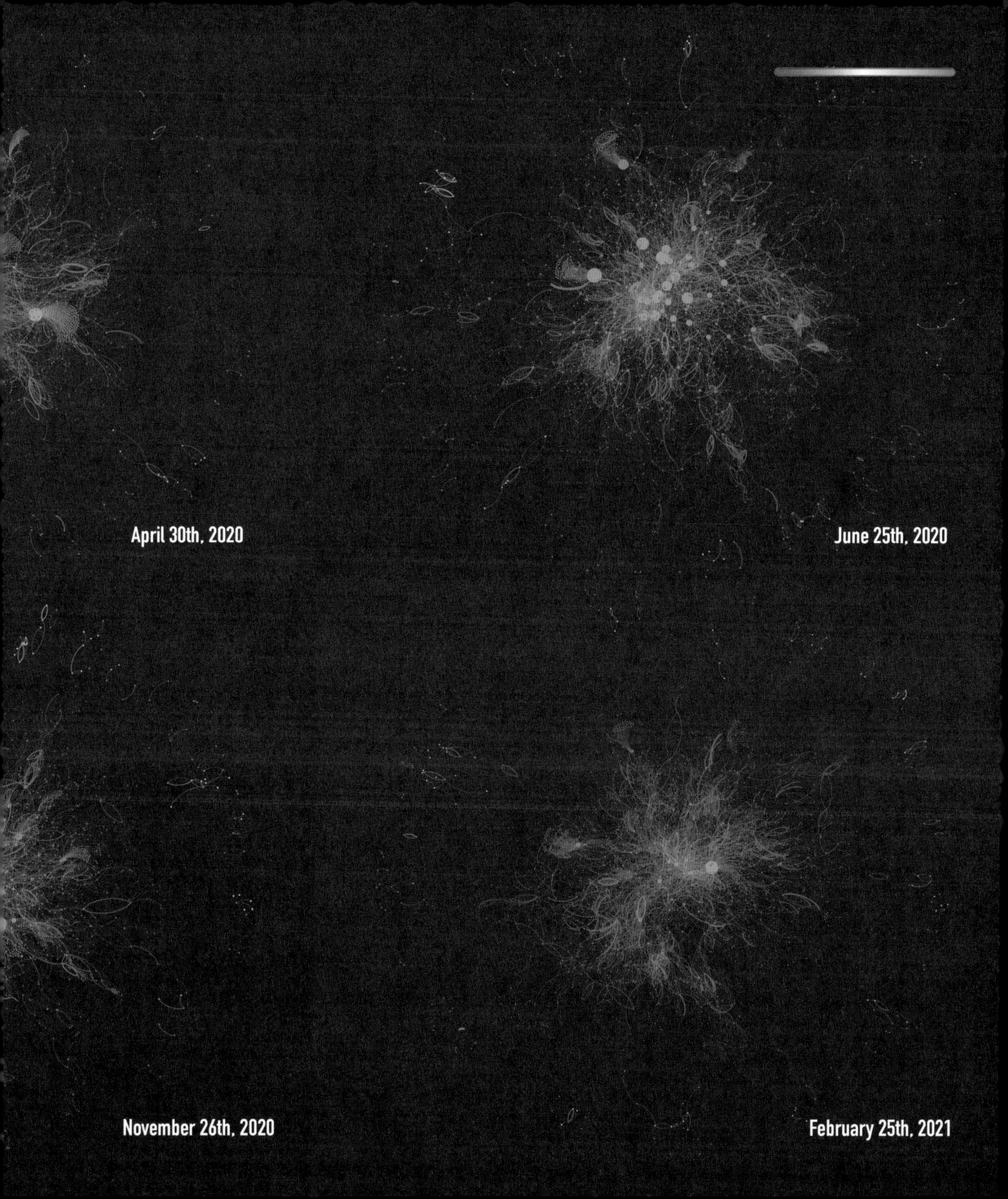
April 30th, 2020
June 25th, 2020
November 26th, 2020
February 25th, 2021

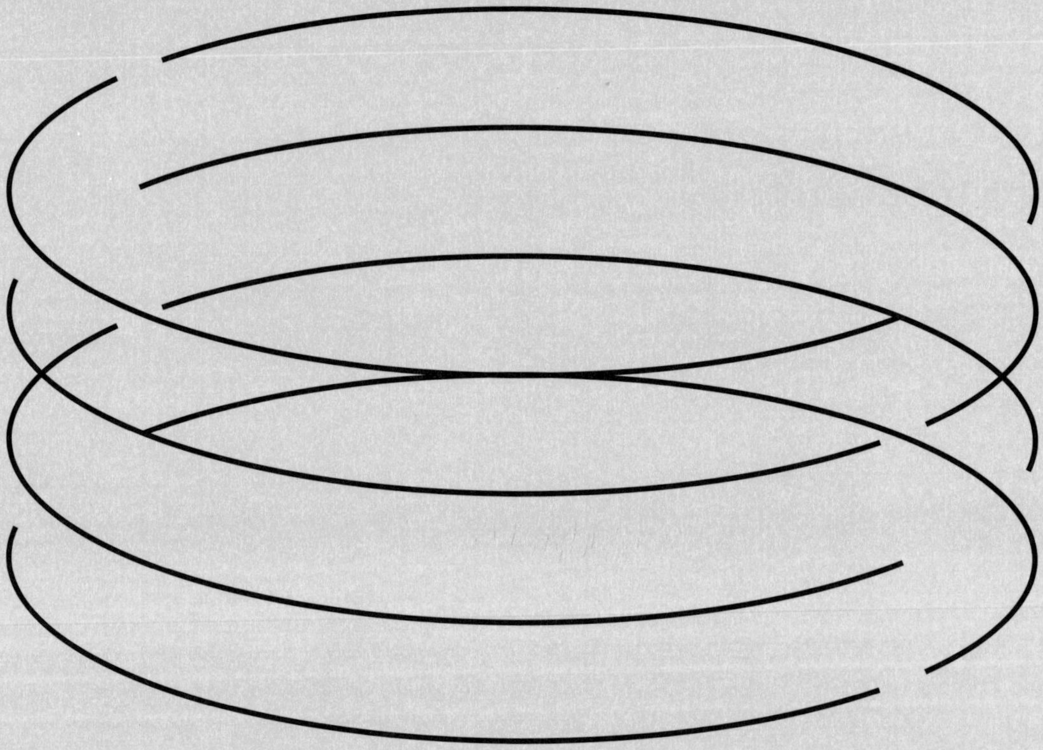

CIRCULATION

CHAPTER — 3

Circulation

During the Industrial Revolution, London was foul, dense, and polluted; disease spread rampantly. As city dwellers watched their neighbors fall sick, the terror of illness was fueled by the mystery of its spread. Prevailing speculations about transmission attributed it to everything from a type of bad air, or "miasma," to divine retribution, and people invented treatments and preventive measures that were no less imaginative.

The physician John Snow, however, approached the question systematically, beginning with what could be empirically charted: the spread of illness across urban space. Using cartography as a diagnostic tool, he identified a cluster of cases surrounding a single water pump and concluded that its well was contaminated.[1] Because of his map, the area was quarantined, the contagion was mitigated, and the standard practices of urban sanitation and utilities management were transformed. Building on this methodology, Snow went on to pioneer modern epidemiology.[2] Beyond mapping sewers or utility infrastructure—a planning tool conceptually no different from an ordinary street map—Snow had set a precedent for depicting flows themselves: the biological metabolism of the city.

A cartographic tradition emerged from the idea of charting flows through urban space, producing such documents as the map of the Great Chicago Fire of 1871, which visualized the origin and spread of the blaze in order to pinpoint vulnerable building types. In the 1950s, a conceptually similar map showed global urban flows from an unprecedented perspective, through high-resolution satellite imaging that captured international light patterns. This revealed population density and energy consumption—proxies for human settlement and development patterns.

1 John Snow, *On the Mode of Communication of Cholera* (London: John Churchill, 1849).

2 Donald Cameron and Ian G. Jones, "John Snow, the Broad Street Pump and Modern Epidemiology," *International Journal of Epidemiology* 12, no. 4 (1983): 393–396.

Fast-forward to recent decades. The birth of the Internet pushed the range of imaging tools to even greater extremes, from large-scale surveys of human activity down to nearly invisible fine-grained sensors. Projects such as Trash Track support a radical notion of "smart dust," tiny geolocating digital tracers running through the trash-removal "blood-stream" and revealing the national metabolism of American waste flows. This case demonstrates the broad implications of atomized computing and its capacity to expose the inner workings of our increasingly patchwork and invisible metropolitan systems. Revealing these circulations—especially those pertaining to less appetizing domains, such as garbage or pollution—may help us feel responsible for their consequences.

As technology continues to advance, sensors continue to shrink and fill daily life, giving us new ways of understanding complex urban and interurban ecologies. Air and water quality, for example, are the subjects of pioneering research at the SCL. To study the air, the SCL exploited the power of mobile sensors—which capture far more data, at a far more reasonable price point, than static devices placed at every corner—mounted on bikes in Copenhagen and on trucks in Cambridge, Massachusetts. Beyond their efficacy, the SCL demonstrated also the narrative power of these technologies with an incisive comparison of commuters' airscapes in Hong Kong and Shenzhen, which revealed profound geographic disparities. To study the water, two sets of scanning devices were invented: sewage collection robots that can be deployed underground, and autonomous fleets of diagnostic water-sampling quadcopters—ecological drones that descend from above.

In the near future, sensors will disperse even further, integrating with urban infrastructure such as the sewer network. Medical science is beginning to address humans' individual microbiomes—the ecologies of living microorganisms that inhabit our bodies—and urban science may yet discover humanity's macrobiome, the bionomic flows that define our collective health patterns. With real-time analysis as granular as the attention we give to our own bodies, we can untangle the metabolic complexity of the "urban biome." For example, studding the sewer system with sensors could allow researchers to have their fingers on the pulse of the city's wellness, pinpointing disease outbreaks, drug use, leakages, or other deficiencies. Across a breadth of scales, digital-biological sensing could become an active network that reports its own metabolic condition and informs its constituents. John Snow's vision—cartography as a diagnostic tool—has been equipped with real-time and multidimensional sensors and projected across cyberspace for anyone who knows where to look. Today, more than ever, we have the power to map, analyze, and improve the health and wellness of our cities.

01

01. JOHN SNOW, MAP OF DEATHS FROM CHOLERA IN AND AROUND BROAD STREET, GOLDEN SQUARE, 1855.

After a dramatic outbreak of cholera hit London's Soho in 1854, the physician John Snow drew a dot map which revealed that the cases were clustered around a specific water pump on Broad Street. Eventually, after members of the city government who worked with statistics were convinced to help Snow collect more information, the pump's well was discovered to be taking water from sewage-polluted sections of the Thames. Before Snow, it was thought that cholera spread in an unspecified way through the air; he, however, was convinced that contaminated water was the culprit. To prove his theory, he did extensive research, mapping the victims' drinking habits and proximity to one another and to the city's wells. Snow's work contributed to the development of the modern germ theory of disease. It also pioneered the idea of diagnostic mapping: by visualizing certain flows, like that of disease, over physical space, important discoveries about a city's ecology and health can be made.

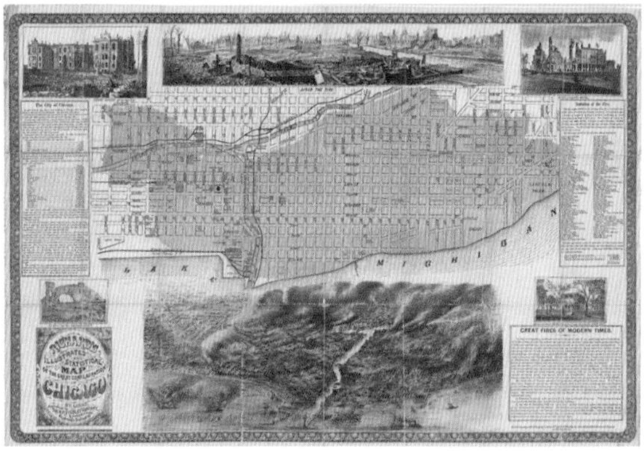

02

02. R. P. STUDLEY COMPANY, RICHARD'S ILLUSTRATED AND STATISTICAL MAP OF THE GREAT CONFLAGRATION IN CHICAGO, 1871.

In October 1871, a dramatic fire left large swaths of Chicago in ruins. A series of detailed maps was produced in the aftermath, like the one to the left by the R. P. Studley Company, depicting the extent and progress of the catastrophe as a large red stain on streets and buildings. These maps turned out to be useful tools during the reconstruction process, helping officials understand how the city's layout and building materials had contributed to the fire's spread. Informed by the missteps that caused the Great Fire, builders now used more fire-resistant materials. This map is thus among the first, alongside Snow's, to demonstrate the merits of tracking the flows of specific events—especially the most drastic ones—instead of just representing the city as a static entity.

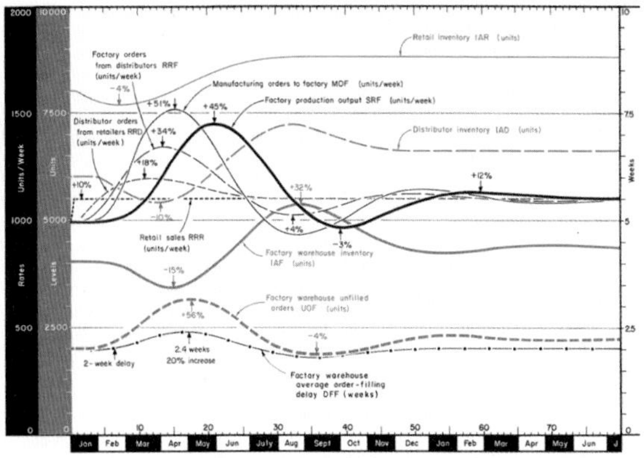

Figure 15-18 (Repeat of Figure 2-2) Response of production-distribution system to a sudden 10% increase in retail sales.

03

03. JAY WRIGHT FORRESTER, RESPONSE OF PRODUCTION-DISTRIBUTION SYSTEM TO A SUDDEN 10% INCREASE IN RETAIL SALES, 1961.

The American computer engineer and MIT professor Jay Wright Forrester designed a modeling program to illustrate cause and effect in complex organizations and systems. By analyzing mid-1950s factories and supply chain dynamics, he laid the basis for a managerial logic known as system dynamics, a complex way of understanding the workings of multivariable systems. Forrester started out as an electric engineer, but when he accepted a professorship at the MIT Sloan School of Management he began investigating how his expertise could inform the running of successful corporations. His resulting research, including books and numerous diagrams, drastically changed corporate management. System dynamics, the field Forrester created, studies the interactions between elements in dynamic systems through simulations, and views the complex, circular, and at times illogical relationships among these elements as just as important to the working of the system as the types of individual elements themselves. Forrester thus brought a new logic to management by adding a dynamic dimension to the mapping of complex systems, based not only on the fixed precepts of rational economic theory but also on the shifting relationships within systems.

04

04. BUCKMINSTER FULLER, DOME OVER MANHATTAN, 1960.

In 1960, the American inventor Buckminster Fuller had the provocative idea of placing a geodesic dome two miles (3.2 kilometers) wide and one mile (1.6 kilometers) high over midtown Manhattan. The dome would alter the urban weather, regulating the climate and reducing the energy output from sources such as heating by 20 percent, thereby also reducing pollution. According to Fuller's plan, the dome would stretch from 62nd to 22nd Street and be composed of shatterproof one-way glass reinforced with wire, so that from the outside it would seem like a bubble-shaped mirror but from the inside would appear as clear as the sky—decreased pollution would compensate for any slight damage to the view from the glass. Although farfetched, Fuller's proposal was also farsighted, in its recognition that in the future our urban biomes would require technological solutions to regulate their ecological flows so as to satisfy the needs of both the environment and the population. In fact, the weather threats facing big cities like New York because of climate change have caused some people to reconsider Fuller's idea: geodesic domes are very efficient temperature-regulating devices, and his proposal for Manhattan would weigh only four thousand tons (3.6 million kilograms).

CHAPTER • 3

Circulation ↓
MIT Senseable City Lab Projects

17.
Trash Track — 2009

18.
Copenhagen Wheel — 2009

19.
One Country, Two Lungs — 2014

20.
Waterfly — 2015

21.
Underworlds — 2015

22.
City Scanner — 2017

23.
Urban Sensing — 2018

24.
Roboat Flows — 2020

17.
Trash Track — 2009

Trash Track was one of the SCL's first projects that sought to track and map the metabolism of a city or country—in this case through its waste system. Inspired by the NYC Green Initiative, the project focused on exposing the challenges of waste management and sustainability and revealing the potential of digital-biological sensing. In collaboration with the city of Seattle, the SCL deployed hundreds of small, location-aware tags. These sensors were a first step in the development of smart dust, or a network of tiny locatable and addressable microelectromechanical systems. Attached to different pieces of trash, the tags revealed the final journey of everyday objects through the city's waste management system—and beyond (17A). Volunteer participants could then trace the trajectory of objects they had thrown away, like an aluminum can (17B) or a plastic container of liquid soap (17C).

Unlike the movements of people, these circulations are less visible to urbanites in their day-to-day lives. Digital maps and other technologies have the chance to expose this important information and reveal the existence of a diverse range of urban metabolisms. Trash Track was an initial investigation into the *removal chain*, equally important but far less visible than the well-studied supply chain. By making its results publicly available, it promoted the adoption of a bottom-up approach to managing resources, encouraging people to modify their behavior thanks to pervasive technologies. The well-designed invisibility of the waste disposal process has caused many of us to live under the illusion that trash vanishes upon being abandoned. Internalizing the contrary reality—our bottle caps are sitting (and not biodegrading) in a dump halfway across the country—may help us to realize the consequences of a throwaway culture whose convenience is destroying our environment. In 2016, the SCL expanded on this research with Monitour, a project that used similar technology to track the international routes of electronic waste leaving the United States.

TATE
COUNTRY
batteries
in Roseville MN
Motorola cell phone
battery recycling
CFL
Louis, Missouri, Total Metal Recycling
Printer cartridge
Recycling Solutions Inc.(La Vergne, TN)
Batteries
Metal Conversion Technologies
Samsung cell phone
EcoPhones

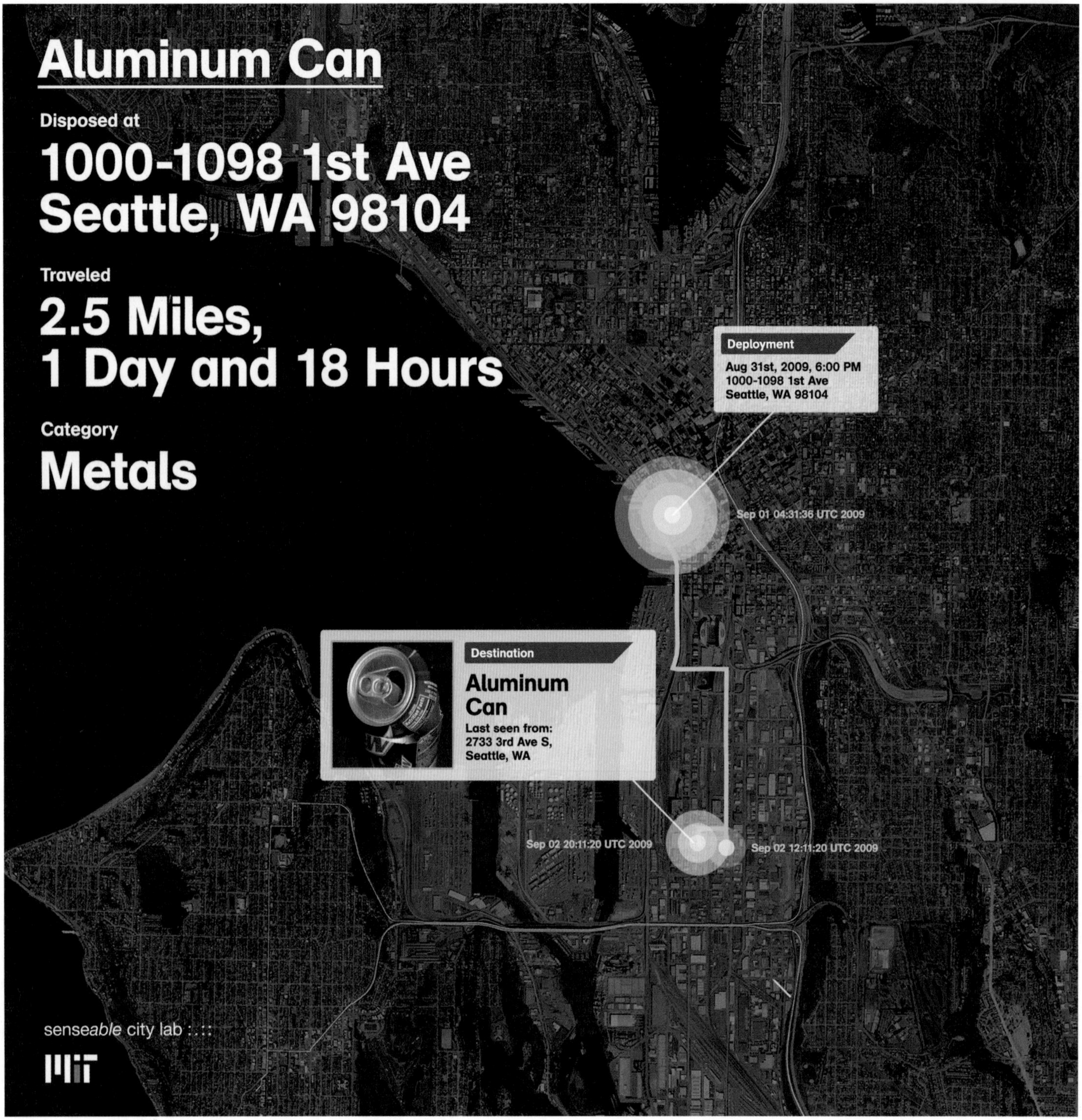
Aluminum Can
Disposed at
1000-1098 1st Ave
Seattle, WA 98104
Traveled
2.5 Miles,
1 Day and 18 Hours
Category
Metals
Deployment
Aug 31st, 2009, 6:00 PM
1000-1098 1st Ave
Seattle, WA 98104
Sep 01 04:31:36 UTC 2009
Destination
Aluminum
Can
Last seen from:
2733 3rd Ave S,
Seattle, WA
Sep 02 20:11:20 UTC 2009
Sep 02 12:11:20 UTC 2009
senseable city lab :.::
MIT

Plastic Container
of Liquid Soap
Disposed at
457 Madison Ave
New York, NY 10022
Traveled
18.3 Miles
Category
Plastic
Leonia
Ridgefield
Park
Fort Lee
Palisades Park
Little
Ferry
Ridgefield
Rutherford
East
Rutherford
Edgewater
North
Bergen
North Arlington
Secaucus
Union City
New York
Hoboken
Green
Point
Sep 5th, 2009, 07:22 AM
Sep 5th, 2009, 09:02 AM
Sep 5th, 2009, 05:19 AM
Sep 5th, 2009, 04:13 AM
Sep 8th, 2009, 07:26 AM
Sep 5th, 2009, 05:02 AM
Sep 5th, 2009, 04:34 AM
Sep 5th, 2009, 04:21 AM
Deployment
Sep 4th, 2009, 2:00 PM
457 Madison Ave
New York, NY 10022
En Route
Plastic Container
of Liquid Soap
Last seen from:
786-798 Bellevue Turnpike
Kearny, NJ 07032
Softsoap
senseable city lab
MIT

18.
Copenhagen Wheel — 2009

One of the most important presences in a city is neither visible nor virtual: air pollution. To map this flow, researchers at the SCL created the Copenhagen Wheel to convert ordinary bicycles into hybrid e-bikes equipped with motors, digital controls, and powerful mobile sensors. Developed with Ducati Energia, the Italian Ministry of the Environment, and the City of Copenhagen, the wheel is a compact device that can be attached to any normal bike—simply swap out of one of its tires (18A). It captures information about personal riding and about the urban environment, including ambient temperature, relative humidity, levels of carbon monoxide and NOx, and noise. Inside the wheel's hub, one can find a sensor kit, a motor, a three-speed internal gear, batteries, a torque sensor, and a general packet radio service (GPRS) device. With a personal smartphone, a user can unlock and lock the bike, change gears, select the amount of assistance from the motor (which pedaling and breaking recharge), and view real-time updates on relevant conditions. Because the wheel is controlled by smartphone, the information it produces can be stored and accessed as a natural extension of our preexisting repositories of personal data.

The data collected for individual use are also anonymized and shared with the public, allowing for a better understanding of the urban environment and how transportation impacts it. Maps and other visualizations of the aggregate data from many cyclists reveal both traffic conditions and air pollution levels in real time, with colors that are more intense where the two datasets overlap (18B–18D). Ultimately, this type of crowdsourced information can influence how a city allocates its resources, responds to environmental conditions in real time, and structures and implements environmental and transportation policies. The Copenhagen Wheel thus advances both the individual and the collective good, allowing users to be better cyclists and helping their city to gain a better understanding of itself.

18A

THE COPENHAGEN WHEEL
ZAFFIRO PRO

18B

18C

18D

19.
One Country, Two Lungs — 2014

One Country, Two Lungs tracks air pollution in two of the major cities in China's highly populated Greater Bay Area. For the project, a team of "human probes" traversed Shenzhen and Hong Kong with an array of sophisticated sensors, collecting data that revealed atmospheric boundaries between the two cities—very real divisions, made of nothing but air. Amid the matrices of towering skyscrapers and dense streets, the people inhabiting these two vertical cities are inhabiting very different airscapes (19A).

In the past, the precision of air quality measurements was limited by the immobility and sparseness of ground-based stations. Thanks to the development of miniaturized networked sensors, we can now accurately zoom down to the individual scale and measure personal exposure to pollutants, the most basic determinant of public health. For One Country, Two Lungs, the team that traversed Hong Kong and Shenzhen followed various commuting patterns while their instruments measured particulate matter (PM10), carbon monoxide (CO), and nitrogen dioxide (NO2), together with personal data associated with travel, such as spatial position, pace, and heart rate. Researchers were then able to draw a dynamic map of Hong Kong and Shenzhen that captures how the people there live in and move through urban space, breath by breath. Initial results showed that air pollution is higher in Shenzhen than in Hong Kong—especially the levels of small aerosol particles that have the most adverse effects on human health. These results also appear in a video shot from the perspective of one of the researchers, i.e., a typical commuter going from Hong Kong to Shenzhen, with red representing high pollution and green low (19B–19C).

Tracking the invisible inequality between these two cities and making it public can empower their residents to take action—either by adjusting daily commutes or advocating for citywide political change. The Chinese central government in Beijing coined the slogan "One Country, Two Systems" in the 1980s, during negotiations with the UK over Hong Kong's sovereignty transfer. Since this project was first developed, Beijing has dramatically tightened its control over the Hong Kong Special Administrative Region, which local pro-democracy activists and international observers see as a potentially irreversible step toward its political assimilation into mainland China. Before these events fully unfolded, One Country, Two Lungs explored how a significant divide still persisted in one of the less visible dimensions of urban life: distinct but interconnected atmospheres.

19A

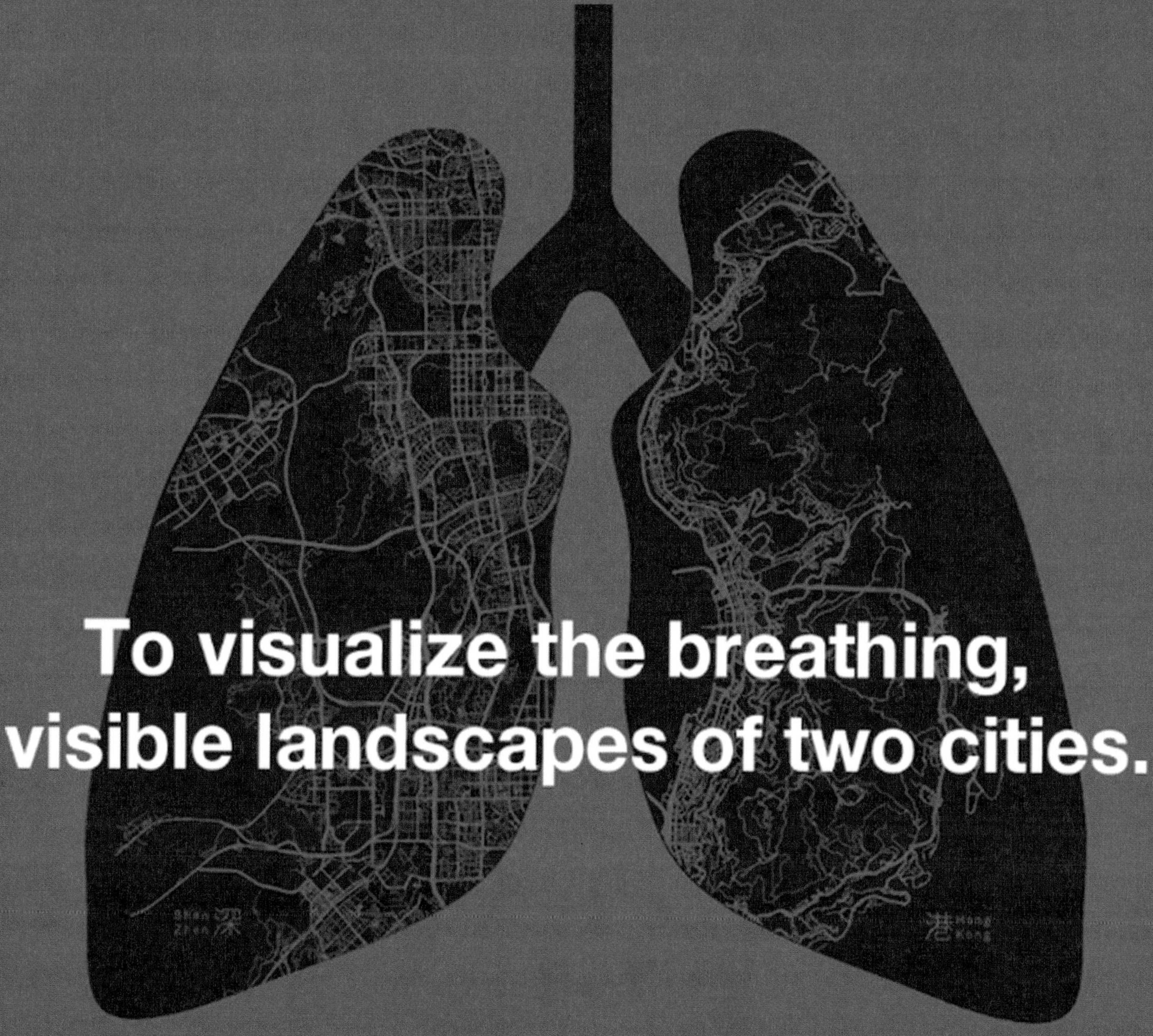
To visualize the breathing,
visible landscapes of two cities.

19B

27.4 °C
26.5%
66.7dB

MONEY CHANGER
2013.12.03
2:18:20
showing how we mov
breath
182.0µg/m³
PM 10
352.1µg/m³
NO2
1373.5µg/m³
CO

Exit Only 出
through urban space,
breath.
26.3 °C
41.3%
80.0dB

20.
Waterfly — 2015

Water quality monitoring is one of the greatest challenges we face today. From toxic cyanobacteria blooms to chemical pollutants, the threats that unmonitored water presents to drinking supplies, wildlife habitats, and public health are significant and growing. By identifying and mapping water quality issues with high precision, we can not only identify problematic areas but eliminate their root causes. The Waterfly project brought a combination of techniques together in one cyberphysical platform, generating high-resolution, geolocated, spatiotemporal datasets for one of the most complex ecologies in any city.

Waterfly is also the name of a small, sensor-imbued drone (or unmanned aerial vehicle, UAV) that gathers information at both macro and micro scales by performing aerial imaging and water probing (20A). Flying in formation, these quadcopters capture data on the health of aquatic ecologies through a collaborative process called swarm sensing. First, the lead vehicle performs high-resolution imaging tasks to procedurally generate maps of the water, which are analyzed in real time to detect and geolocate problem areas (20B). The supporting UAVs then carry full probing equipment to the detected area, which the lead UAV uses to collect spot readings. All the probing acts can be mapped in real time (20C) to capture the flows of bacteria and other polluting elements in the water, and the drones can be easily controlled through a web-based interface on a laptop or tablet.

The first Waterfly prototype employed two drones to perform aerial imaging and probing tasks in Boston's Charles River. Researchers used hyperspectral imaging to detect photosynthetic activity on the water—a cue to the presence of cyanobacteria, which convert sunlight into chemical energy. Probes were then deployed to determine the presence and concentration of phycocyanin, a pigment-protein complex found in cyanobacteria and a direct indicator of the presence of algae. The proof-of-concept flight demonstrated the successful coordination of the two vehicles.

UAV COMPONENTS

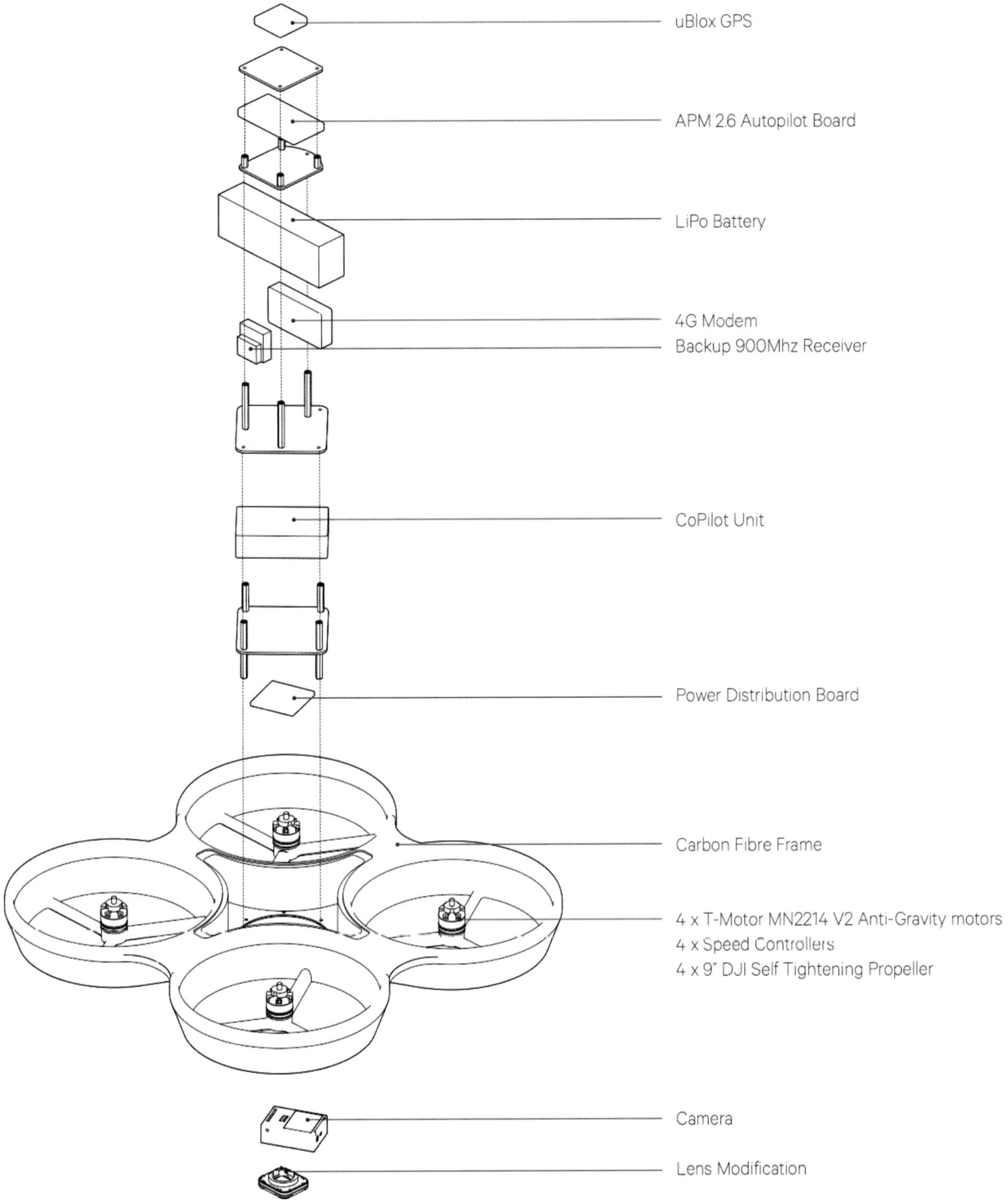

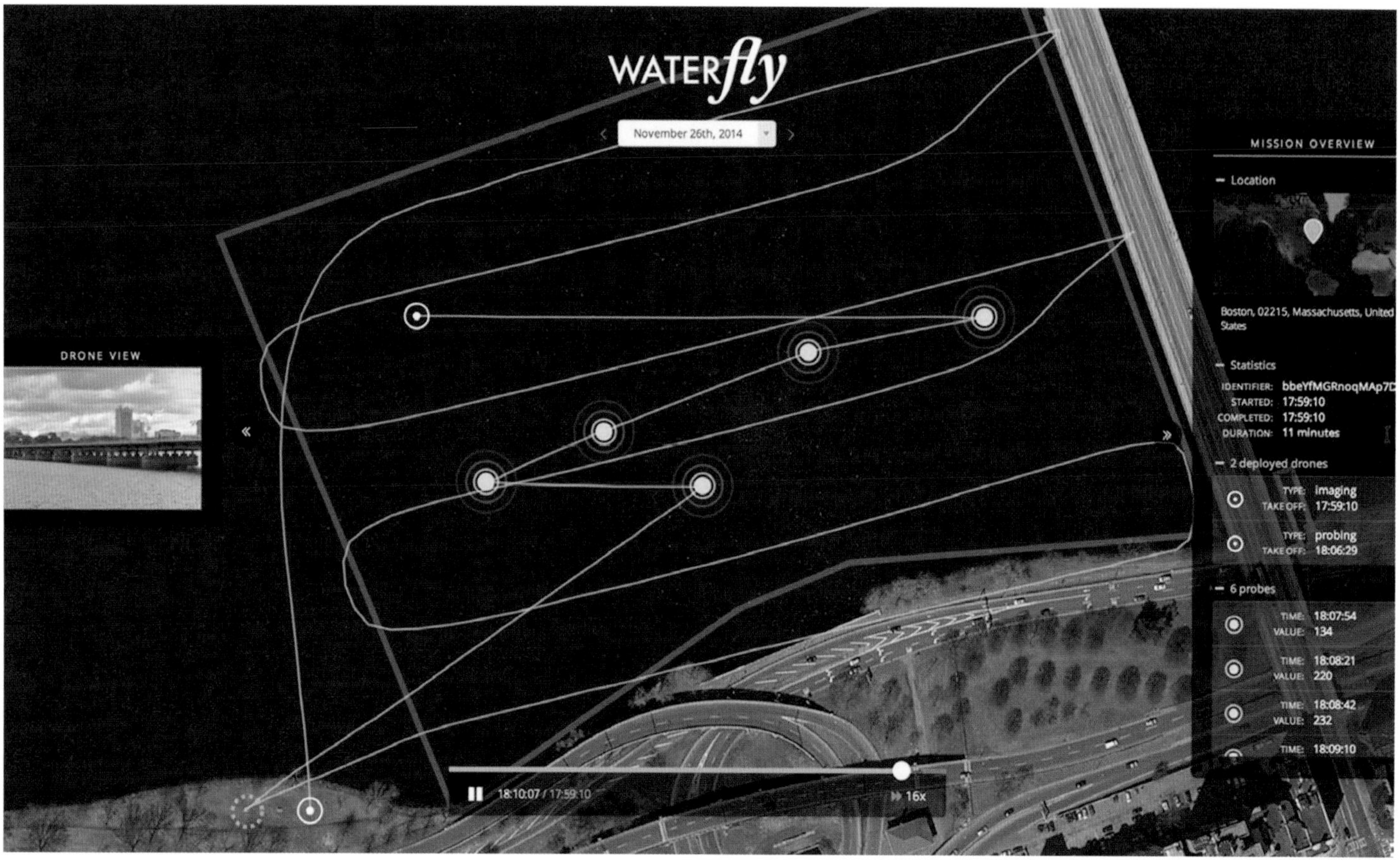
WATERfly
November 26th, 2014
DRONE VIEW
MISSION OVERVIEW
Location
Boston, 02215, Massachusetts, United States
Statistics
IDENTIFIER: bbeYfMGRnoqMAp7D
STARTED: 17:59:10
COMPLETED: 17:59:10
DURATION: 11 minutes
2 deployed drones
TYPE: imaging
TAKE OFF: 17:59:10
TYPE: probing
TAKE OFF: 18:06:29
6 probes
TIME: 18:07:54
VALUE: 134
TIME: 18:08:21
VALUE: 220
TIME: 18:08:42
VALUE: 232
TIME: 18:09:10
18:10:07 / 17:59:10
16x

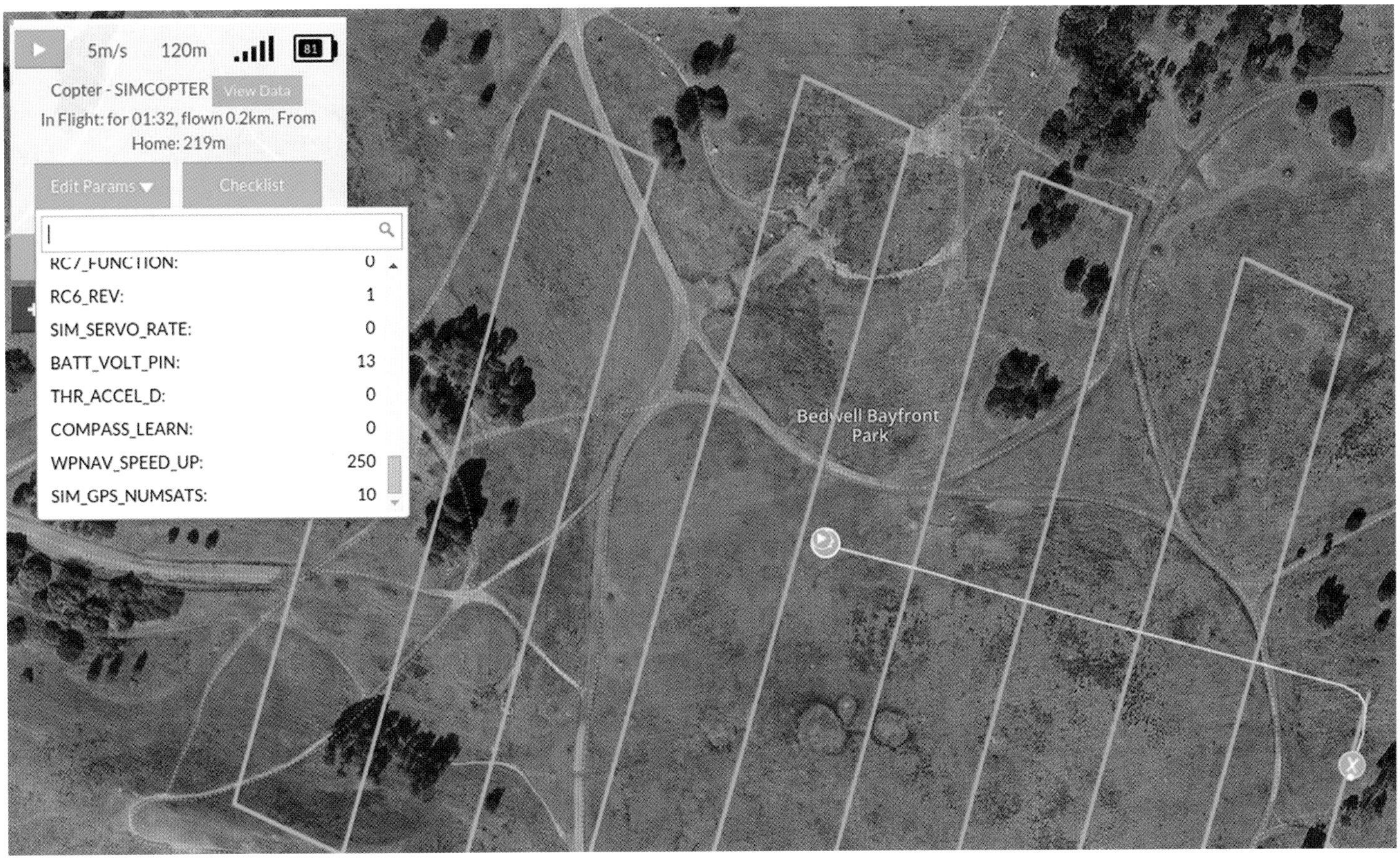
5m/s
120m
81
Copter - SIMCOPTER
View Data
In Flight: for 01:32, flown 0.2km. From Home: 219m
Edit Params
Checklist
RC7_FUNCTION: 0
RC6_REV: 1
SIM_SERVO_RATE: 0
BATT_VOLT_PIN: 13
THR_ACCEL_D: 0
COMPASS_LEARN: 0
WPNAV_SPEED_UP: 250
SIM_GPS_NUMSATS: 10
Bedwell Bayfront Park

21.
Underworlds — 2015

Underworlds digs deep (and quite literally deeper than cities' air and water levels) into urban circulations by exploring sewage systems. This project used three iterations (nicknamed Mario, Luigi, and Yoshi) of an advanced filtering and data-processing robot to collect real-time information on collective health conditions by mining sewage in select neighborhoods, and then released that data on an open, cross-disciplinary platform. In this way, Underworlds can monitor urban health patterns, shape more inclusive public health strategies, and push the boundaries of urban epidemiology, a contemporary, metaorganism-based version of what John Snow pioneered with cholera. But unlike Snow, who could operate only after the fact, smart sewage technology offers real-time infectious disease surveillance and thus—perhaps the most apparent application—the possibility to predict outbreaks. Early warnings about new flu strains in urban centers, for instance, could significantly reduce economic and human costs.

The Underworlds platform can reveal which microorganisms, such as specific bacteria and viruses, are present in a sewage sample (21A), and give users the opportunity to learn more about their properties (21B). In addition, biomarkers for diseases such as obesity and diabetes can be measured at unprecedented scale and temporal resolution.

The implications of this platform, and of the urban maps and other visualizations it creates, extend beyond disease surveillance, to the development of a new type of health census. Used in tandem with demographic data, Underworlds can shed light on the aggregate health of a city as well as on the particular health of a neighborhood. With sponsorship from the Kuwait-MIT Center for Natural Resources and the Environment, the SCL and MIT's Alm Lab developed a prototype smart sewage platform, consisting of physical infrastructure, biochemical measurement technologies, and the downstream computational tools and analytics necessary to interpret the data and act on the findings. The Underworlds project ran experiments in Boston, Cambridge (Massachusetts), Kuwait City, and Seoul (21C), and resulted in the launch of a startup, Biobot Analytics.

21A

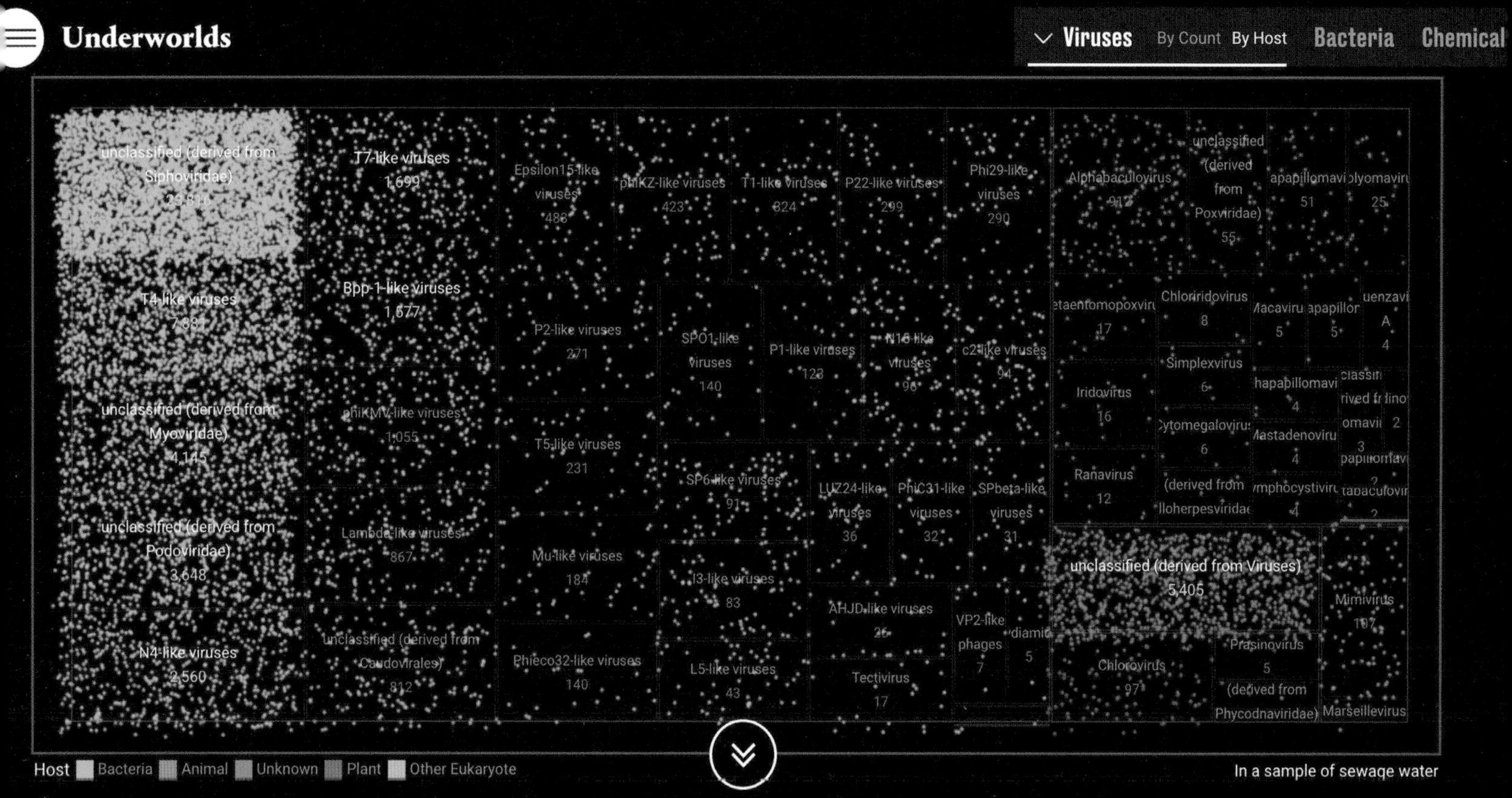

Underworlds
Viruses
By Count
By Host
Bacteria
Chemical
unclassified (derived from Siphoviridae)
T4-like viruses
unclassified (derived from Myoviridae)
4,145
unclassified (derived from Podoviridae)
3,648
N4-like viruses
2,560
T7-like viruses
1,699
Bpp-1-like viruses
1,677
phiKMV-like viruses
1,055
Lambda-like viruses
867
unclassified (derived from Caudovirales)
812
Epsilon15-like viruses
486
phiKZ-like viruses
423
T1-like viruses
324
P22-like viruses
299
Phi29-like viruses
290
P2-like viruses
271
T5-like viruses
231
Mu-like viruses
184
Phieco32-like viruses
140
SPO1-like viruses
140
P1-like viruses
128
N15-like viruses
96
c2-like viruses
94
SP6-like viruses
91
I3-like viruses
83
L5-like viruses
43
LUZ24-like viruses
36
PhiC31-like viruses
32
SPbeta-like viruses
31
AHJD-like viruses
26
Tectivirus
17
VP2-like phages
7
5
Alphabaculovirus
912
unclassified (derived from Poxviridae)
55
51
25
Chloriridovirus
8
Simplexvirus
6
Iridovirus
16
Ranavirus
12
unclassified (derived from Viruses)
5,405
Mimivirus
107
Chlorovirus
97
Prasinovirus
5
(derived from Phycodnaviridae)
Marseillevirus
Host
Bacteria
Animal
Unknown
Plant
Other Eukaryote
In a sample of sewage water

Underworlds

Lachnospiraceae
GREEN GENES ID 708680
PHYLUM Firmicutes
CLASS Clostridia
ORDER Clostridiales
FAMILY Lachnospiraceae
GENUS unknown
NO OF TAXIMONIAL HITS
4966
5.38 % OF TOTAL
It is one of the most abundant families found in the mammalian gut and it is relatively rare elsewhere. They grow in
Lachnospiracea
10%
8%
6%
4%
2%
0%
00 h
01 h
02 h
03 h
04 h
05 h
06 h
07 h
08 h
09 h
10 h

BY AMOUNT
BY CATEGORY
All
Human
Non Human
Show me how it works!
13 h
14 h
15 h
16 h
17 h
18 h
19 h
20 h
21 h
22 h
23 h

Firmicutes and Bacteroidetes make up over 98% of the bacteria in our gut.

Firmicutes
Bacteroidetes

The remaining bacteria present are likely from other sources.

Proteobacteria
Actinobacteria
Fusobacteria
Candidatus
Saccharibacteria
Synergistetes

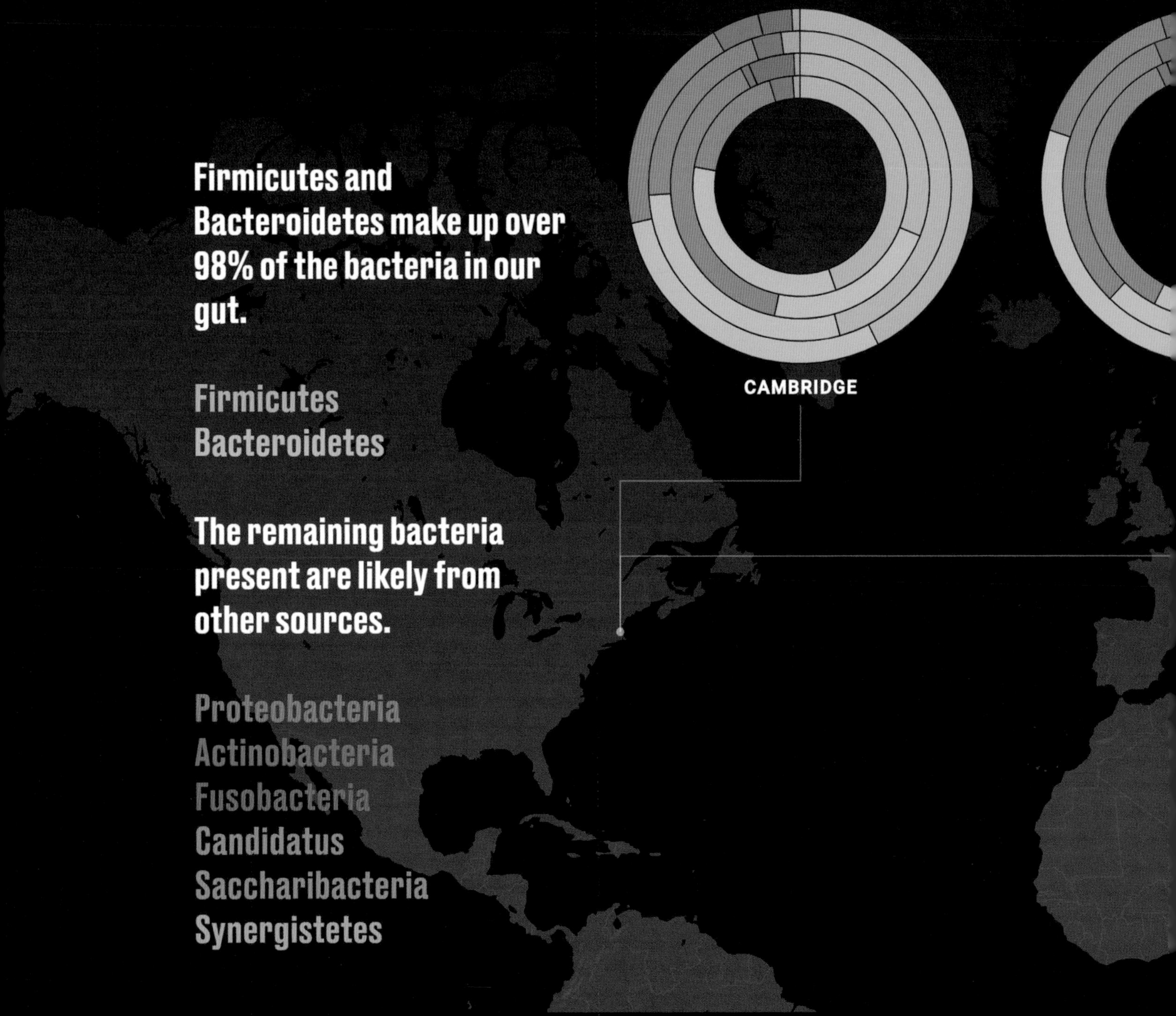

KUWAIT CITY
SEOUL

22.
City Scanner — 2017

By hitching a ride on already present urban infrastructure, portable sensors have the potential to revolutionize the work of data collection. In the City Scanner project, the SCL and Cisco collaborated to create lightweight dynamic sensors that can be unobtrusively attached to taxis and garbage trucks. Mounted to these vehicles—whose daily routes cover predictably broad areas—a relatively small number can capture an entire city's worth of data. This follows the same basic principle as the Google Street View car, whose mobility makes it far more efficient than blanketing every corner on the planet with stationary security cameras. City Scanner devices are not only small enough to attach to existing vehicles but also dynamic enough to capture a wide variety of variables.

The first map below shows thermal imaging data, which can help us track the human-made causes of urban heat islands—from the energy output of buildings to concentrations of black asphalt (22A). Another important metric, amount of particulate matter, can help researchers analyze the block-by-block realities of air pollution (22B). The densities of traffic, industrial buildings, and other drivers of bad air quality vary immensely in different parts of a city—and are often greater in poor and minority neighborhoods. While using garbage trucks as cheap replacements for fixed sensors, City Scanner captures data from mobility itself: each sensor's built-in accelerometer measures the vibrations of the truck it's attached to as it moves across the city, providing a good estimate of road quality (22C).

City Scanner's devices initially captured four data dimensions simultaneously: thermal imaging, matter levels, temperature and humidity readings, and road quality. In the future, even more can be incorporated and compared. When shifting from academic research to the everyday realities of urban management—especially on razor-thin budgets—this adaptability is essential. Dynamic and affordable, these devices are a first step toward making big data analysis possible in every community.

22A

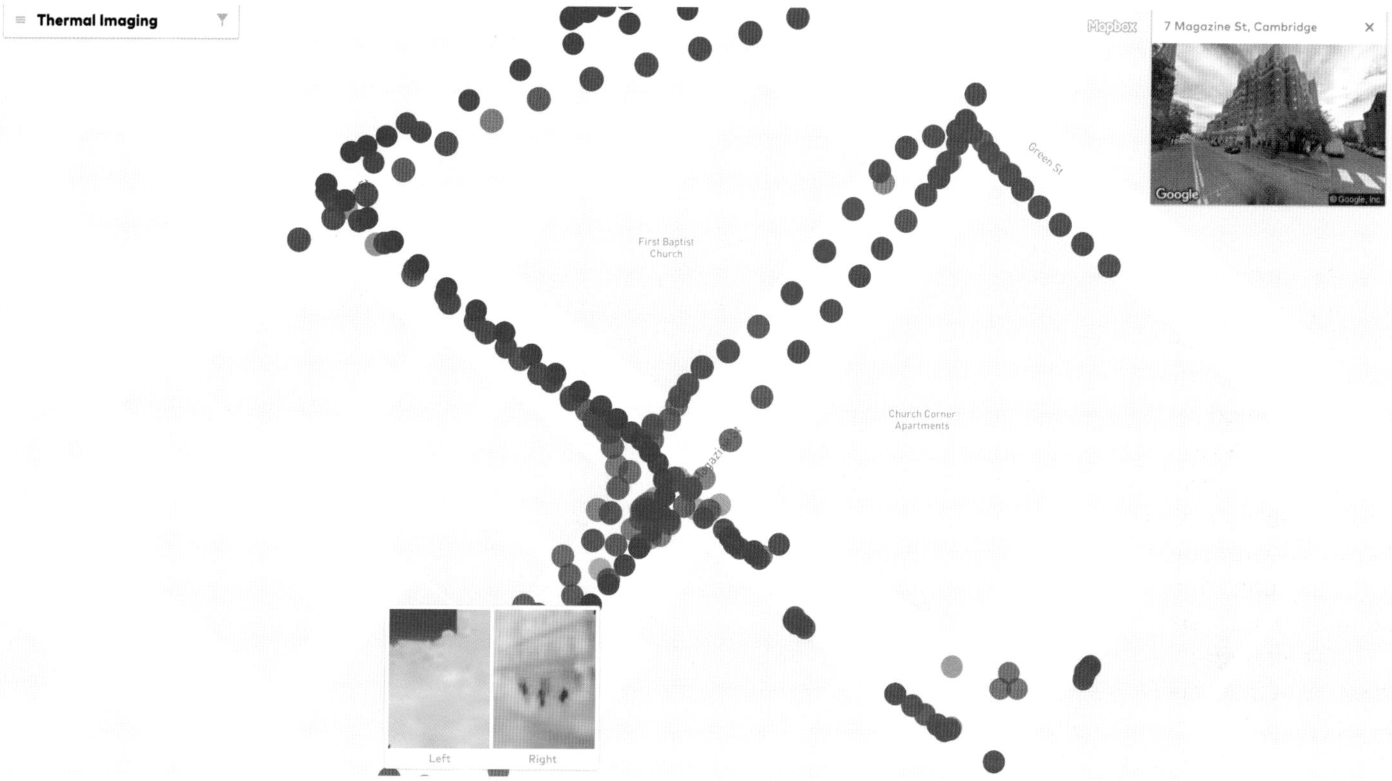

Thermal Imaging
Mapbox
7 Magazine St, Cambridge
First Baptist Church
Green St
Church Corner Apartments
Left
Right

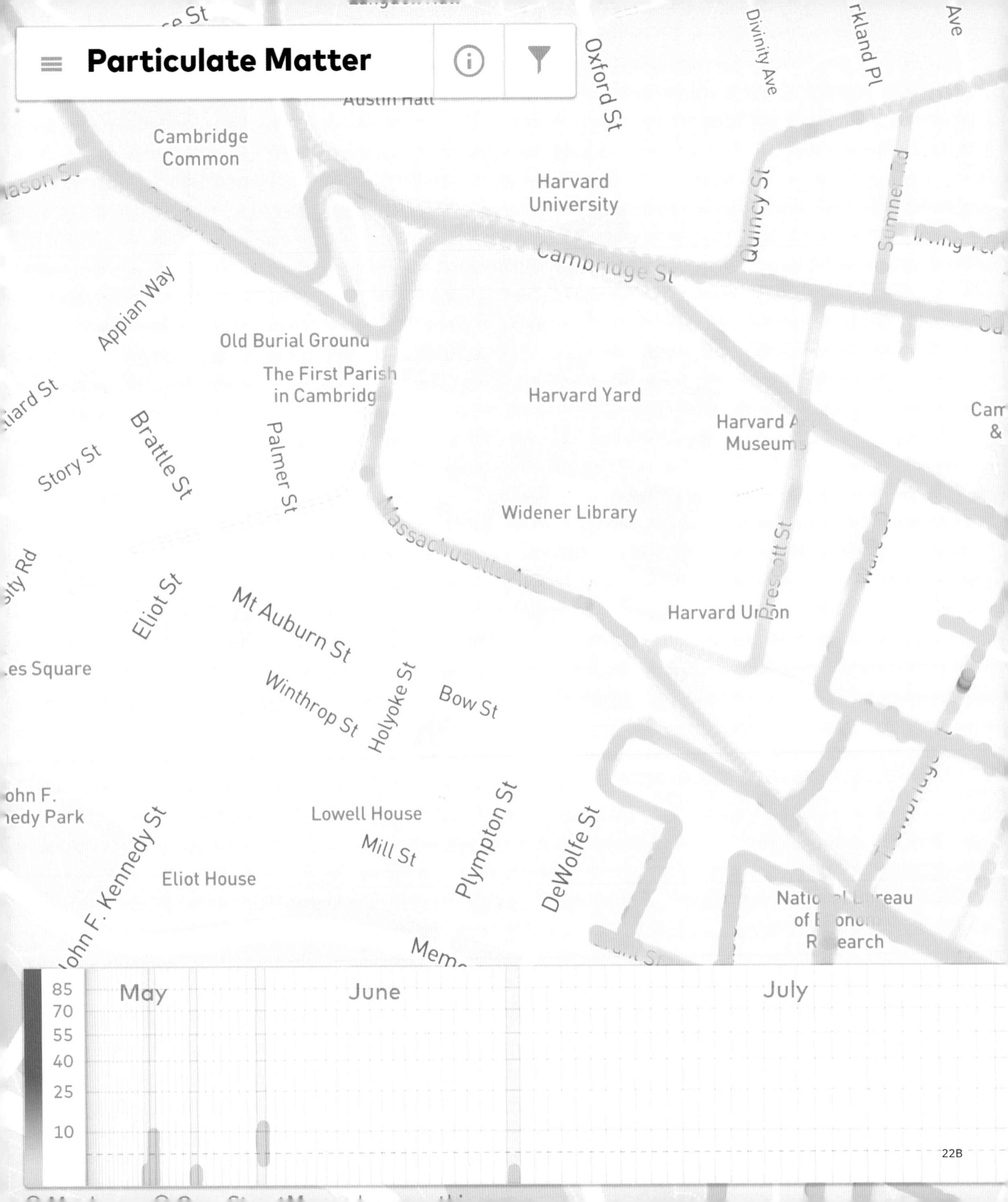
Particulate Matter
Oxford St
Divinity Ave
Cambridge Common
Harvard University
Quincy St
Cambridge St
Appian Way
Old Burial Ground
The First Parish in Cambridg
Harvard Yard
Story St
Brattle St
Palmer St
Widener Library
Harvard Union
Eliot St
Mt Auburn St
Winthrop St
Holyoke St
Bow St
Lowell House
Mill St
Plympton St
DeWolfe St
Eliot House
85
70
55
40
25
10
May
June
July

22B

Lewis St
Search Address
Roberts Rd
Myrtle Ave
Trowbridge St
Dimick St
Concord Ave
Concord
Spaulding Hospital
Cambridge
Cambridge
Hospital
Houghton St
Ellery St
Highland Ave
Inman St
Fayette St
Murdock St
Amory St
August
Histogram
Value
3.58
avg. in µg/m³

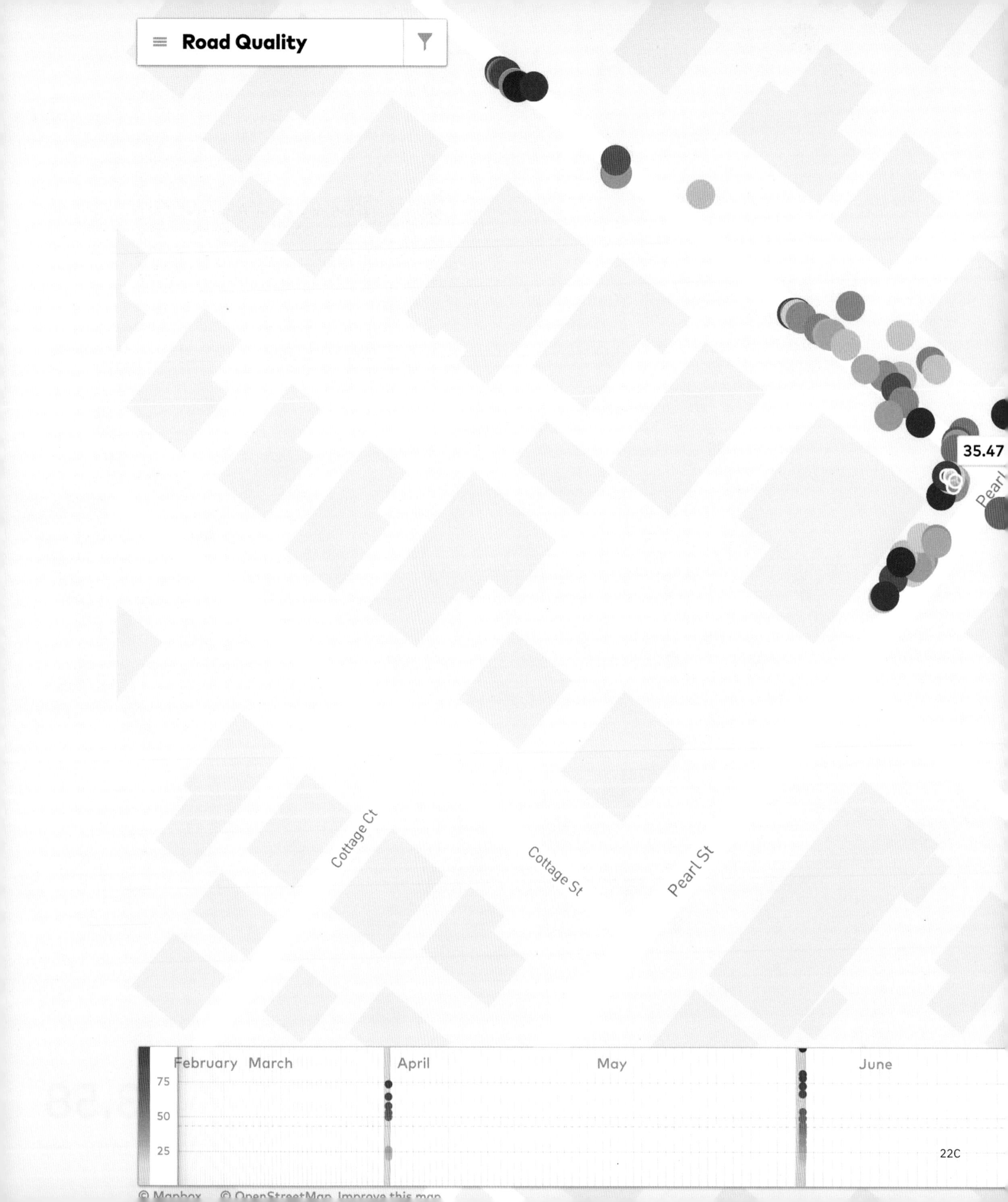
Road Quality
35.47
Pearl
Cottage Ct
Cottage St
Pearl St
February
March
April
May
June
75
50
25
© Mapbox © OpenStreetMap Improve this map

22C

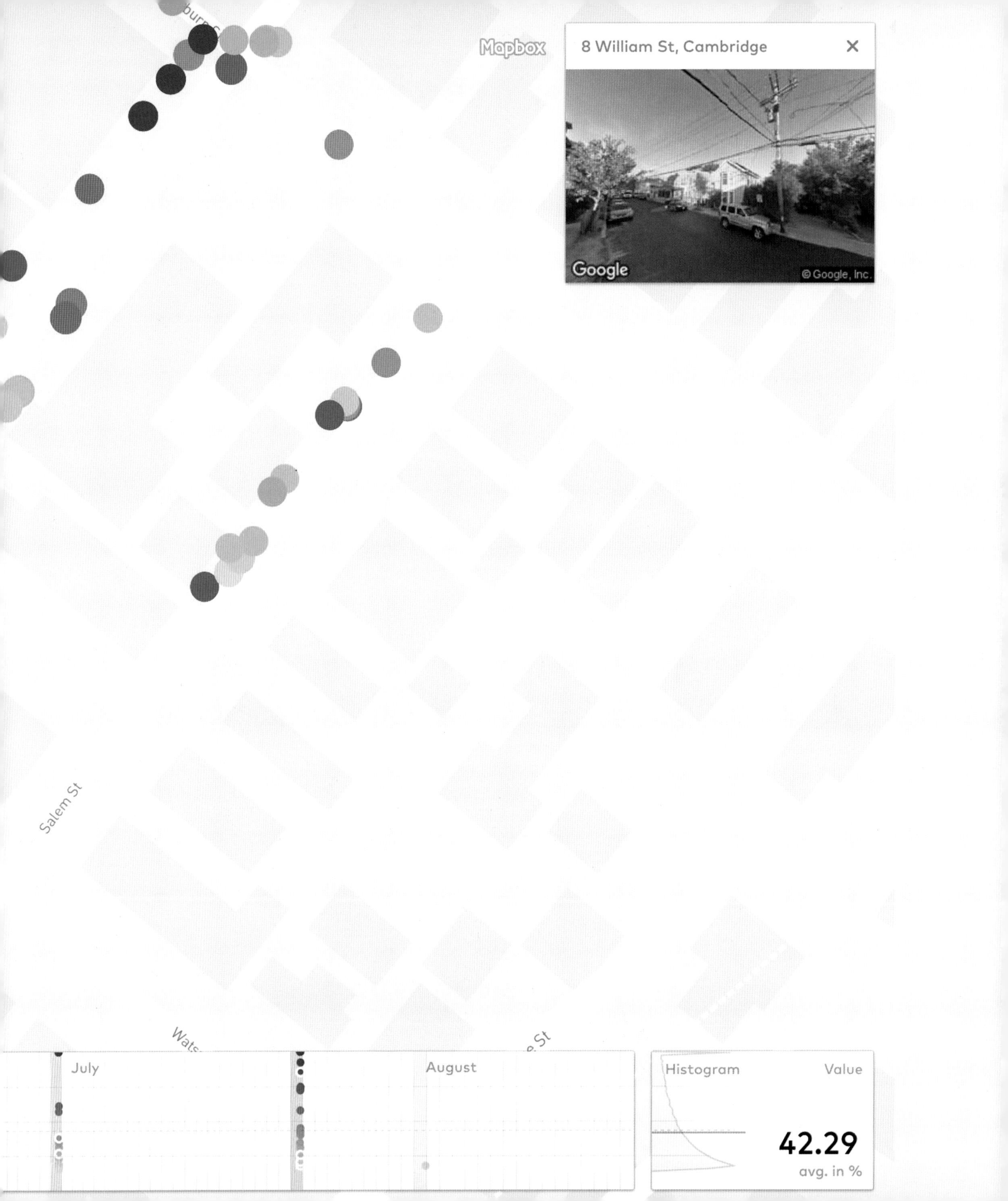
Mapbox
8 William St, Cambridge
Google
© Google, Inc.
Salem St
July
August
Histogram
Value
42.29
avg. in %

In Urban Sensing, the SCL set out to quantify how many mobile sensors it would take to collect data throughout an entire city—and got a surprising result. Attaching devices to only ten random taxicabs, researchers found that they could scan a third of Manhattan in a single day. With a tiny investment, a huge amount of the target area was covered. Only twenty additional taxis, for a total of thirty, were needed to capture half the borough. Reaching 85 percent, however, required more than one thousand mobile sensors. Because taxi routes overlap, every additional cab was less likely to capture a new street. The first map below, which is animated online, shows the city's outlines emerge as ten vehicles pump through its veins over the course of a normal day (23A).

This extraordinary relationship between the number of taxis and the amount of coverage was even more surprising when it held up in a variety of settings. Vienna's ancient streets are nothing like Manhattan's orderly grid, but a similarly comparatively small number of taxi trips captured a huge swath of the Austrian capital (23B). Everywhere the SCL carried out this experiment (Chicago, New York, San Francisco, Shanghai, Vienna, and Singapore), the same result emerged: one can scan up to half of a city before a large fleet becomes necessary. This consistent curve of data acquisition could allow planners across the world to estimate how many mobile sensors it would take to scan their own cities—and reap incredibly valuable information. Although perfectionists will eventually face diminishing returns, much of the urban environment is apparently low-hanging fruit. Just as the innovations of City Scanner (project 22, above) make it practical to measure a variety of variables, the findings of Urban Sensing reveal that affordable scanning is a statistical reality, simply waiting to be employed in cities worldwide. Our streets are practically begging to be understood—we need only hail a few cabs to begin.

23A

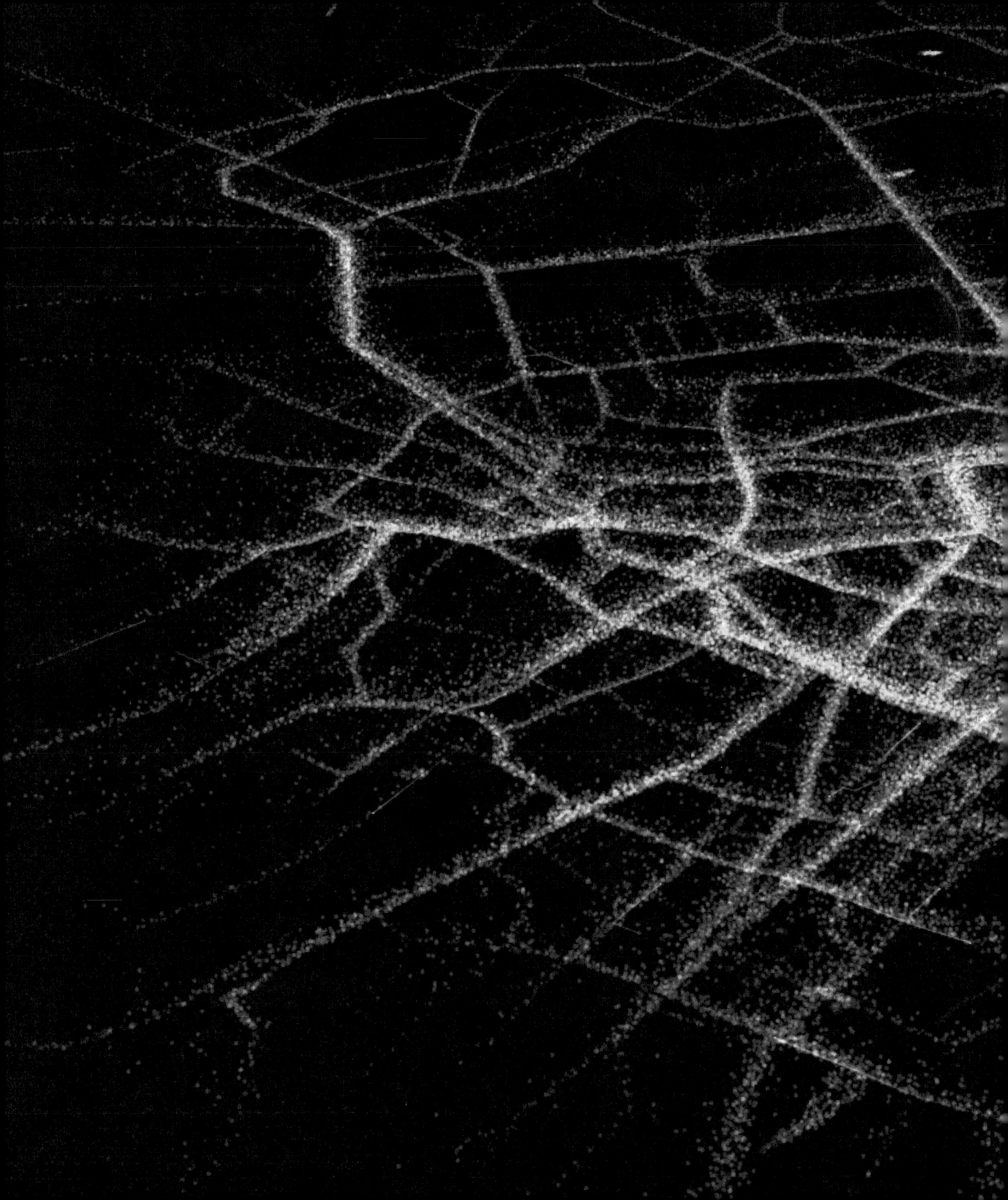

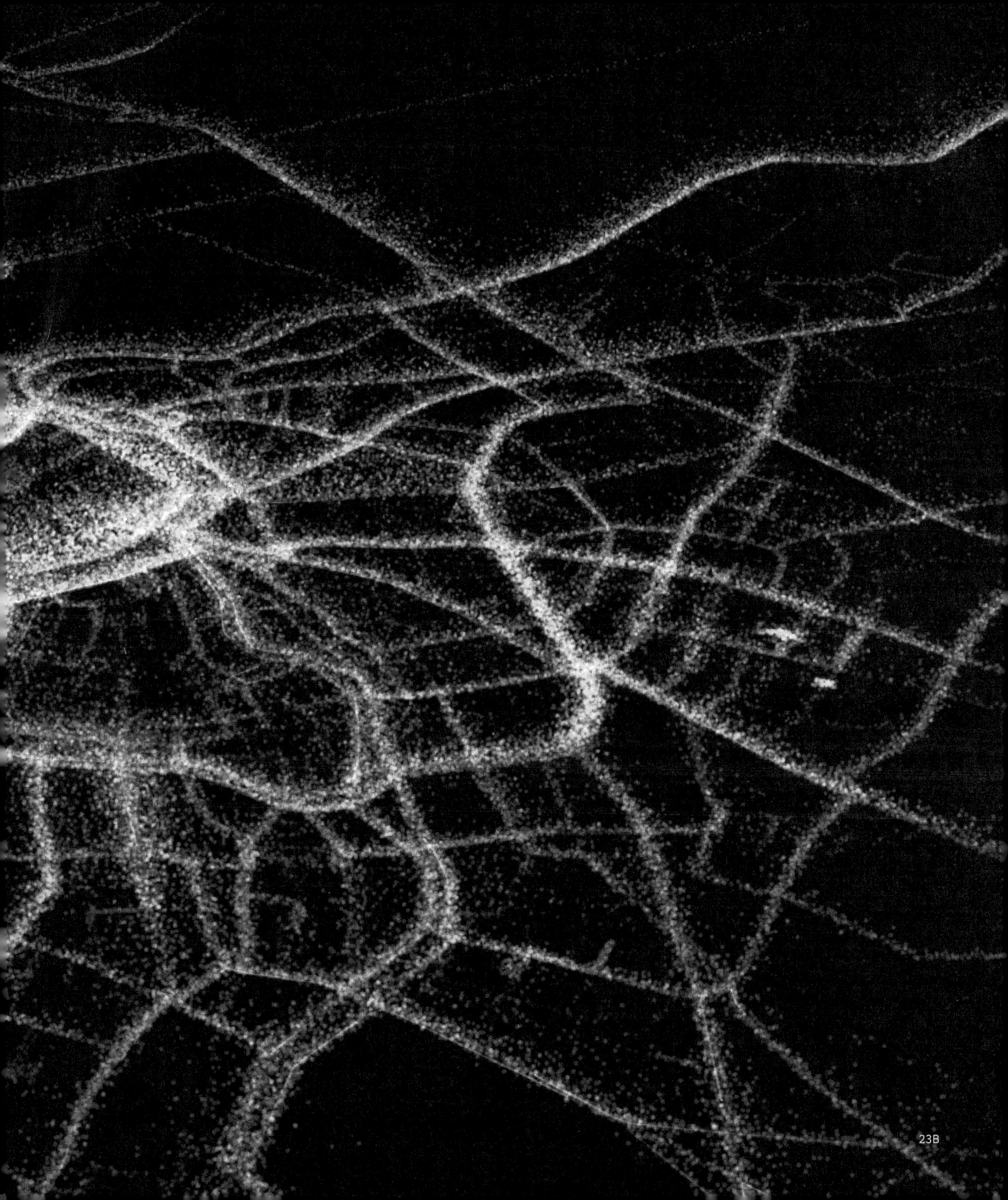
23B

24.
Roboat Flows — 2020

Amsterdam is famous for its network of canals: about one-quarter of the city's surface area is covered with water. In the picturesque central district, this presents residents and visitors alike with an array of mundane logistical challenges, including the management of waste from households and hotels. Other parts of the city use underground containers for trash, but the fragile quays of the central district rely on curbside receptacles that are often difficult to access. To replace these terrestrial trash cans, the SCL, in collaboration with the Amsterdam Institute for Advanced Metropolitan Solutions (AMS Institute), developed the Roboat, a high-tech "floating dumpster."

A Roboat is a small autonomous vehicle that uses LiDAR (light detection and ranging) scans to sense the world and artificial intelligence to recognize objects, as in the first image below (24A). Because so much of Amsterdam's central district is close to water, a small fleet of Roboats could easily service the vast majority of the city with automated weekly routes (24B), eliminating the need for trash receptacles on dry land—and thereby removing an eyesore, pest magnet, and waste of valuable space.

Other possibilities are endless. Roboats are equipped with water quality sensors that can provide real-time updates of ecology and public health conditions. They can also be used as self-driving taxis (24C), pop-up miniature storefronts, and temporary footbridges. Thus, the Roboat has the power to transform Amsterdam's canals into a dynamic new platform for urban infrastructure and design solutions, changing with the needs of the city and the flows of its water.

24A

Korte Niezel | 172.76 m
Car | 140.31 m
Boat | 133.02 m
Boat | 107.74 m
Car | 52.19 m
Boat | 95.59 m
Boat | 52.19 m
Bikes | 43.99 m
Light | 41.81 m
Oudekennissteeg | 33.43 m
Others | 22.49 m
Car | 23.78 m
Boat | 17.96 m

SLOTERDIJK
Haarlemmerweg
Haarlemmerweg
STAATSLIEDENBUURT
Bosleeuw
BOS EN
LOMMER
WEST
Marnixstraat
Lindengracht
Westerstraat
Nassaukade
Bilderdijkstraat
Da Costakade
Bilderdijkkade
Prinsengracht
Keizersgracht
OVERTO
VEL
Overtoom
Van Eeghenstraat
roboat.org
roboat.org

part of the **Roboat** project

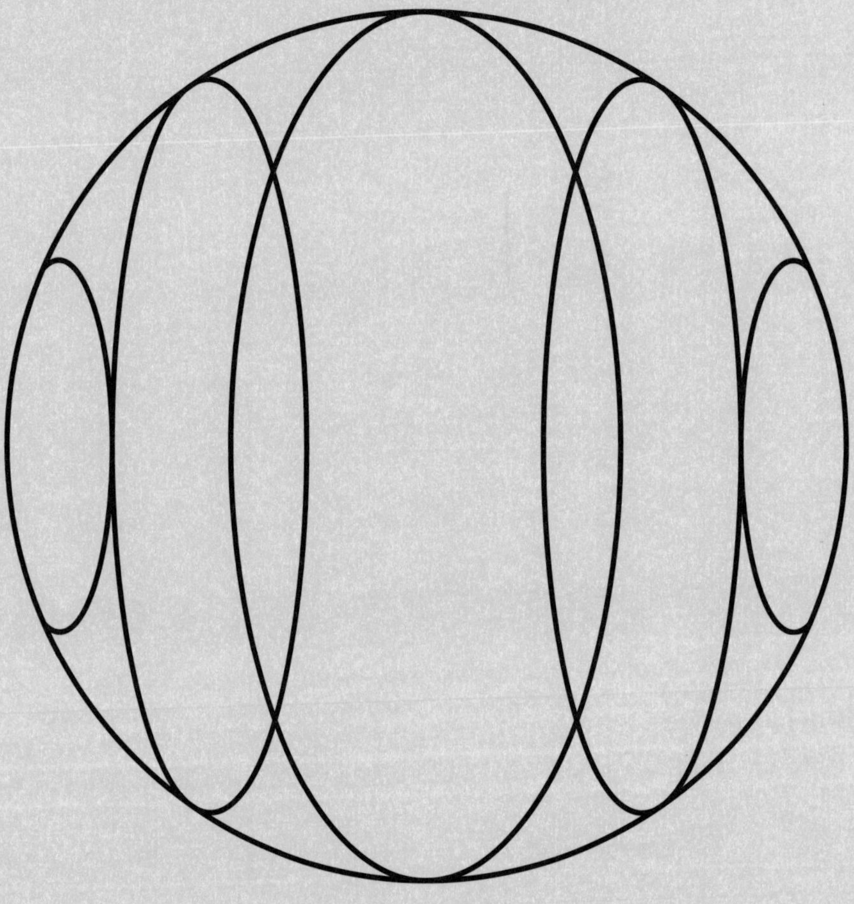

EXPERIENCE

CHAPTER — 4

Experience

"Asia includes many provinces and regions," wrote Isidore of Seville, a seventh-century archbishop known as the last scholar of the ancient world.[1] "I shall briefly list their names and locations, starting with Paradise." Beliefs have long been intertwined with facts in the practice of cartography, and together they informed maps of the ancient world's untrodden extent. But as the Far East was traversed in the era of the great explorers, the unknown diminished. Fact outweighed emotion in the newly resolved world map, even if subjective preferences led many Westerners to prefer projections that inflated the size of Europe and simplified ethnic and political boundaries in Asia and Africa. Still, the explorer's mentality ushered in a new regime of cartography. Beginning with the Greek periplus, essentially a sailor's logbook, maps became tools for documenting objective but individualistic events—such as an explorer's personal journey. Centuries later, in the 1950s, the Situationists implemented a similar idea, stitching together urban fragments through subjective experience: this group of radical creatives developed the practice of "urban dérive," emotional and intuitive wanderings through a city to elucidate personal "psychogeographies." The iconic *Guide psychogéographique de Paris* by Guy Debord, for example, documents instinctual links and flows between noncontiguous locations.[2]

Senses and emotions knit compelling urban portraits together, but they are nonetheless impressionistic. With the introduction of sensing technologies, collective perceptions may reveal something deeper than the dizzying and sublime enjoyment of what Balzac called "the gastronomy of the eye."[3] Some experiential maps have already evolved from impressionistic collages to become true perceptual cartographies of a city. Christian Nold's Bio Mapping project (2004–), based on galvanic skin response, aggregates "emotion tracks" across a city to understand how a population physiologically responds to its urban space.[4]

If perceptions can be charted from a human vantage point, they can also be woven into a comprehensive sensory cartography. In 1998, Gordon Bell embarked on the first 24-7 full-resolution experiment in life logging: MyLifeBits.[5] What he initially outlined as a 1:1 scientific and sociological study is now almost the default condition of an Internet generation. The emergence of wearable technologies and the "quantified self" movement have foregrounded personal data, gathered in real time, all the time. Almost anyone can see where they have traveled, with whom they have connected, and how many calories they have both expended and taken in. Daily life becomes data. In parallel, a profound shift from the individual to the collective has introduced progressive cartography at the scale of the global population. High-definition cameras in the guise of smartphones, for example, have become nearly prosthetic, and snapping a photo almost a reflex. With the experiential big data that they create, we can see through humanity's collective eyes.

1 Isidore of Seville, quoted in Toby Lester, "When Paradise Was on the Map," *Boston Globe*, 12 January 2014, https://www.bostonglobe.com/ideas/2014/01/12/when-paradise-was-map/B9vnu5ASb1CyFS16AoN1zO/story.html, accessed 12 May 2022.

2 Guy Debord, *Guide psychogéographique de Paris* (Orléans : Frac Centre-Val de Loire, 1957).

3 Honoré de Balzac, *Physiologie du mariage; ou, Méditations de philosophie éclectique, sur le bonheur et le malheur conjugal* (Brussels: Louis Hauman, 1834), vol. 1, 37.

4 *Emotional Cartography: Technologies of the Self*, ed. Christian Nold (self-pub., 2009), http://emotionalcartography.net/.

5 Gordon Bell and Jim Gemmell, *Your Life, Uploaded* (New York: Penguin, 2010).

Researchers at the SCL have been using big data to map individual and group experiences in their most subjective dimensions. When mapping urban greenery, we used street-level images rather than aerial scans to capture tree coverage as residents, not satellites, see it. The SCL has also derived valuable information from user-created content on Flickr and other photo platforms, employing color pattern recognition to identify drought hot spots, for example. Similarly, in a project at the building scale, sensors across the Louvre Museum picked up visitors' movement patterns and clustering to show which works of art we love and, just as important, how we interact with them. Even smaller, car-based sensors can quantify emotions on the road to reveal the personal experiences of daily commutes—data as valuable as travel duration or traffic—which can be stitched together into a collective road frustration index and visualized on a map. Such data-informed maps show how thinking and feeling humans collectively use space. We can also chart how a society holds its breath before reacting explosively in moments of high drama—whether tweeting after a dramatic stroke at the Masters Tournament in golf or calling friends and family after Barack Obama's inauguration as president. These new maps can become crucial guides for understanding society and history as they are lived and felt—what better tool is there to explain, for instance, the COVID-19 pandemic than a sound map of an eerily quiet park during the first lockdown of 2020?

Belief guided Isidore of Seville's map of paradise in Asia, and emotions influenced the psychogeographies of the Situationists' Paris. Today, feelings themselves are becoming the subject of cartographic inquiry, marking a profound shift from emotional maps to maps of emotions.

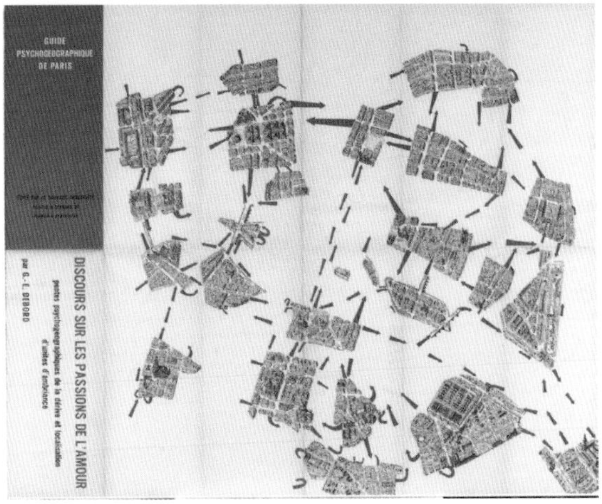

01

02

01. GUY DEBORD, PSYCHOGEOGRAPHIC GUIDE TO PARIS: DISCOURSE ON THE PASSIONS OF LOVE, 1957.

This map is one of five prepared by Guy Debord on the occasion of the *Première exposition de psychogéographie (First psychogeography exposition),* at the Taptoe Gallery in Brussels in 1957. It represents the *dérive,* a concept invented by the French avant-garde movement the Letterists to disrupt daily practices—like walking—and allow for the spontaneous experience of cities. It is one of the first articulations of a purposeful mapping of emotions, as opposed to an (accidentally) emotional map that fails to achieve objectivity. The Letterist International, a Paris-based collective of radical thinkers and artists who broke away from the Letterists and were led by Debord and Gil J. Wolman, was responsible for the influential idea of psychogeography, the playful exploration of urban environments based on individuals' feelings and whims. The dérive was an experimental behavior intended to bring about a more spontaneous, emotional, and human relationship with urban space: one walked around a city based on the attractions one felt, in that moment, for elements of the landscape itself. This map by Debord traces the movements of one such drifter through Paris, with the arrows joining certain areas of the city based on the individual's personal and intuitive conception of them and not according to any logical or practical sequence.

02. ANDRÉ BERTRAND, COVER OF THE INTERNATIONAL TIMES, 1968.

The Situationist International (SI), founded in 1957, is emblematic of an approach to urban space and mapping that prioritizes human experience and emotion and the links and flows that people make as they use and live their cities. Over the decade following its founding, the SI developed an increasingly incisive and coherent critique of both Western multinational capitalism and its pseudo-opposition (as the SI saw it), Eastern bureaucratic communism. In its early days, the movement's focus was more artistic than political, and it was during that time that it brought forward explorations in psychogeography, as in Debord's map above. This focus eventually shifted from the subjectivity of urban experience to politics, as the SI became a largely antiauthoritarian Marxist group. Its two most famous texts, *The Society of the Spectacle* by Debord and *The Revolution of Everyday Life* by Raoul Vaneigem, were influential in the French insurrections of May 1968. Bertrand's cartoon (which uses a medium that has long been popular in France) is an attack on consumerism, which the Situationists viewed as the century's dominant paradigm. Society's collective efforts aim only to "raise the standard of BOREDOM," and it is our task to leave consumerism behind (shown in the first few panels), overthrow the old order, and realize our profound desires. This process begins by replacing a daily commute with a dérive.

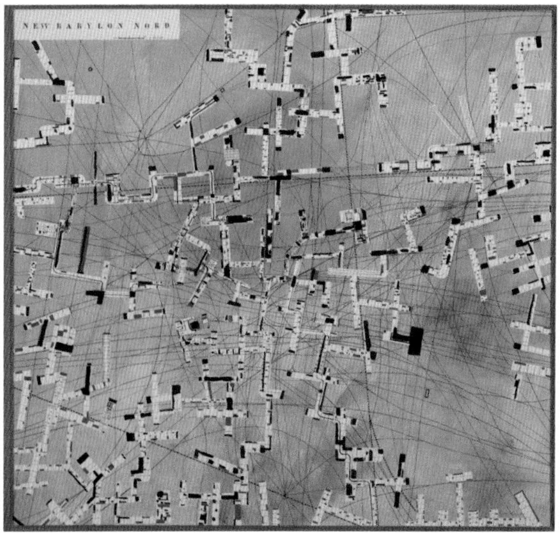

03

04

03. CONSTANT NIEUWENHUYS, SYMBOLISCHE KAART NEW BABYLON NORD, 1958.

New Babylon is an urban utopia conceived by the Dutch artist Constant Nieuwenhuys, who was a close correspondent of Debord's and a member of the SI. Initially known as Dériville (from *ville derivée*, or "drift city"), it is embodied in a series of often abstract paintings, sketches, texts, and architectural models. It represents Nieuwenhuys's anti-capitalist theories of urban development and the future of human interaction. As described by the critic Sarah Williams Goldhagen, New Babylon "would literally leave the bourgeois metropolis below and would be populated by *homo ludens*—man at play."[6] For Nieuwenhuys, the creation of such a utopist vision depended on architecture to influence people's daily realities—in particular, large megastructures that would rise above the previous trappings of civil society, giving people the freedom to enjoy a nomadic life of creativity and play. His colorful and radical artworks show the extreme of a city imagined by its residents, upending traditional ideas of urban planning. Nieuwenhuys wrote, "It is obvious that a person free to use his time for the whole of his life, free to go where he wants, when he wants, cannot make the greatest use of his freedom in a world ruled by the clock and the imperative of a fixed abode."[7]

04. GORDON BELL, PHOTO COLLAGE FROM "LIFELOGGING", 1998-2010.

In recent years, maps based on subjective experience have proliferated, because the collection of data about our actions and habits has become much easier and even ubiquitous. The computer scientist Gordon Bell began exploring this reality as early as the 1990s. Using himself as a case study, he has investigated our ever-increasing access to electronic personal memories, whether stored in cloud services such as Facebook or on personal hard drives. But Bell's is the rare case in which the collection of personal data is fully intentional. In 1998, he began the first full-resolution experiment in so-called *lifelogging*, with himself as the subject: hardware and software that he created captured every moment and every action of his life through photos (as in the collage to the left), computer activity, biometrics, and more. This study has continued as MyLifeBits, a Microsoft Research project, for which Bell is trying to collect a true lifetime store of information about himself. What he initially set out to do as a full-scale scientific and sociological study, however, is now the default condition of the Internet generation. Creating a paperless digital trail of every single action and document in one's life no longer requires the conscious effort of a computer scientist like Bell but instead is something we all do, wittingly or not: unlike Bell with his life logging, we often do not know what we are "choosing" to record or where our recordings are stored.

6 Sarah Williams Goldhagen, "Architecture: Extra-Large," *New Republic*, 31 July 2006, https://newrepublic.com/article/93273/sarah-williams-goldhagen-architecture-extra-large, accessed 30 May 2022.

7 Constant Nieuwenhuys, *New Babylon*, exhibition catalog., ed. J. L. Locher (The Hague: Haags Gemeentemuseum, 1974).

CHAPTER • 4

Experience ↓ MIT Senseable City Lab Projects

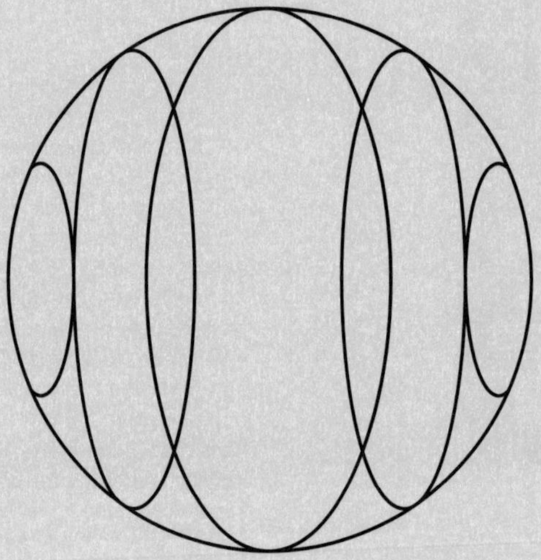

25.
Los Ojos del Mundo — 2007

26.
Obama | One People — 2009

27.
Road Frustration Index — 2013

28.
Art Traffic — 2014

29.
Tweet Bursts — 2014

30.
Treepedia — 2016

31.
City Ways — 2017

32.
AI Station — 2019

33.
Favelas 4D — 2021

25.
Los Ojos del Mundo — 2007

Los Ojos del Mundo shows photos taken by visitors to Spain, revealing a perceptual cartography from the perspectives of tourists, who experience the country very differently from its residents. Spain has undergone one of the world's most impressive urban facelifts in recent decades, overtaking the United States to become the world's second-most-visited country in the 1990s. Beyond these big numbers, though, the tourism that has radically transformed it is difficult to quantify, as visitors leave minimal tangible traces of their stays. Yet who they are, what they see, and why they come are important questions for both citizens and local authorities.

Through data mining of digital photos publicly shared on Flickr and visualization of the results, Los Ojos del Mundo provided insights into these questions, uncovering the evolutions of tourists' presence and experiences: where people visit, where they come from, and what they are interested in capturing and sharing. The analysis and mapping of these data allow us to understand the points of interest of some of Spain's most visited cities, illustrating their attractiveness to visitors. Mapping also reveals empty spaces: Spain's least photographed regions, still free from the buzz of tourists.

The SCL made several visualizations based on the photos it mined. One depicts the photographed Spain by mapping the places with the highest densities of images (25A). Thanks to the ability to disclose one's home country on Flickr, which about 60 percent of users choose to do, the photographic trails of locals can be distinguished from those of visitors. Researchers were thus able to create a map of Barcelona that collects Britons' perceptions (25B) while unveiling their movements around the city. When posting to Flickr, users also often attach descriptions and tags to their photos, which allow us to infer the kinds of activities that these images capture. For instance, the SCL searched for tags related to "partying" in summer 2007 to locate the city's heart for carousers and cavorters. There turned out to be three answers: the old town, the bohemian district of Gràcia, and the Fòrum area, with its music festivals (25C).

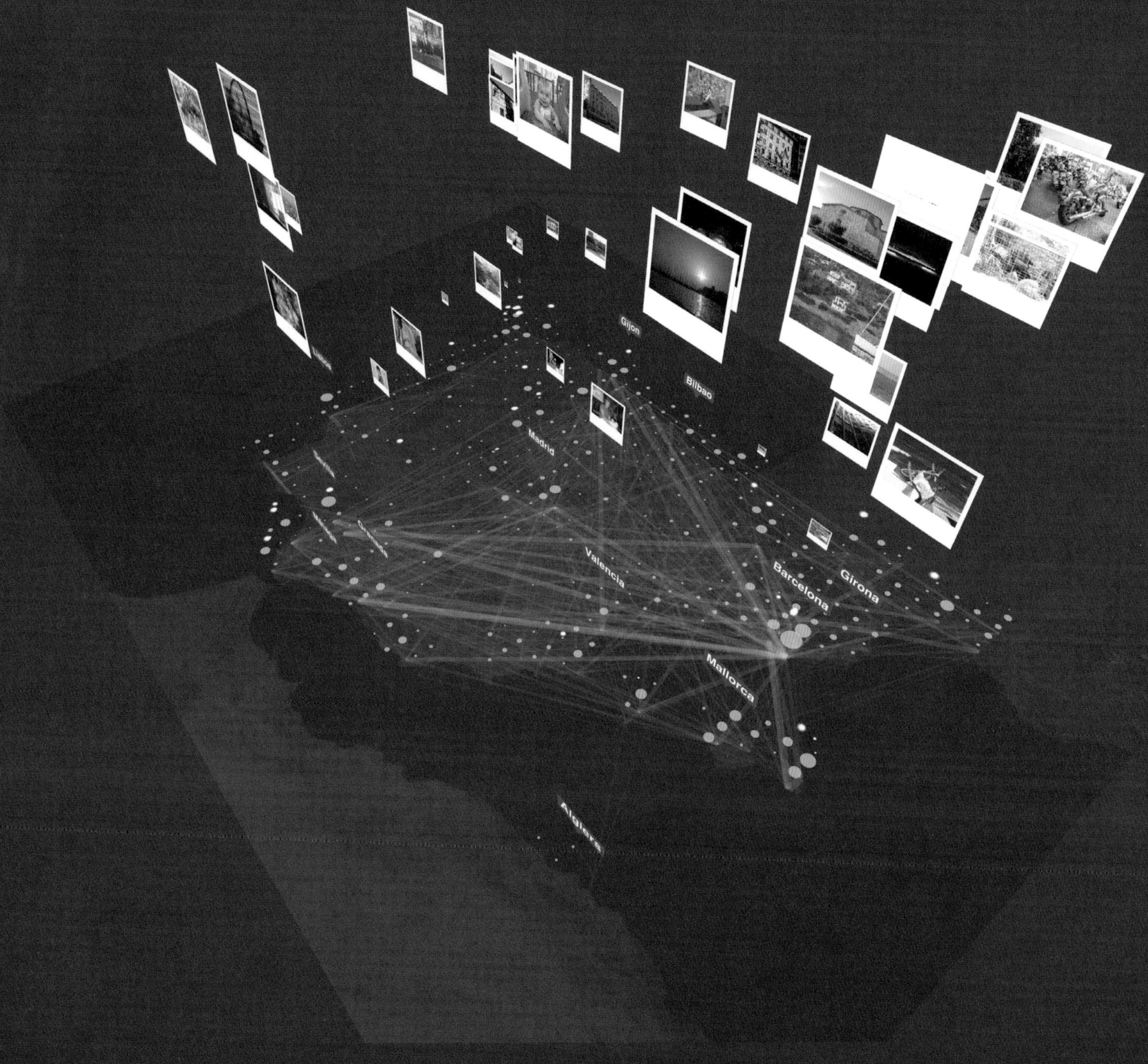
Gijon
Bilbao
Madrid
Valencia
Barcelona
Girona
Mallorca
Algiers

25A

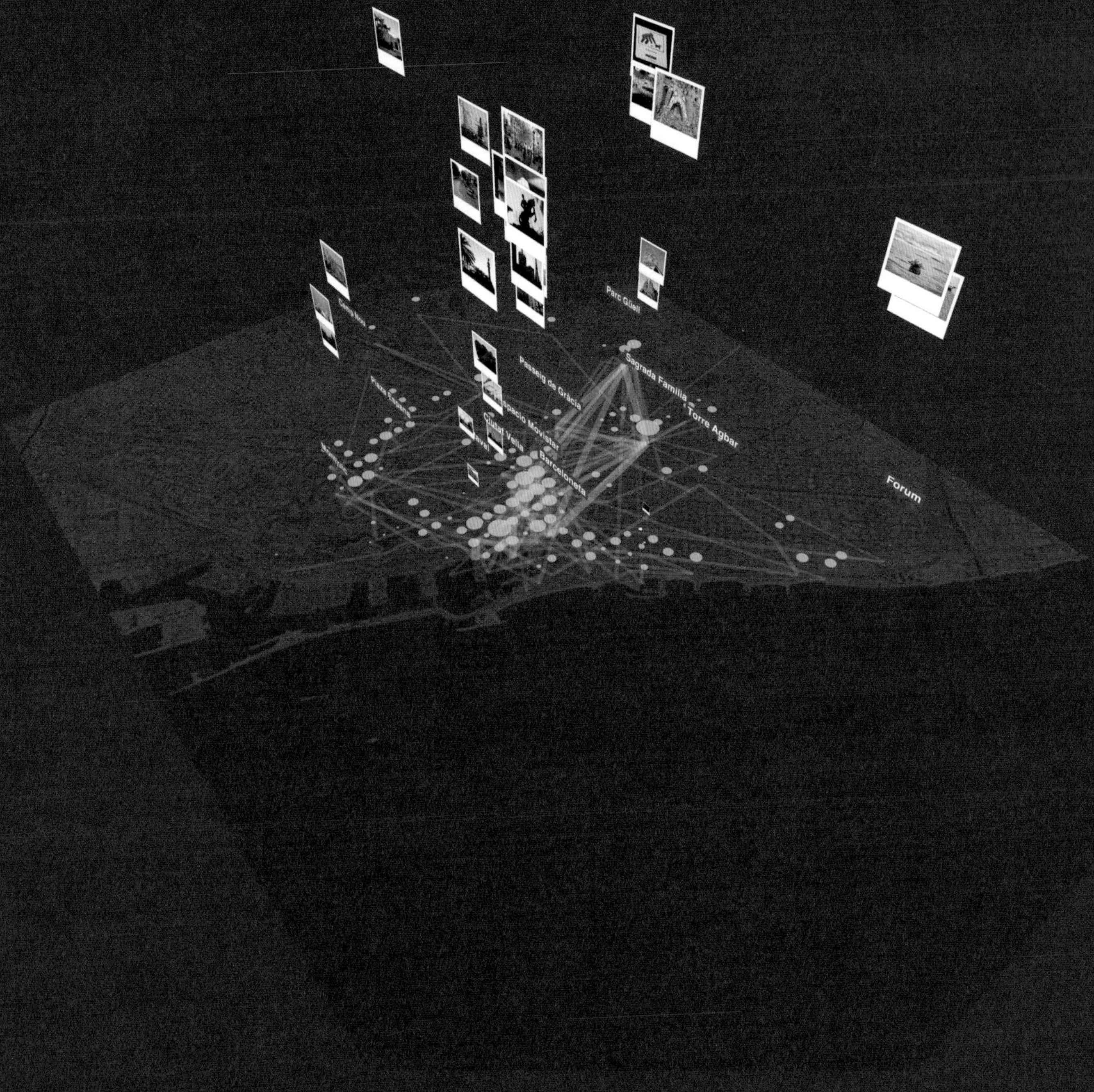
Parc Güell
Passeig de Gràcia
Sagrada Familia
Torre Agbar
Plaza España
Ciutat Vella
Barceloneta
Forum

25B

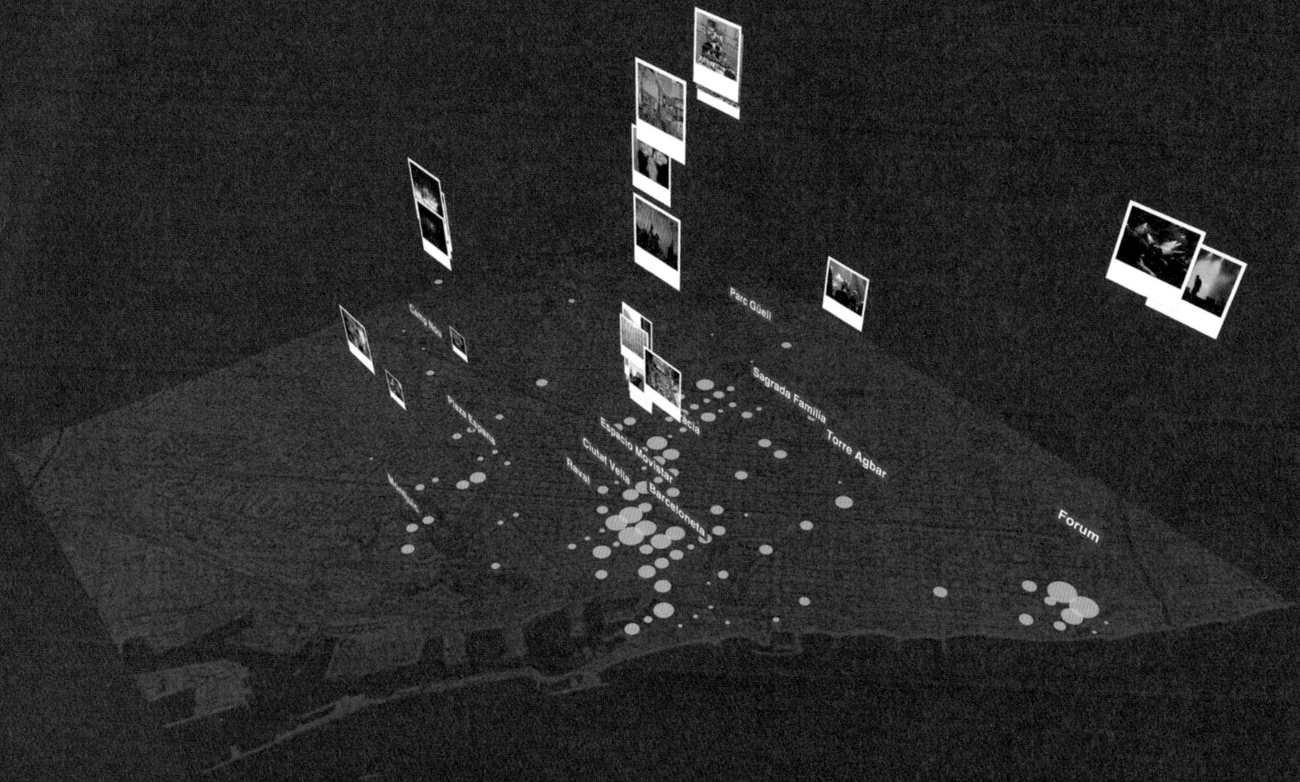
Parc Güell
Plaza España
Sagrada Familia
Espacio Movistar
Torre Agbar
Ciutat Vella
Raval
Barceloneta
Forum

26.
Obama | One People — 2009

On the morning of 20 January 2009, call activity in Washington, DC, was two to three times higher than usual. Around 2 PM, the number of calls rose further, reaching five times the normal level. It was the day of Barack Obama's inauguration as president.

By analyzing the number of mobile phone calls made in the city and the state or country where each phone was registered, the SCL was able to track the emotions of people from around the world on a historic day and record them in visual form. For instance, anticipation before Obama's oath of office coincided with higher than usual call activity, while the gravitas of the moment when the newly elected president began his inaugural address was underscored by a sudden drop in calls, which peaked again in the early afternoon, when celebrations commenced.

The SCL adopted three approaches to represent these trends. In the first figure, mobile call data are superimposed on a map of Washington in which the areas around the Mall and Pennsylvania Avenue, where most inaugural activities took place, are highlighted with yellow blocks (26A). In the animated version online, the surface rises and turns red as call activity intensifies. The timeline at the bottom shows the overall trend for inauguration week, while the bar chart on the left breaks call traffic down by geographic origin. In the next figure, a map of the United States (likewise animated online) appears in the background to replace the majority of the sidebar and better engage the viewer (26B). As it reveals, President Obama's home states, Illinois and Hawaii, were especially attentive as their native son became the leader of the free world. The last map below shifts the focus away from Washington, illustrating the event's international nature (26C). This visualization shows the variation in call activity between US states and foreign countries as flows of people from 138 nations traveled to and from the capital to celebrate the new president.

26A

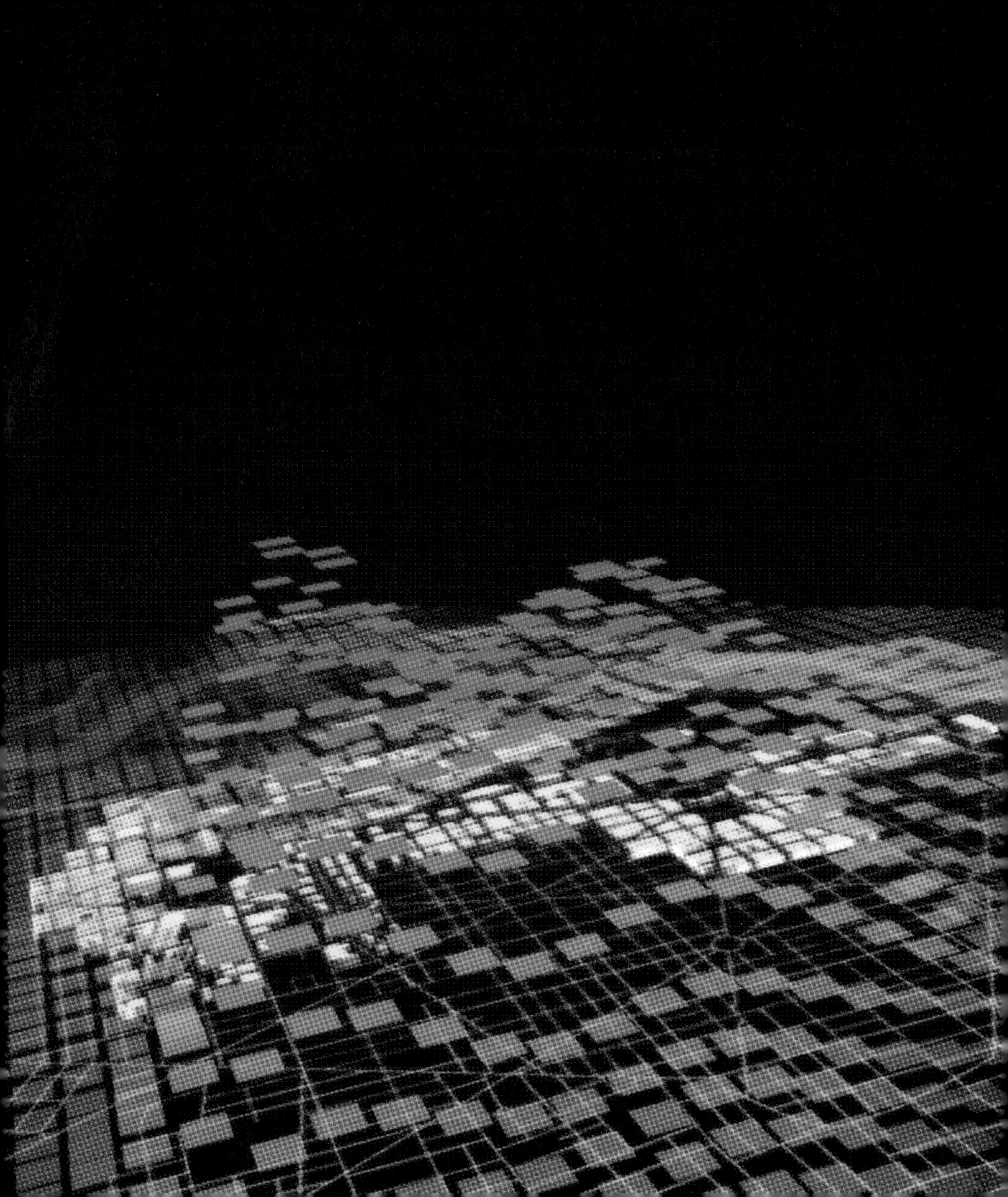

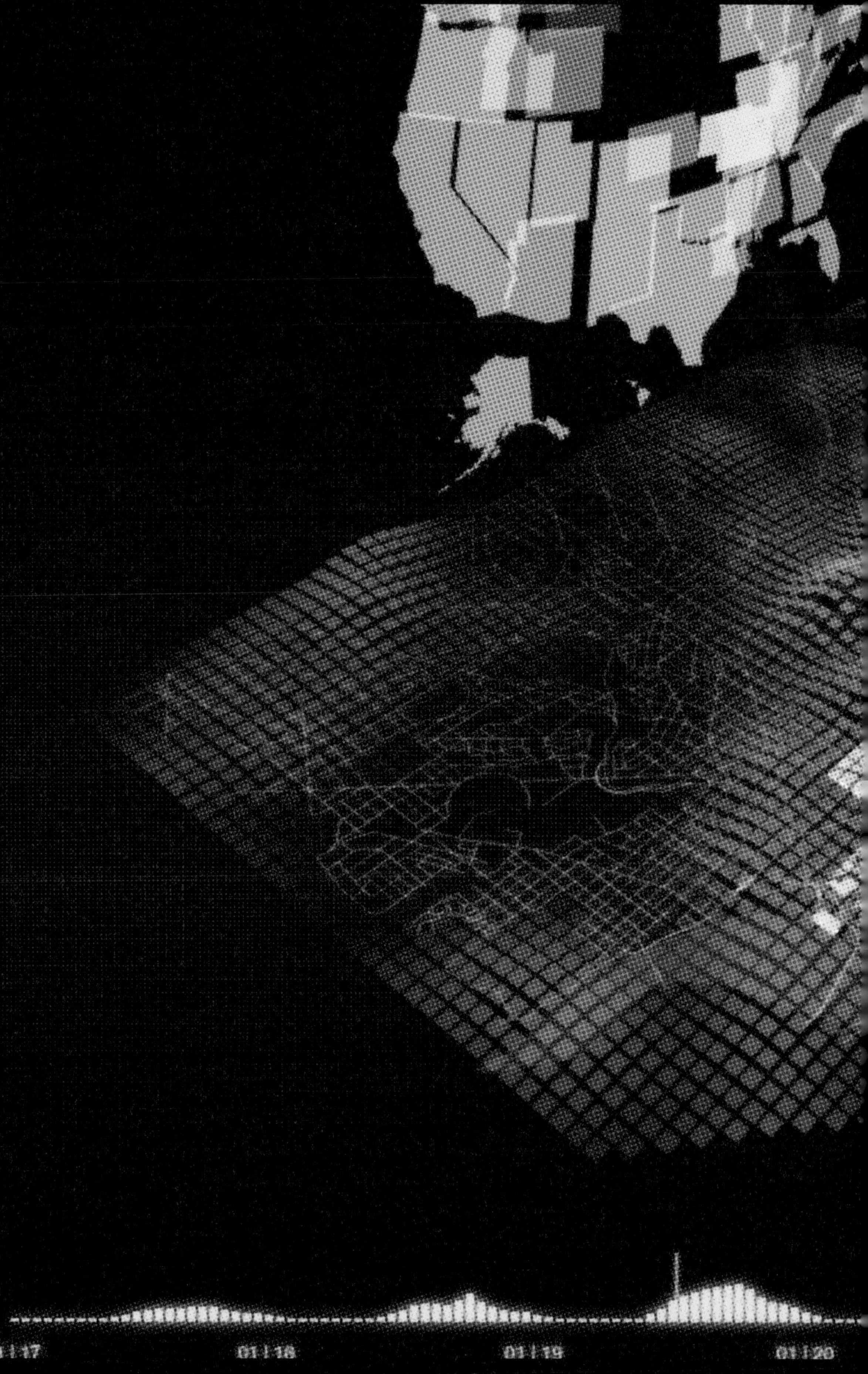
01 | 17
01 | 18
01 | 19
01 | 20

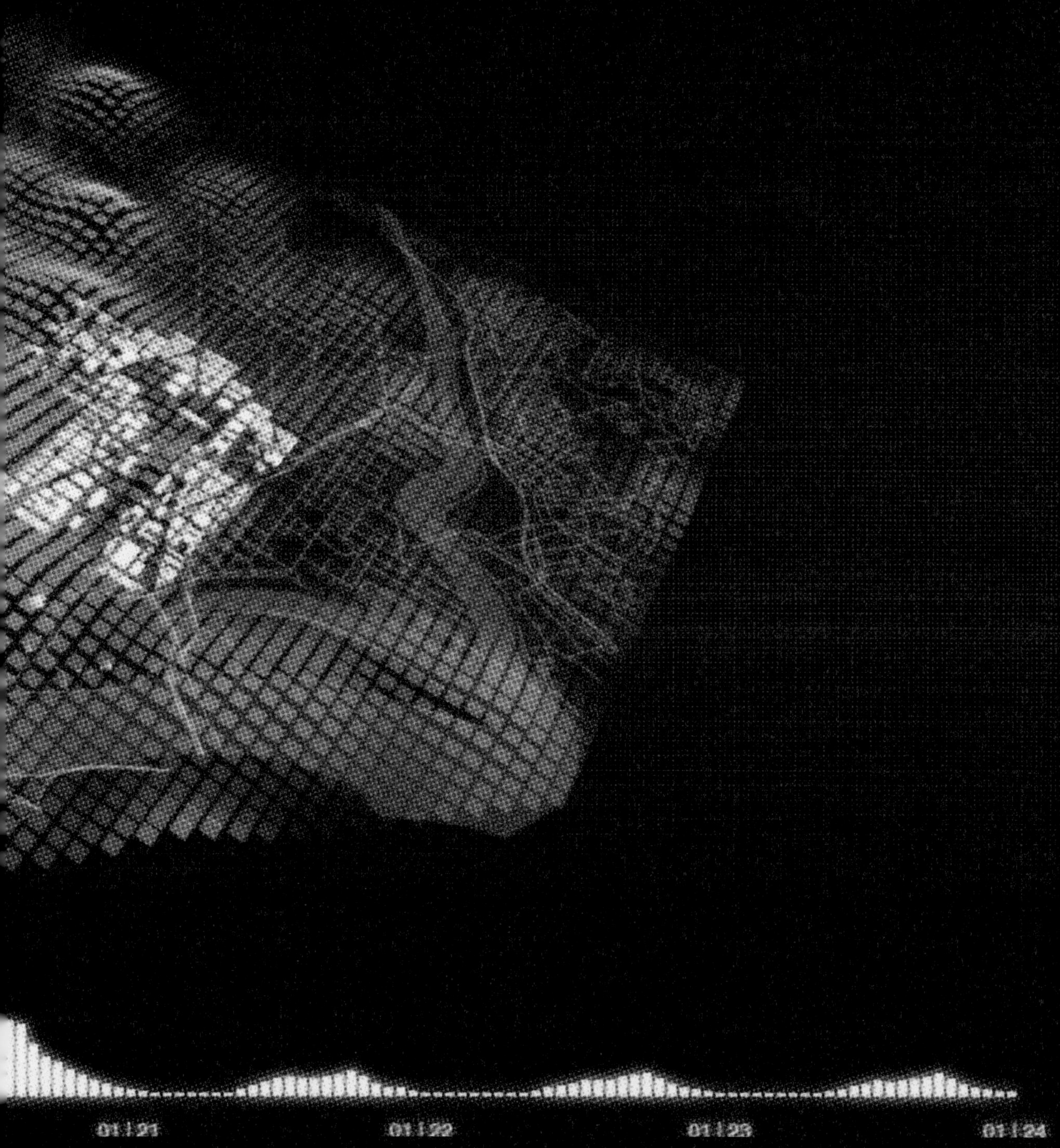

26B

01 | 17
01 | 18
01 | 19
01 | 20

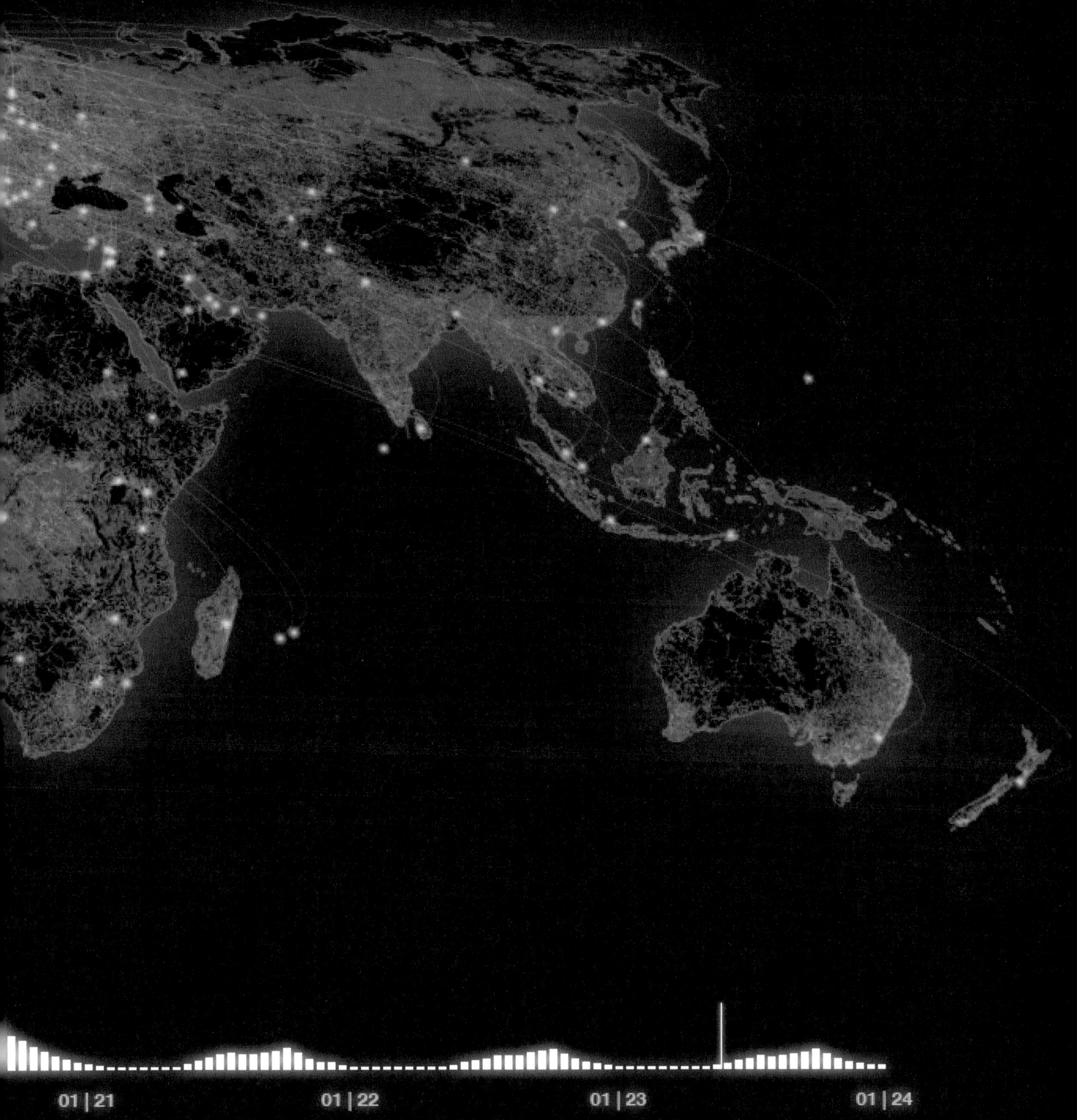
01 | 21
01 | 22
01 | 23
01 | 24

27.
Road Frustration Index — 2013

Road Frustration Index is a project from the SCL and Audi that combined real-time data on traffic, accidents, weather, and driver sentiment across thirty US metropolitan areas to approximate the level of road-induced stress, or road rage, in each. Maps of streets and the ways people use them usually do not include the subjective and emotive aspects of driving, which can involve large amounts of frustration or stress that change the way one experiences a city. Road Frustration Index incorporated these emotional responses into street-level cartography, producing maps far truer to life than mere geometric renderings.

The project aimed to home in on individual factors that frustrate drivers, in principle allowing Audi and other car manufacturers to work toward solutions to minimize those things and make driving more enjoyable. To calibrate its frustration algorithm, the SCL team designed a series of experiments to measure stress and aggravation during real-world driving tasks, using physiological sensors and an array of face-and-body-tracking technologies (including a Microsoft Kinect) placed by the steering wheel in the vehicles involved (27A).

A sensory map created by the project documents the first trial: a chaotic drive through the congested streets of Boston during peak traffic (27B). On the bottom, a graph demonstrates the level of frustration over time. Spikes came with traffic, honking, and being sideswiped. The project also demonstrated just how stressful driving can be when compared to other ordinary and not-so-ordinary activities (27C): from bottom to top, giving a presentation, sitting in an economics lecture, and driving. Dwarfing even the most intense road rage, but not pictured in this figure, was an afternoon of skydiving.

27A

CAMERA 1
00;00;09;35
CAMERA 2
00;00;09;35
KINECT
00;00;09;35
CAMERA 3
00;00;09;35

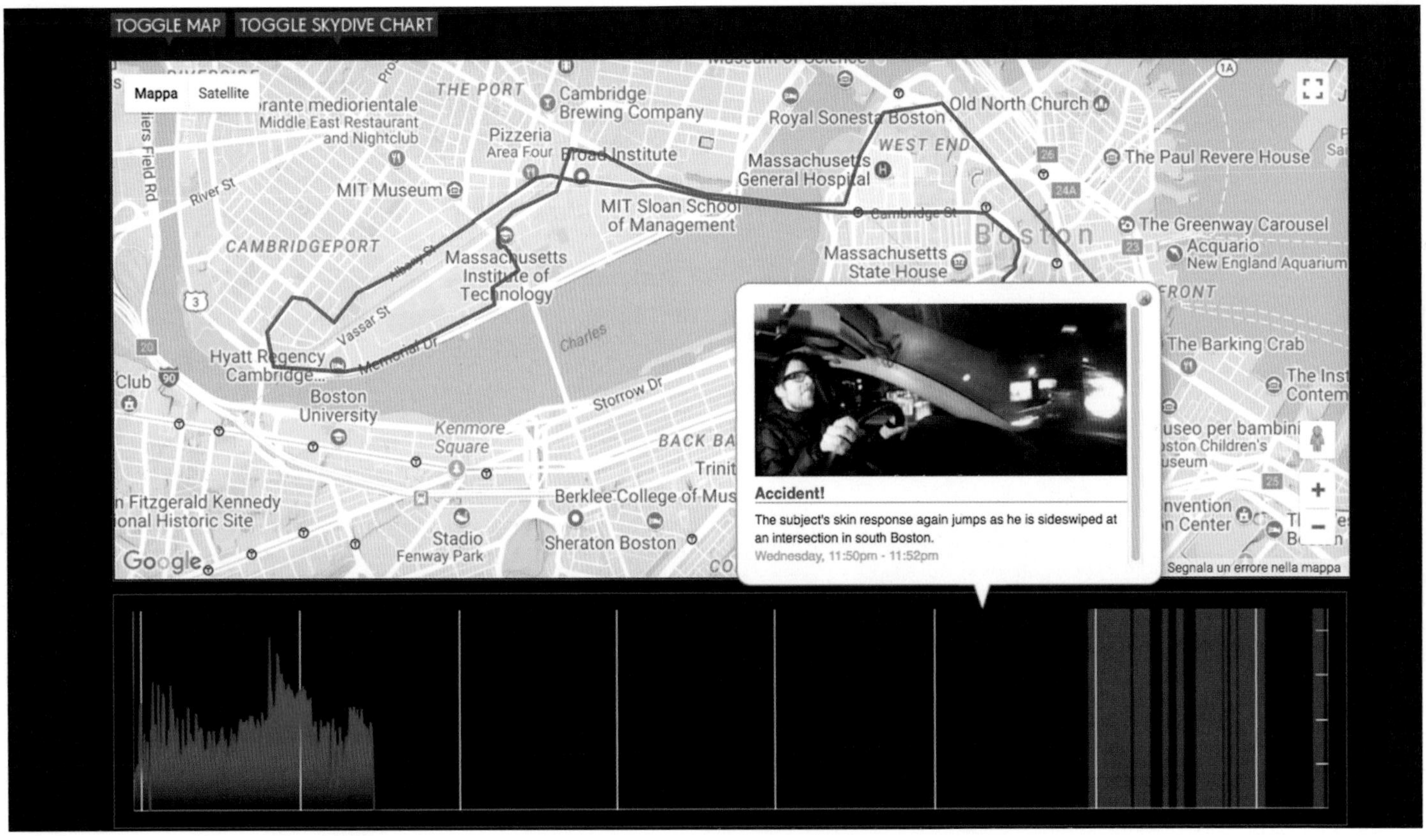
TOGGLE MAP
TOGGLE SKYDIVE CHART
Mappa
Satellite
Accident!
The subject's skin response again jumps as he is sideswiped at an intersection in south Boston.
Wednesday, 11:50pm - 11:52pm
Segnala un errore nella mappa

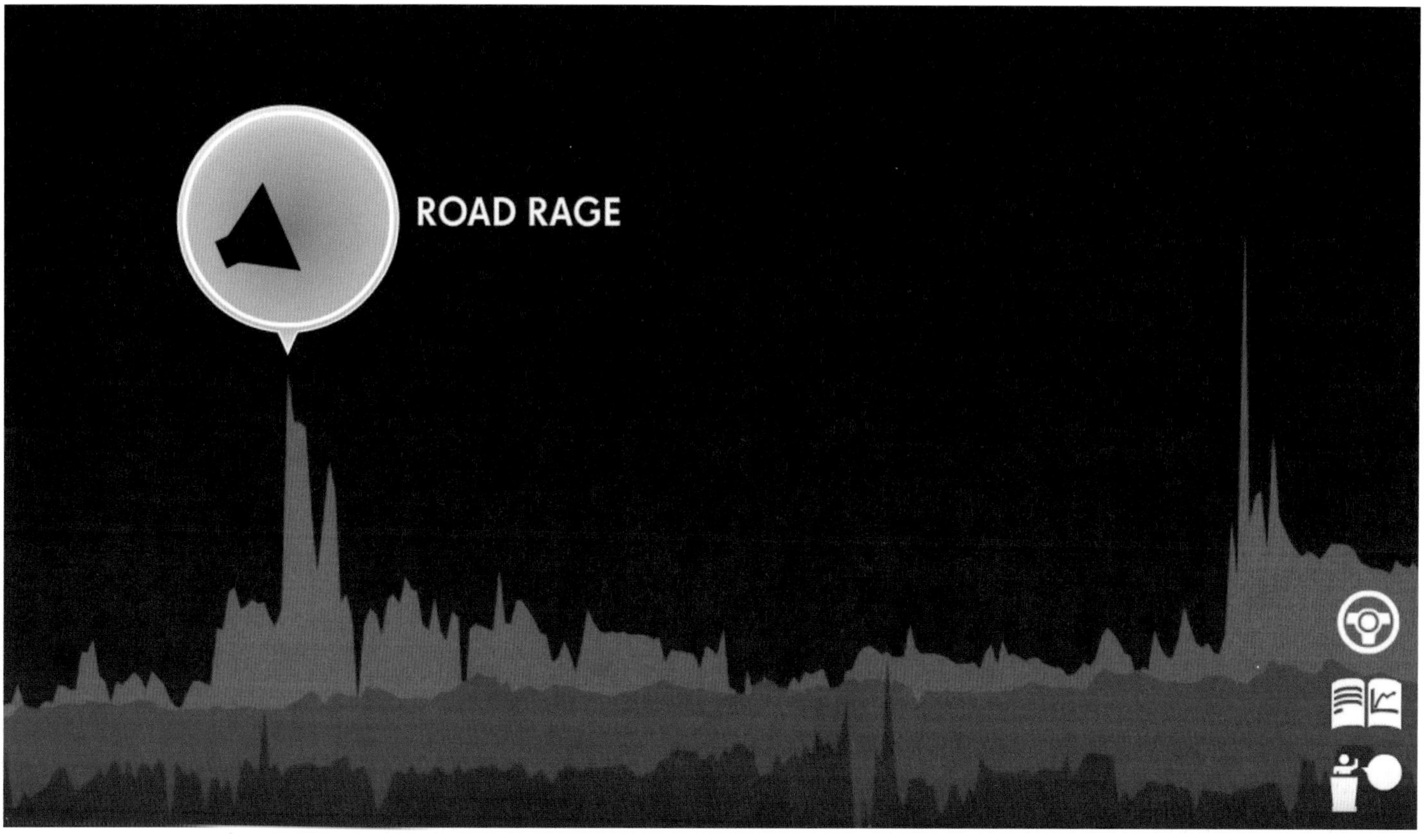
ROAD RAGE

28.
Art Traffic — 2014

How long do you take to smile back at the *Mona Lisa*? Today, sophisticated Bluetooth tracking allows us to map how visitors move through a museum like the Louvre in Paris: which galleries they visit, what path they take, and how long they spend in front of each piece of art. With perceptual cartography we can focus on a museum, a space much smaller than a city but similarly defined by the perspectives of its users.

Visitor behavior and experience are among the most important factors informing museum management curators have usually relied on traditional observations and surveys to understand them. Yet surveys gather only self-reported perspectives on personal experience—useful, but incomplete. The Art Traffic project used newly available large datasets—in this case, anonymized longitudinal visitation patterns captured by noninvasive Bluetooth sensors—to offer new tools for computational and comparative analysis of visitors' behavior in one of the world's largest museums, the Louvre.

The analysis discovered that short-stay (less than ninety minutes) and long-stay (more than six hours) visiting styles are not significantly different. Visitors of both categories tend to go to a similar number of key locations in the museum, yet those who stay longer tend to spend more time at them. This disproves an initial hypothesis that short-stay visitors explore fewer of the popular places. The analysis implies that visitors follow a limited set of distinct trajectories, a few emergent "elephant's paths" that people tend to move along without instruction. Individual variations are sometimes found, especially in repeat visits to striking works of art. The project's visualizations reveal the different kinds of visitors and their paths through the museum to see its most famous works, such as the Venus de Milo, the paintings in the Big Gallery, and, of course, the *Mona Lisa* (28A–28C).

28A

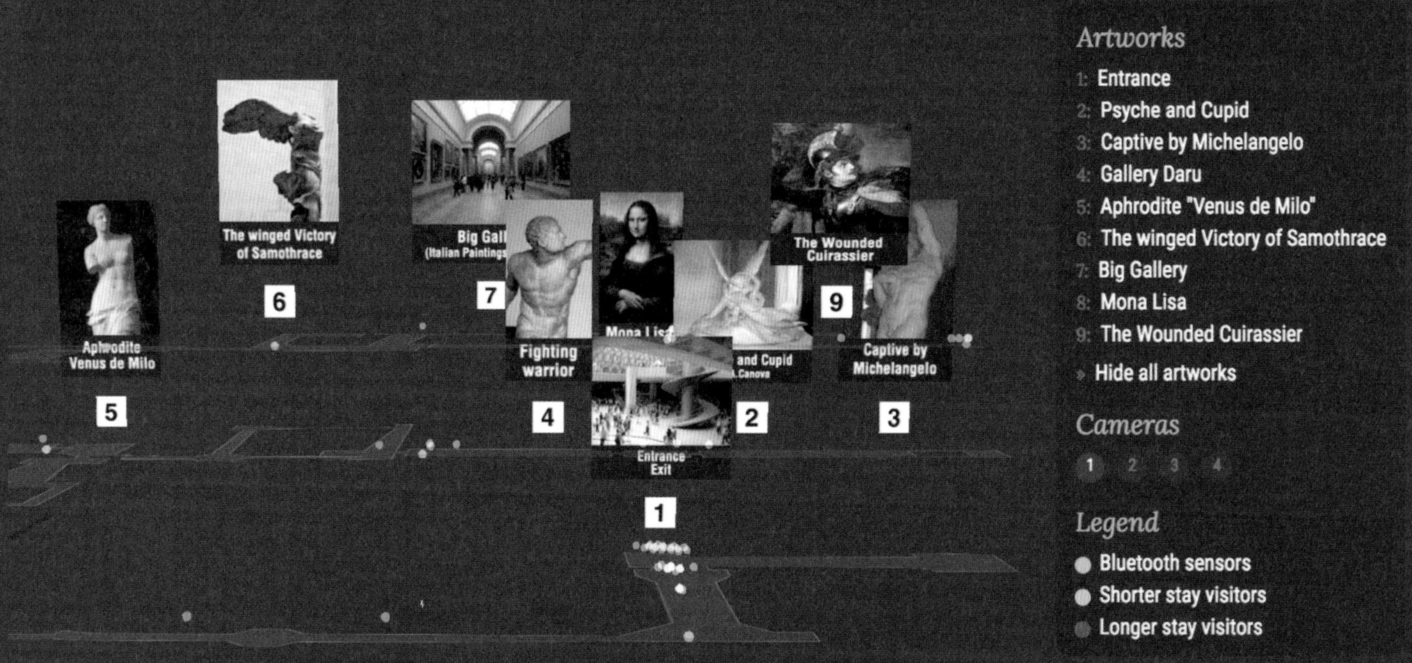
Aphrodite
Venus de Milo
5
The winged Victory
of Samothrace
6
7
Fighting
warrior
4
Mona Lisa
Entrance
Exit
1
and Cupid
2
The Wounded
Cuirassier
9
Captive by
Michelangelo
3
Artworks
1: Entrance
2: Psyche and Cupid
3: Captive by Michelangelo
4: Gallery Daru
5: Aphrodite "Venus de Milo"
6: The winged Victory of Samothrace
7: Big Gallery
8: Mona Lisa
9: The Wounded Cuirassier
» Hide all artworks
Cameras
1 2 3 4
Legend
Bluetooth sensors
Shorter stay visitors
Longer stay visitors

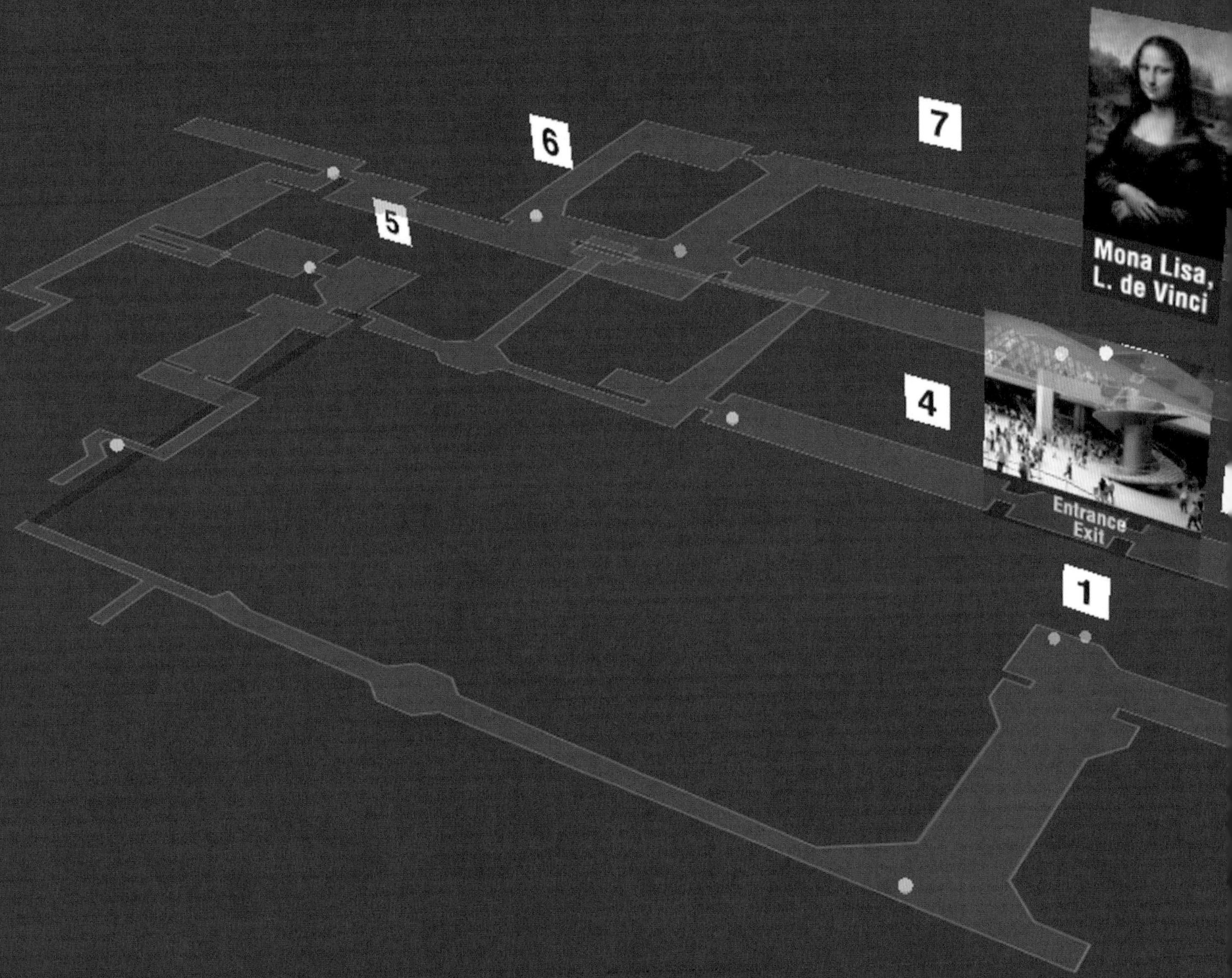

7
6
5
Mona Lisa,
L. de Vinci
4
Entrance
Exit
1

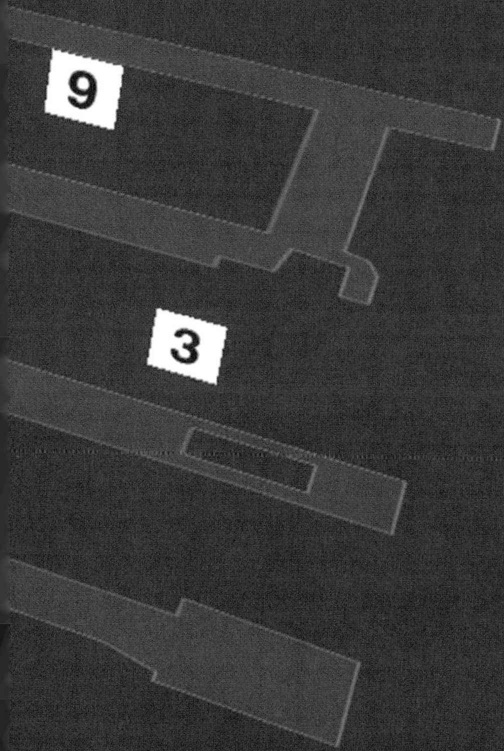

Artworks

1: Entrance
2: Psyche and Cupid
3: Captive by Michelangelo
4: Gallery Daru
5: Aphrodite "Venus de Milo"
6: The winged Victory of Samothrace
7: Big Gallery
8: Mona Lisa
9: The Wounded Cuirassier

» » Hide all artworks

Cameras

1 2 3 4

Legend

- Bluetooth sensors
- Shorter stay visitors
- Longer stay visitors

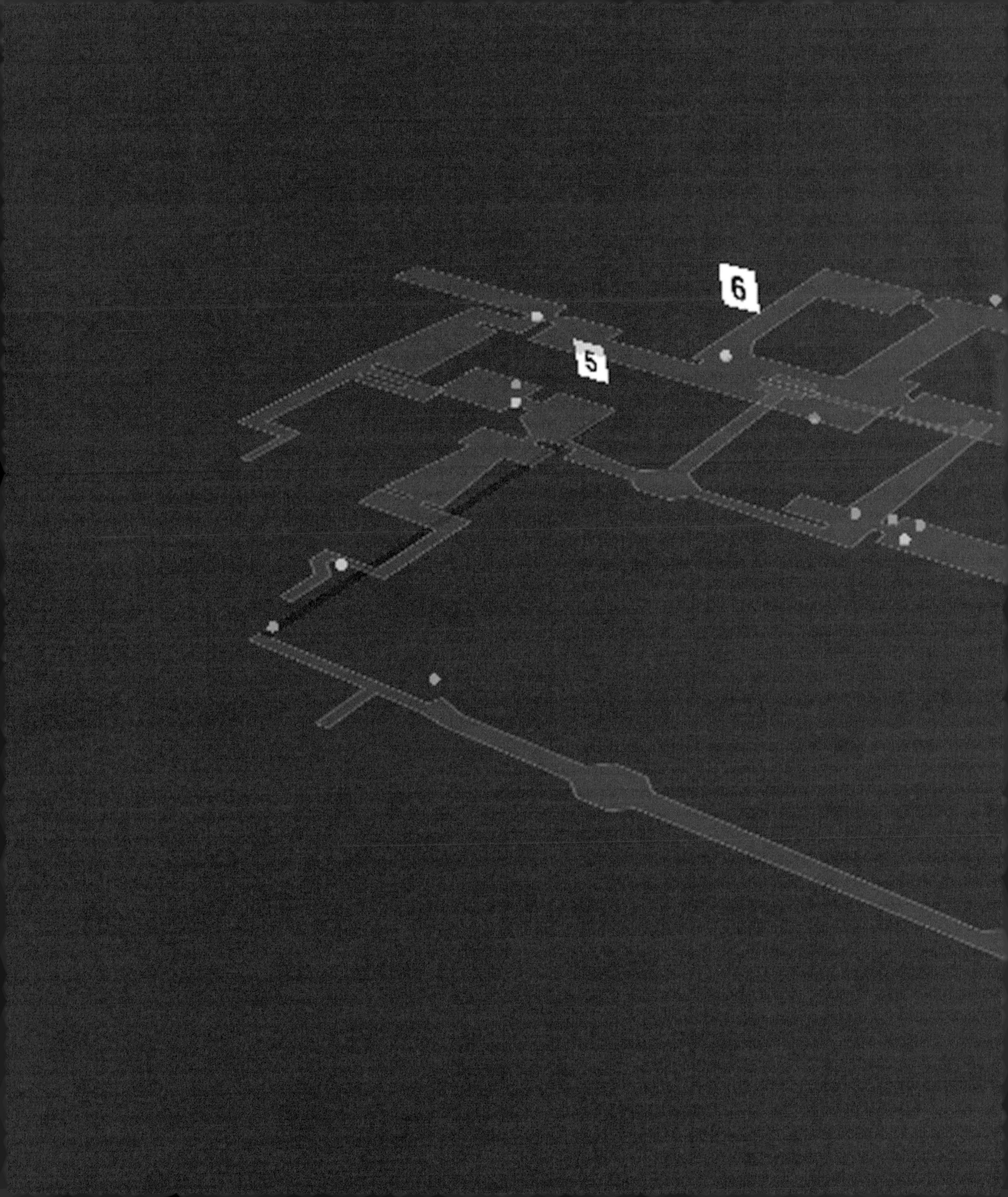
6
5

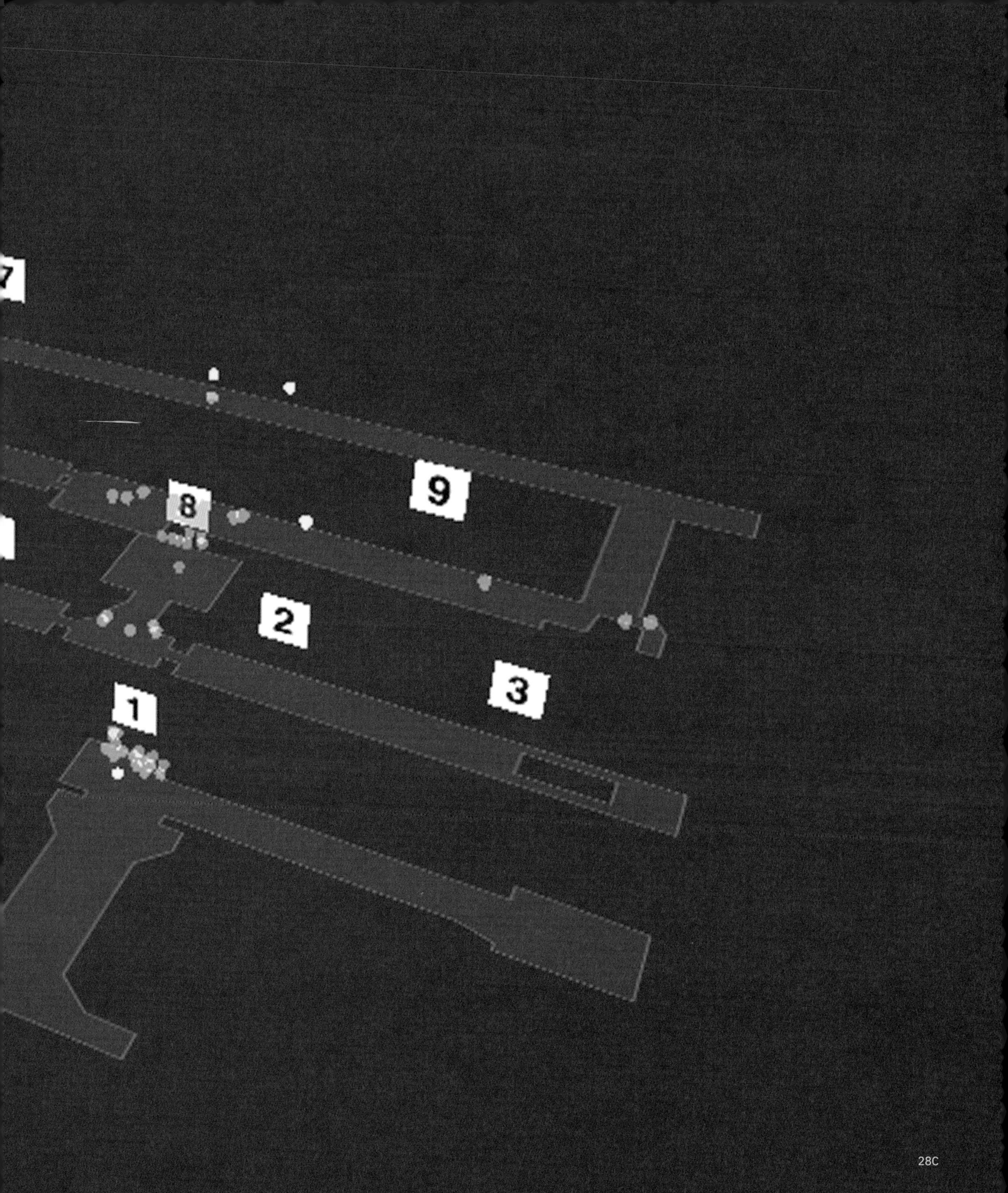
7
8
9
2
3
1

29.
Tweet Bursts — 2014

The mapping of emotions would be incomplete without taking into account the ways that people's feelings and perceptions of physical space shape virtual spaces. This is all the more true as the use of social media has fully pervaded our lives: we exchange emotions of love or hate on Facebook and react to important political affairs, exciting sports events, and natural catastrophes by racing to Twitter. In Tweet Bursts, the SCL, in partnership with Ericsson, undertook a visual and scientific exploration of how our tweets express our excitement, in order to collect new insights and improve our understanding of human behavior.

In one case, the project's researchers homed in on the 2012 Masters Tournament, a four-day thrill ride, from 5 to 8 April, for golf fans across the world. More than 40 million tweets related to the competition were posted as a global audience tuned in. On a longer graph mapping Twitter activity, this flurry of tweets stands out among otherwise relative regularity. Reactions to the Masters followed a daily rhythm: a constant stream of tweets intensified during the rounds featuring famous players, especially on the day of the final. They also followed a more general rule: the more excited Twitter users grew, the more intense the flurry of their tweets and the shorter each message became (29A). Emotional bursts are faster and more impulsive online, revealing that our aggregate passions manifest with striking, mathematical regularity. During exciting moments, when Twitter is bursting with emotional tweets, the average message length drops from ninety to sixty characters (29B).

This study raises several important questions: Are people making these changes independently, or are they following the herd? Are they competing to be the first to post, or are they too emotional to string more characters together? Might we use these insights to learn more about financial bubbles by measuring impulsive responses? The hope is to address these questions and expand the research to other social media platforms.

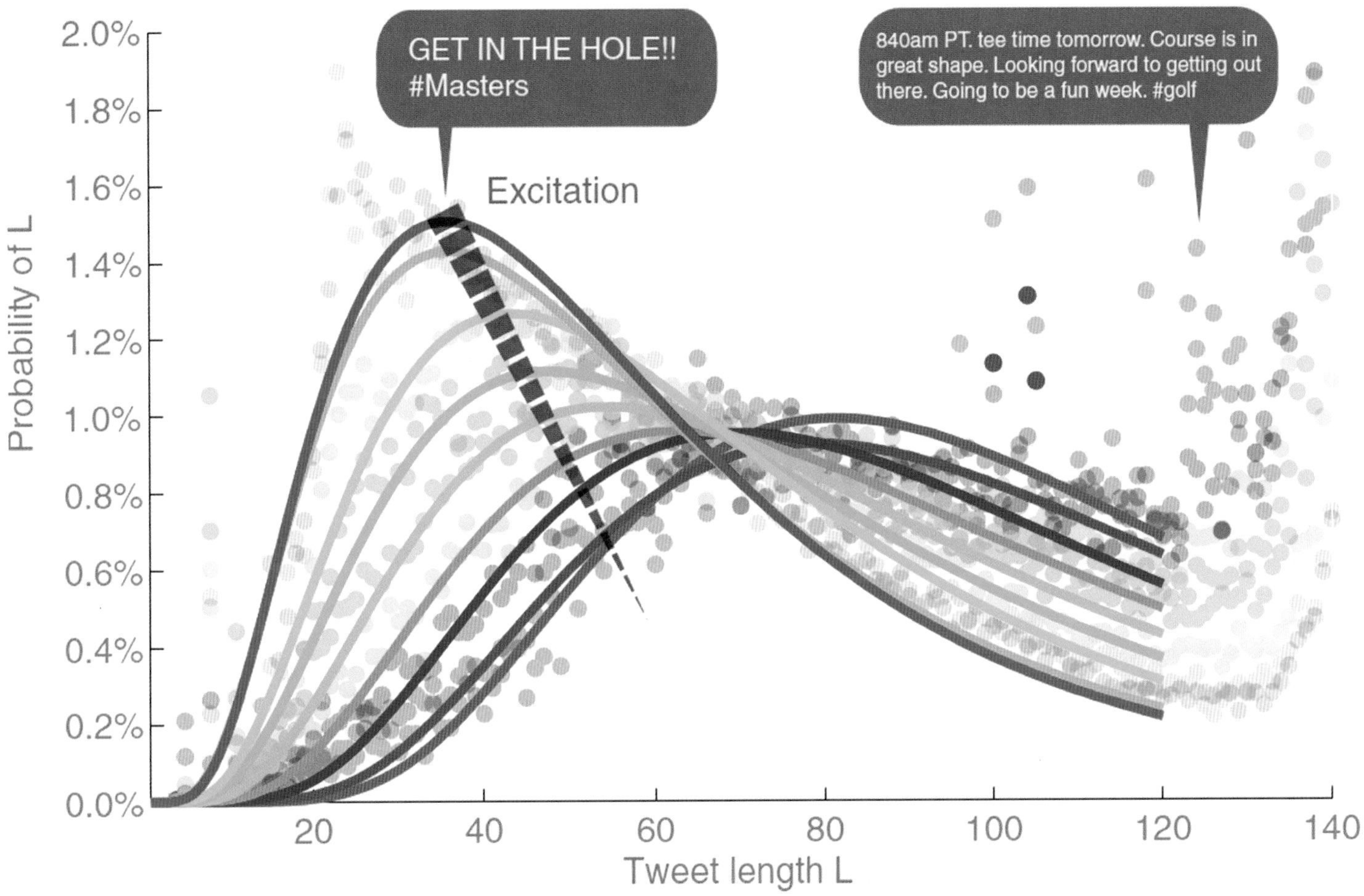
GET IN THE HOLE!! #Masters
840am PT. tee time tomorrow. Course is in great shape. Looking forward to getting out there. Going to be a fun week. #golf
Excitation
Probability of L
2.0%
1.8%
1.6%
1.4%
1.2%
1.0%
0.8%
0.6%
0.4%
0.2%
0.0%
20
40
60
80
100
120
140
Tweet length L

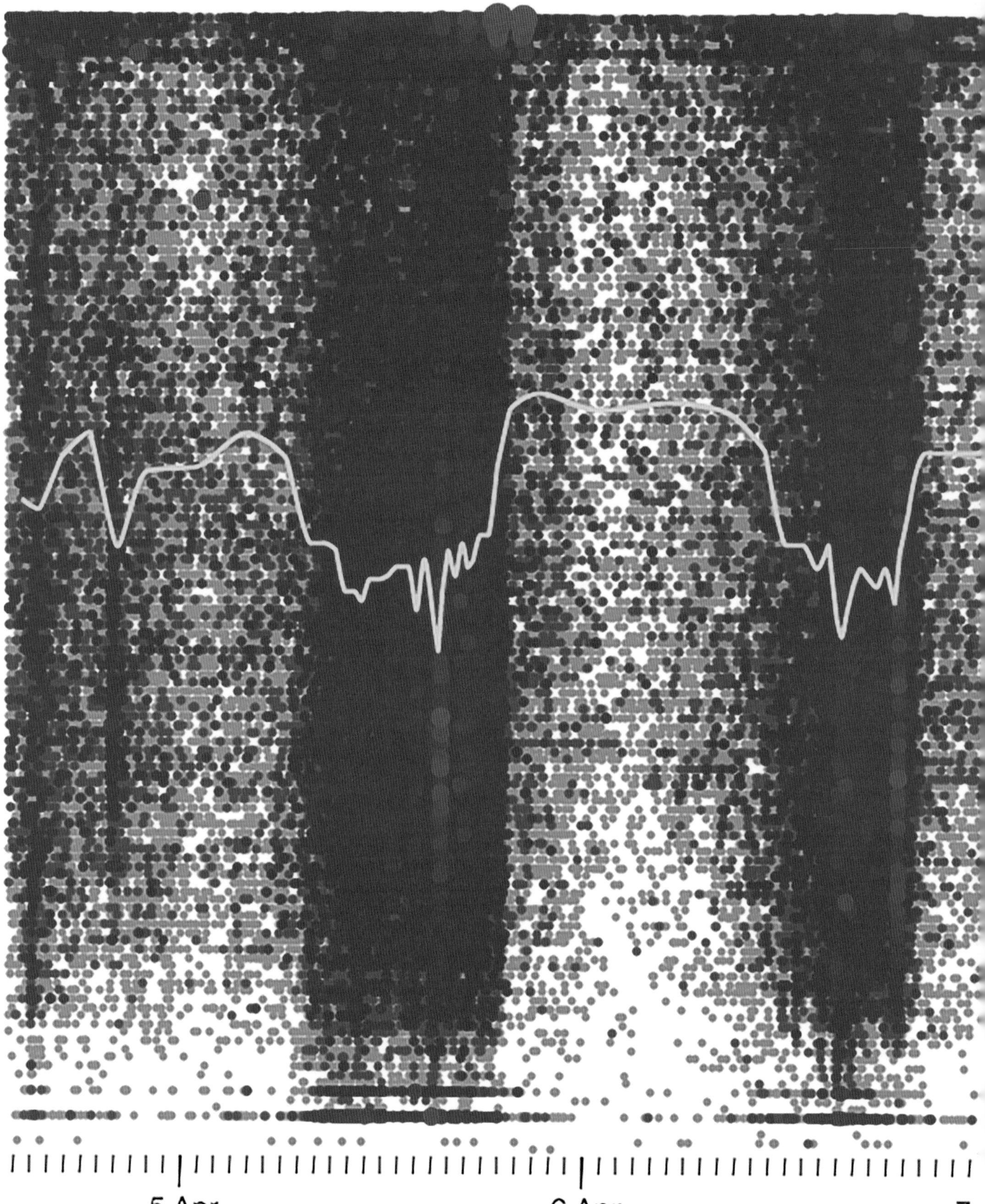

5 Apr
6 Apr
7

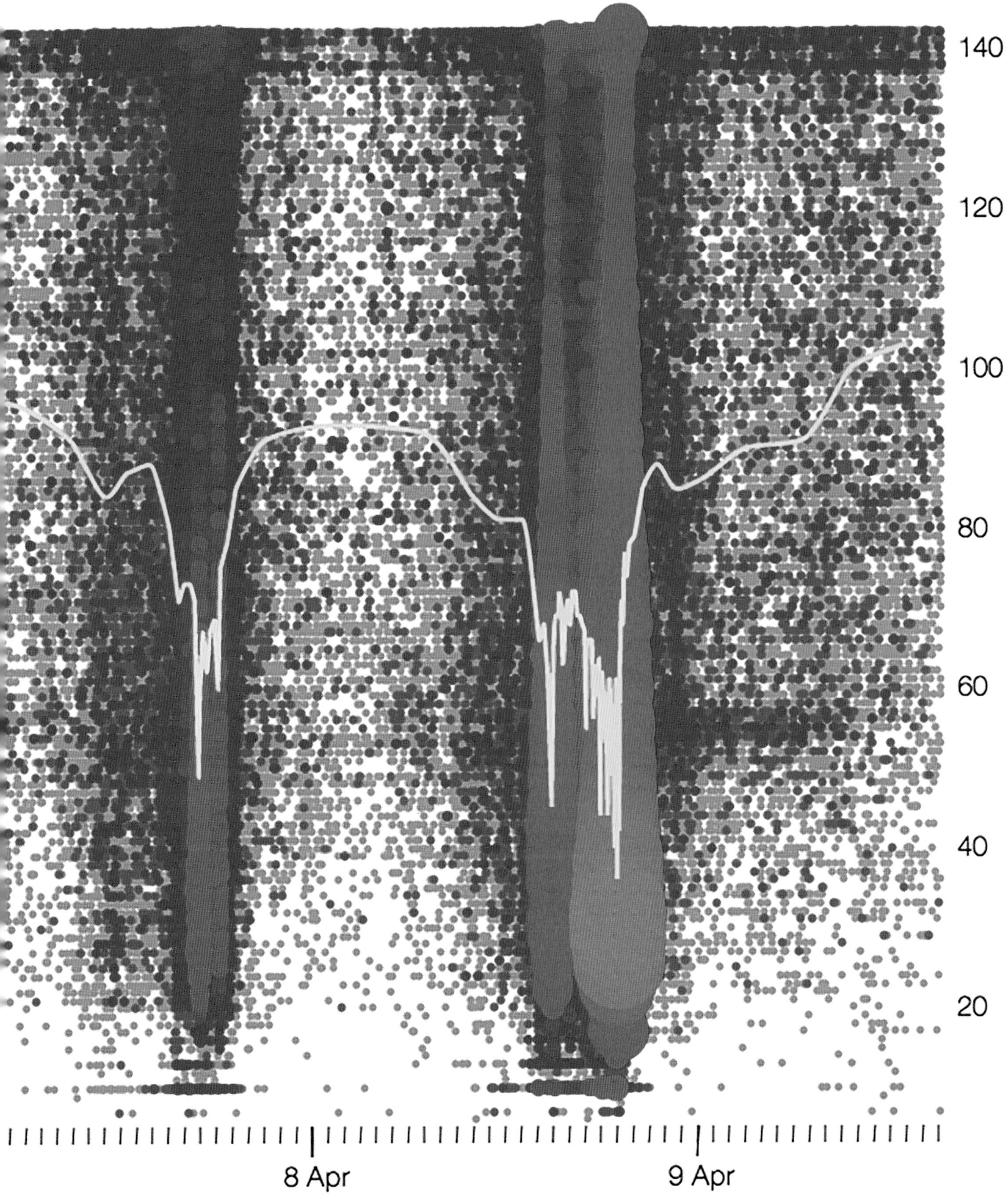

29B

30.
Treepedia — 2016

When we think about urban vegetation, we usually think about parks. But have you ever noticed how green your street is? A city's tree canopy helps lower its temperature, improves air quality, boosts flood resilience, and increases people's well-being. In 2015, the World Economic Forum's Global Agenda Council on the Future of Cities (chaired by one of this book's authors) included increasing canopy cover in its list of "Top Ten Urban Innovations."[8]

One year later, the SCL launched Treepedia, a project to record and measure canopy cover at street level. Using Google Street View panoramas rather than satellite images, as if gazing up through the eyes of human beings instead of spying down with a superimposed definition of what a green urban center should look like, researchers calculated a green view index for each city they investigated, quantifying the number of trees along its streets and the amount of cover that their leaves provided to the people who walked under them every day (30A).

The ultimate goal of the Treepedia database is to raise awareness of the state of urban vegetation around the world and to spark bottom-up change. Green and brown interact uneasily on the maps that the SCL produced for this project (30B–30C), reminding us that the most verdant, well-covered areas exist side by side with neighborhoods that have barely any trees. The residents of different blocks experience completely different urban ecologies, an inequity that must be rendered visible before it can be remedied. These data visualizations can help city planners and planters optimize future efforts, but they can also be tools of education and empowerment for locals and community groups. Seeing a database affirm their day-to-day frustrations can encourage and support people who want to push back against unequal access to green spaces. The project also includes an open-source Python library so anyone can calculate their own city's green view index. By creating maps that capture a small slice of the human condition, Treepedia can help people collectively navigate the long, winding path toward social and environmental justice.

8 Global Agenda Council on the Future of Cities, "Top Ten Urban Innovations" (October 2015), 6, https://www3.weforum.org/docs/Top_10_Emerging_Urban_Innovations_report_2010_20.10.pdf.

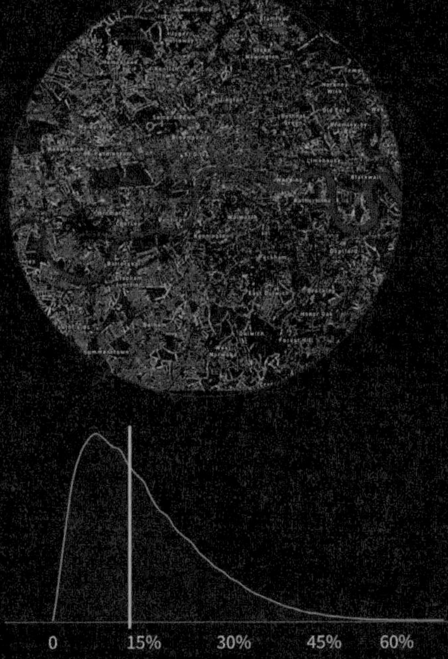

London

Green View Index	12.7%
Population Density	5,518/km^2

New York

Green View Index	13.5%
Population Density	10,831/km^2

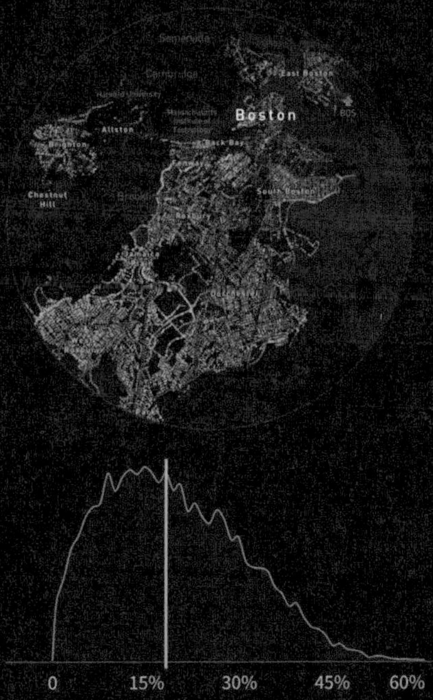

Boston

Green View Index	18.2%
Population Density	5,344/km^2

Geneva

Green View Index	21.4%
Population Density	1,873/km^2

Clichy
de Saint-Ouen
Courbevoie
Île de la Jatte
Levallois-Perret
Tour Areva
Défense
Tour First
Neuilly-sur-Seine
Île de Puteaux
Hyatt Regency Paris Étoile
Jardin d'Acclimatation
Louis Vuitton Foundation
Plaine de jeu de Bagatelle
Bois de Boulogne
16th arrondissement of Paris
Trocadero gardens
Guimet Museum
Passy
Auteuil Hippodrome
Auteuil
Stade Roland Garros
Stade Jean-Bouin
Parc des Princes
ogne-
ncourt
Parc Suzanne Lenglen
Île Saint-Germain
Issy-les-Moulineaux
Cité Scolaire Michelet
Montmartre Cemetery
Montmartr
Arron
17th Arrondissement
Saint-Jean-de-Montmartre
Quartier Pigalle
Monceau
8th Arrondissement
9th Arrondisseme
Champs-Élysées
Elysée Palace
La Madeleine
Palais Garnier
Opéra
Palais Brongniart
Hotel Ritz Paris
Hôtel de Crillon
Notre-Dame-des-Victoires
Grand Palais
Galerie nationale du Jeu de Paume
1st Arrondissement
National Assembly
Louvre Palace
Saint-Germain l'Auxerrois
Ministry of Defence
New Bridge
7th Arrondissement
Palace of
Champ de Mars
Musée Rodin
Saint-Germain-des-Prés
La Seine
École Militaire
6th Arrondissement
5t Arrondis
Grenelle
musée Bourdelle
Montparnasse
Montparnasse Tower
15th Arrondissement
Église du Val-de-Grâce
Gare Montparnasse
Montparnasse Cemetery
Paris Observatory
Église Notre-Dame-du-Travail
La Santé Prison
14th Arrondissement
Alésia

Vignes
départemental de la Bergère
Pantin villette
La Folie
Gare de triage Noisy-le-Sec
La Chapelle Charbon
Technicentre est européen
Pantin
La Géode
parc de la Villette
La Chapelle
19th Arrondissement
Noisy-le-Sec
Parc République
Base de loisirs de la Corniche des Forts
Romainville
Cité des Auteurs
Le Pré-Saint-Gervais
Fort de Noisy
Parc des Buttes Chaumont
Les Lilas
10th Arrondissement
Hôpital Saint-Louis
Belleville
Ménilmontant
Bagnolet
République
3rd Arrondissement
Parc départemental Jean-Moulin - Les Guilands
Montreuil
Saint-Ambroise
Père Lachaise Cemetery
Le Marais
11th Arrondissement
Saint-Blaise
Parc des Beaumonts
Carnavalet Museum
place des Vosges
Charonne
Hôtel de Sully
Bastille
Opéra Bastille
Bassin de l'Arsenal
Arab World Institute
Pierre and Marie Curie University
Vincennes
Paris-Gare de Lyon
Jardin des Plantes
Château de Vincennes
Saint-Mandé
Fort Neuf de Vincennes
12th Arrondissement
AccorHotels Arena
Hôpital Universitaire Pitié-Salpêtrière
Parc floral de Paris
Bercy
parc de Bercy
13th Arrondissement
Paris Zoological Park
bois de Vincennes
INSEP
Parc de vincennes
Institut national des langues et civilisations orientales
Stade Per

30B

Senoko
Woodlands
Mandai
Lim Chu Kang
Sungei Kadut
Choa Chu Kang
Bukit Panjang
Bukit Batok
Jurong West
Jurong East
Pioneer
Boon Lay
Clementi
Queenstown
Tuas South
Jurong
Alexandra

Yishun
Seletar
Punggol
Sengkang
Buangkok
Hougang
Serangoon North
Ang Mo Kio
Sin Ming
Bishan
Serangoon
Kovan
Serangoon New Town
Lorong Ah Soo
QPG
Pasir Ris
Loyang
Changi Village
Tampines
Changi Airport
SIN
Simei
WSAC
Tai Seng
Kaki Bukit
Joo Seng
Toa Payoh
Potong Pasir
Balestier
Whampoa
Kallang Way
Geylang
Chai Chee
Bedok
Bedok South
Tanah Merah
Changi Bay
Kampong Ladang
Newton Circus
Kallang
Orchard
Little India
Beach Road
Tanjong Katong
Marine Parade
Kampong Amber
East Coast
Bugis
Bras Basah
City Hall
Singapore
Raffles Place
Outram
Marina South
Shenton Way

30C

31.
City Ways — 2017

To unite the four themes of this atlas—motion, connection, circulation, and experience—consider the simple act of going out to exercise. By definition, walking, running, and cycling involve human motion. Also, athletes often record, share, and occasionally boast about their progress on digital tracking and communication platforms. In addition, exercise is critical for human health, and urban design has a part to play in making it possible. Finally, although biologists and doctors have much to say about its importance, we all know that our primary motivators for moving around—the compulsion to hit ten thousand steps, the joy of walking a dog, or the random craving to visit a convenience store, for instance—are emotional.

With City Ways, the SCL explored all of the above. Taking advantage of the extraordinary ubiquity of fitness apps on phones and watches, this project analyzed data from thousands of people in Boston (31A) and San Francisco (31B–31C), measuring every time they—or rather, their devices—traveled more than fifteen meters (forty-nine feet) over the course of a year. The results can be broken down into a variety of categories, such as type of activity and the gender of participants. They can also be compared with atmospheric conditions at the time, such as temperature and precipitation.

The results are a window onto the social and physical determinants of movement. Certain spots, like Jamaica Pond and the banks of the Charles River, are clearly beloved by Boston's runners. Colder temperatures decrease rates of going outside, but Bostonians appear to have a far higher tolerance of winter than San Franciscans do. Researchers were especially interested in people's preferences when choosing their routes. How valuable is the shortest path relative to the number of intersections, steepness of hills, or quality of bike lanes, for instance? The answers to such questions differ from place to place: the availability of sidewalks increased the volume of foot traffic in Boston but had little to no effect in San Francisco, for example. To plan cities against the backdrop of human subjectivity, big data is clearly no substitute for specific data.

31A

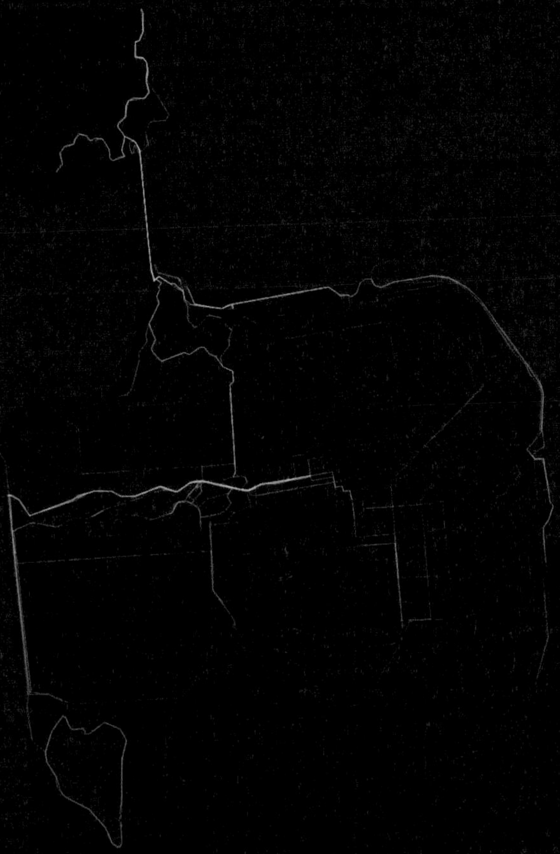

City	Date	Weather	Av. Dist.	Gender	Age
San Francisco Cycling	February 17 2015	13°C	7,590 m	Female 16% Male 84%	13-24 4% 25-44 45-99 17%

City	Date	Weather	Av. Dist.	Gender	Age
San Francisco Running	February 17 2015	13°C	5,808 m	Female 40% Male 60%	13-24 6% 25-44 78% 45-99 16%

32.
AI Station — 2019

The human experience of navigating a train station—thick crowds of daily commuters and bewildered tourists lugging heavy suitcases and groaning over delayed departures—cannot be communicated with blueprints. Working with the French rail company SNCF Gares & Connexions, the SCL used big data and artificial intelligence (AI) to create unconventional maps of how passengers navigate two of Paris's busiest train stations, Gare de Lyon and Gare Saint-Lazare.

The first metric that researchers evaluated was spatial legibility, an area's ability to be identified and understood. Designers have traditionally struggled to be sure that their spaces are legible to users, but today AI can recognize images—just as self-driving cars identify stop signs—in a way that simulates human perception and can help us evaluate spatial legibility across large areas. The first visualization above shows how the AI fared at recognizing different spaces in the Gare Saint-Lazare (32A). On the left side, heat maps reveal that both algorithms and human volunteers referenced similar items of interest—pillars, signs, staircases—in making their identifications. The AI was quite adept at recognizing shops, hallways, and waiting areas, but the places where it struggled—where construction materials were aesthetically vague or architectural elements repetitive—suggest which places might confuse real people and what strategies might help them find their bearings.

The second metric analyzed was navigability, the capacity to help users get around. Anonymized Wi-Fi signals from thousands of cell phones let researchers track how long individuals tended to stay in a given spot and where they tended to go next. Beyond overall trends, the resulting visualization shows the unique movement patterns of arrivals, departures, and layovers (32B). With knowledge of these experiences, we can build and rebuild our transit hubs to promote the greatest ease in traveling—and wandering, when the opportunity presents itself.

32A

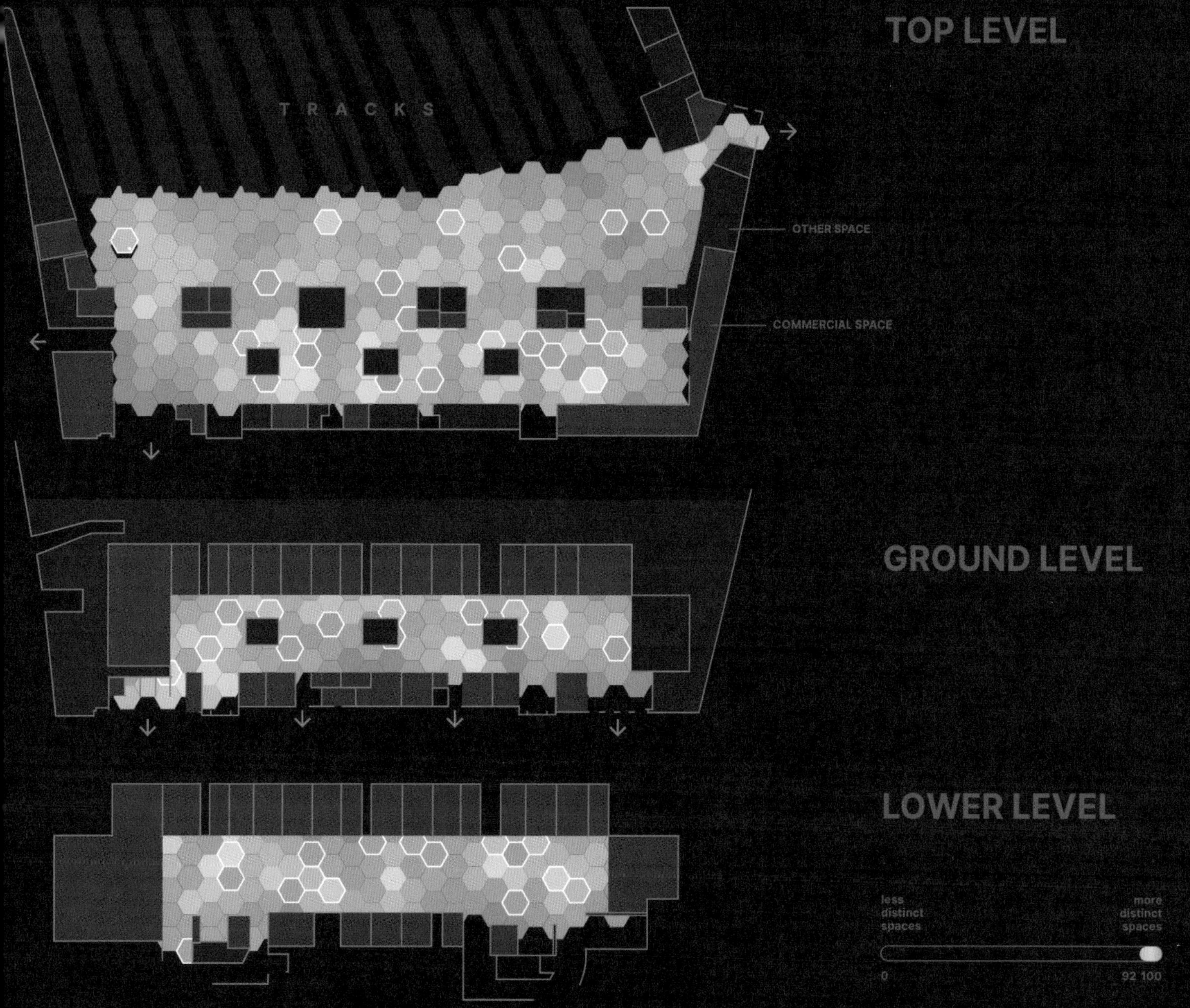
TOP LEVEL
TRACKS
OTHER SPACE
COMMERCIAL SPACE
GROUND LEVEL
LOWER LEVEL
less distinct spaces
more distinct spaces
0
92 100

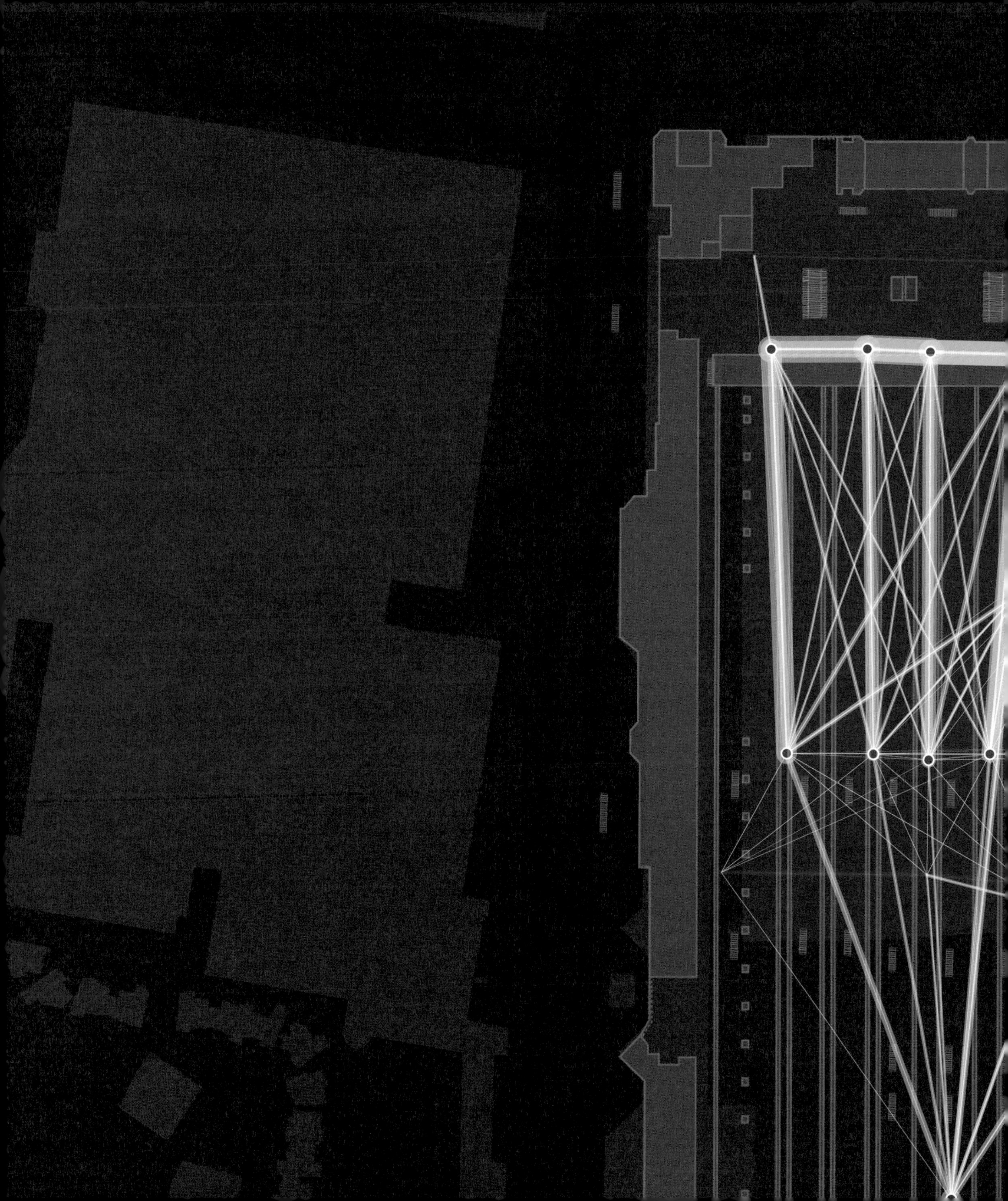

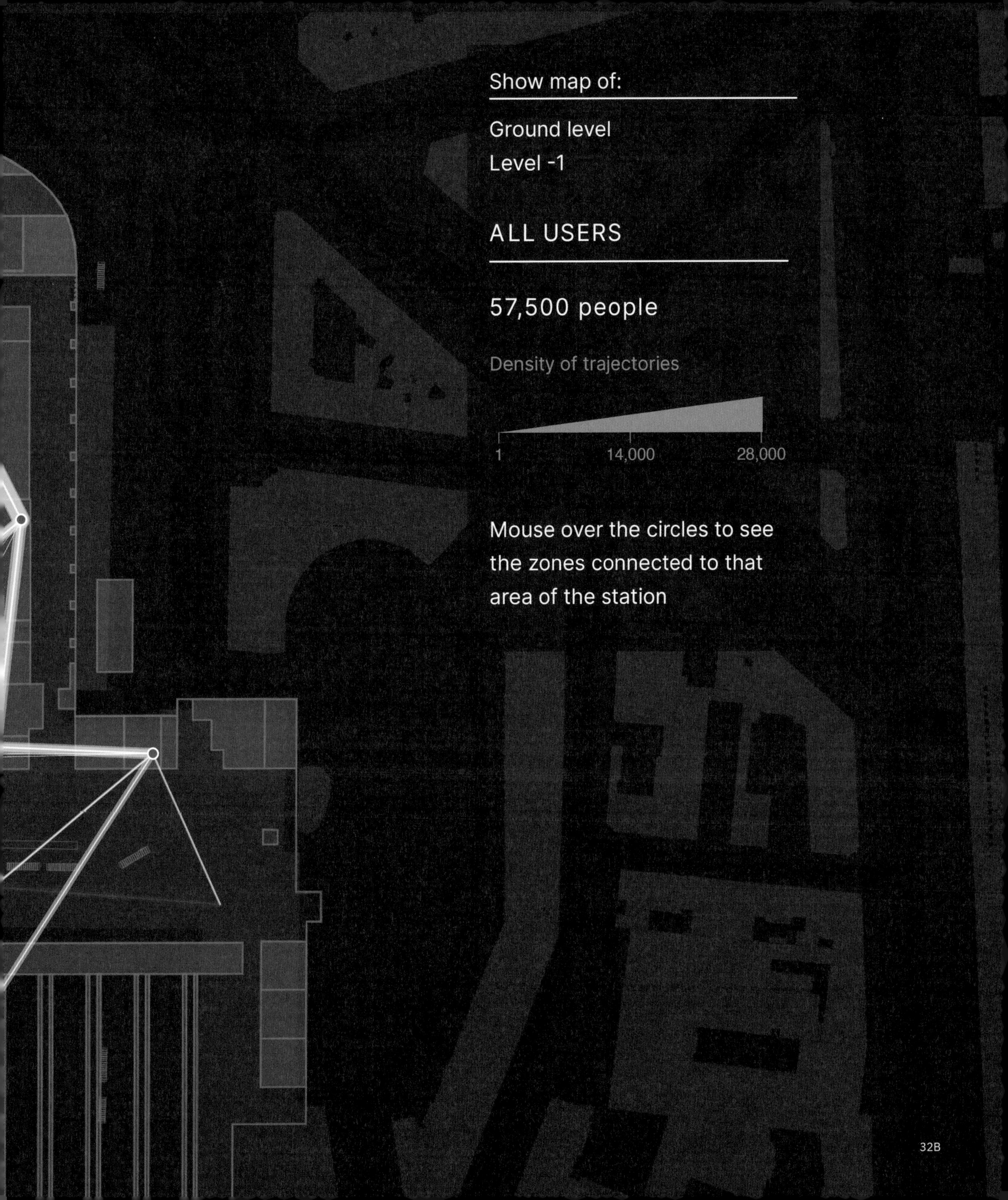
Show map of:
Ground level
Level -1
ALL USERS
57,500 people
Density of trajectories
1
14,000
28,000
Mouse over the circles to see the zones connected to that area of the station

33.
Favelas 4D — 2021

We often imagine the city of tomorrow as a place of futuristic high-rises and precise master plans, but in doing so we forget that nearly a quarter of the world's four billion current urbanites live in informal settlements. These shantytowns and slums are often cut off from city services and experience profound challenges in security, opportunity, and accessibility. In Brazil, informal settlements are called favelas. Governments there have tried to ignore or destroy them, but with the rapid growth of urbanization far outpacing the construction of affordable housing, it is clear that favelas and other informal settlements are here to stay. As part of a growing movement to integrate favelas into cities, the SCL collaborated with Rio de Janeiro's city planning commissioner Washington Fajardo to create 3-D maps of Rio's previously uncharted neighborhoods.

Even those seeking to understand or assist the hundred thousand residents of Rocinha, Rio's largest favela, have never had a very precise map of their homes. Instead of relying on traditional surveying methods or satellite imagery, SCL researchers traveled on foot through Rocinha's winding streets. They carried LiDAR scanners to measure distances between structures and changes in elevation with previously unfathomable precision. The below images show reconstructions of different slices of Rocinha as many millions of dots of LiDAR information (33A–33C). Such data can help policymakers address the many challenges that the favela faces—from resolving ambiguity in property ownership to detecting possible sites for landslides—and just as important, learn from the ingenious strategies that its residents have developed over the decades. Mapping this informal settlement reveals informality as an integral part of urban life. For all of our futuristic reveries, the city of tomorrow looks a lot like Rocinha.

33A

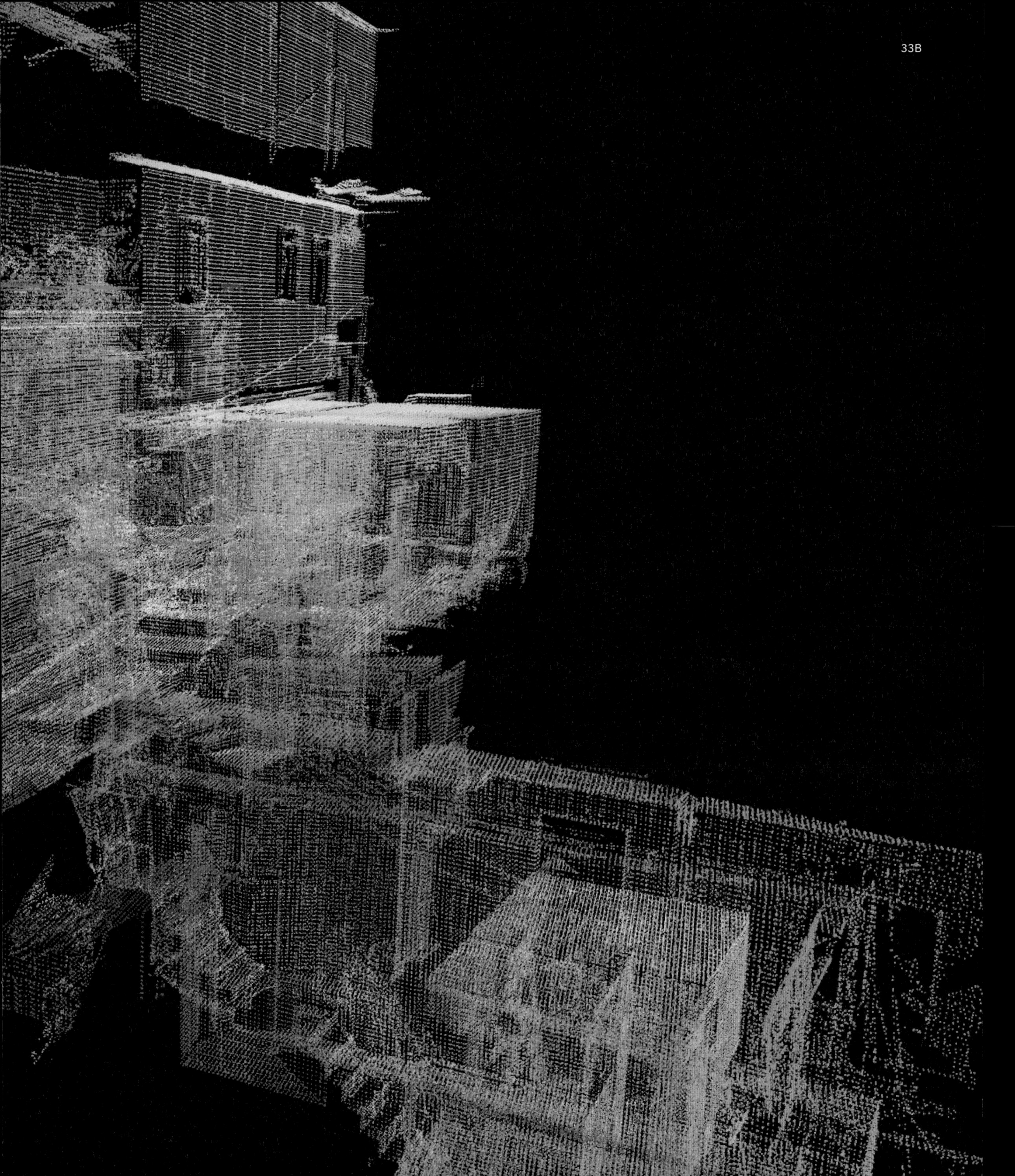

33C

Conclusion: From the Smart to the Senseable City

A new city is emerging before our eyes, a city made of both atoms and bits. In this atlas, we have approached it through digital maps relating to four of its key dimensions: motion, connection, circulation, and experience. Having reached the end of our journey, we must now ask ourselves what can be said about such a city from a more synthetic point of view. To start with, what name should we use to convey some of its essential features?

Since the dawn of the computer age, various expressions have been proposed as shorthand for the possible consequences of information and communication technologies. In the 1960s, the English avant-garde architectural group Archigram called one of their projects that dealt with such consequences the Computer City.[1] In the 1980s and 1990s, the term *digital city* became relatively common. Amsterdam activists, for instance, used it to tag an initiative meant to complement the physical Dutch metropolis by offering a digital public space and a series of online services.[2] At the time, the physical and electronic realms were still seen as fundamentally distinct, although potentially complementary.

The digital urban maps that we have reviewed suggest a very different perspective, that of the increasing inseparability of bits and atoms. Relatedly, a new expression, *smart city*, has emerged in the past ten years. In scientific and professional urban planning literature and in advertising materials, the smart city now often replaces the digital city. Initially used by companies like IBM and Cisco to develop an urban market for software products, the expression has gained momentum among various stakeholders, from municipal authorities to startups and from urban platforms to traditional civil engineering and construction companies.[3]

1 Peter Cook et al., *Archigram* (New York: Princeton Architectural Press, 1999).

2 Peter van den Besselaar, "The Life and Death of the Great Amsterdam Digital City," in *Digital Cities III, Information Technologies for Social Capital: Cross-cultural Perspectives*, Third International Digital Cities Workshop, Amsterdam, The Netherlands, September 18-19, 2003, Revised Selected Paper.

3 See, e.g., Anthony Townsend, *Smart Cities: Big Data, Civic Hackers, and the Quest for a New Utopia*; Antoine Picon, Smart Cities; Andrew Karvonen, Federico Cugurullo, Federico Caprotti eds., *Inside Smart Cities: Place, Politics and Urban Innovation* (Milton Park, Abingdon: Routledge, 2019).

The term smart city has been all the more successful in that it has aggregated a number of concerns that used to be somewhat distinct. The adjective *smart* was initially intended to convey the idea of a city made more efficient and practical through the intensive use of digital technology. The multiplication of sensors and the Internet of Things were among the technological developments that were supposed to improve the management of water and sanitation systems, energy use, and mobility. In recent years, the expression has expanded its scope to encompass notions of livability and the quest for greener and more resilient cities. Today, *smart* has to do with the opportunities to lead more fulfilling lives in cities—a preoccupation generally inseparable from the desire of cities to attract members of the *creative class*, to use Richard Florida's characterization of the various professionals who contribute to our contemporary, knowledge-based economy.[4] *Smart* is also supposed to describe the means of better answering environmental challenges, by enabling a tighter monitoring of natural resources, the weather, and of course our carbon emissions.

Despite these promises, the smart city movement has so far had difficulty when faced with articulating what is truly revolutionary in the mobilization of digital technology. It has been easy for critics to denounce the vagueness of the term *smart*. After all, because they bring people together, allowing them to connect and be more productive than they would be in isolation, cities have always been smart.[5] And in practice, *smart* often means only incremental improvements of existing infrastructure or piecemeal experiments in domains like mobility, parking, or the management of urban greenery. Is there something more decisive at play beyond the catalogs of improvements and innovations claimed all over the world as *smart*—and if so, what? The maps gathered in this atlas suggest a series of possible answers.

4 Richard Florida, *The Rise of the Creative Class: And How It's Transforming Work, Leisure, Community, and Everyday Life*, (New York: Basic Books, 2002). On the closely related theme of the rising knowledge economy, see, e.g., Edward Glaeser, *Triumph of the City: How Our Greatest Invention Makes Us Richer, Smarter, Greener, Healthier, and Happier* (New York: Penguin Press, 2011).

5 See, e.g., Richard Sennett, "No One Likes a City That's Too Smart," *The Guardian*, 4 December 2012, https://www.theguardian.com/commentisfree/2012/dec/04/smart-city-rio-songdo-masdar, accessed 13 June 2021; Adam Greenfield, *Against the Smart City: A Pamphlet* (New York: Verso, 2013).

From Objects to Flows, and from Flows to Events

A first answer has to do with what many of these maps actually show us. Even if urban fabric and street layouts appear on many of them, the information that they provide fundamentally has to do with what *happens* in cities, beginning with the motions, connections, and circulations that give cities their rhythm. As for the experience of cities, nowadays it so often starts with the blue or red "you are here" dot that pops up on the screens of our smartphones, once again a phenomenon akin to an occurrence, an elementary event that literally takes place.

Late nineteenth- and early twentieth-century urban mapping had already tried to go beyond the visible urban fabric to describe what was happening within networks; what was moving, connecting, and circulating in the streets; the copper wires of telegraphs and telephones; and metro and railway lines. But its approach remained holistic, without much detail, and above all based on the hypothesis of a certain stability of movements and flows. In other words, it was a relatively permanent urban regime that was mapped in publications such as the *Atlas de statistique graphique de la ville de Paris* (*Atlas of graphical statistics of the city of Paris*), published in 1889 and 1891 by Jacques Bertillon, the brother of the famous criminologist Alphonse Bertillon. With its plates devoted to public transportation traffic and telegraph use, the Bertillon *Atlas* illustrates what was at stake at the time: understanding the city's overall rhythm without entering into details that were considered irrelevant to planning.[6]

Thanks to geolocation, today's digital maps take a much more precise approach to what is going on in cities. Many digital platforms could not function without such detailed information, which they use to organize the services that they provide. The Uber and Lyft apps, for instance, connect riders to nearby drivers, pending acceptance of the fare's request. What these platforms organize are meetings between supply and demand — which can be interpreted as events built from circumstances such as your position and those of nearby service providers.

While not intended to provide this type of information (but rather to promote reflection on cities and to orient planning decisions), the Senseable City Lab maps are often based on the same extremely detailed approach, paying special attention to motion, connection, circulation, and experience. They testify to the possibility of passing from an overall description in terms of flows—as in the type of cartographic production epitomized by Bertillon's *Atlas*—to an atomistic grasp of individual movements and other actions, even if the data on which they rely are anonymized before being processed.

This shift is inseparable from two features of our contemporary technological and urban world. The first is the importance of big data. In this regard, it is worth noting that what we call big data is often nothing but the recorded traces left by circumstances and events ranging from people's position, as evidenced by the signals sent by their smartphones, to energy consumption in buildings, and from purchases on the Internet to posts on

6 On Bertillon's *Atlas*, see Antoine Picon, "Nineteenth-Century Urban Cartography and the Scientific Ideal: The Case of Paris," *Osiris*, 2nd ser., vol. 18 (2003): 135–149.

social networks. As the French philosopher Pierre Lévy once noted, a bit of information is not a thing but an occurrence, an atomistic event.[7] It corresponds to something that happens rather than to something that can be placed in a traditional ontological category. This profound characteristic explains the pervasiveness of gaming culture throughout the history of computers, from early developments to contemporary digital culture. Games are not sets of objects but rather systems of possible events that arise from rules.

The second feature is the abandonment of the presumption that good regulating practices can keep infrastructure and cities as a whole in proper equilibrium. Ideally, well-run factories, networks, and cities were places where nothing unusual happened, where disruption remained exceptional, where evolution was gradual, like with sea tides. From smart grids to logistical chains, contemporary management of technological resources tends to assume the opposite—namely, that irregularity and disruption are natural conditions, to be addressed with flexible tools and systems. The ideal of passive automatism has been systematically replaced by an imperative of agile adaptation to an ever-changing context replete with incertitude and unexpected events. Similarly, cities are no longer thought to be in relative equilibrium. They are instead defined by all that can happen, including the sometimes brutal inflection of their trajectories—hence the inevitable development of simulation as a means of anticipatory preparation.

These shifts should lead us to a different perspective on what matters in cities. By "what matters" we mean what we consider truly vital, what we ultimately try to improve, the substance that rational thought is working on when envisaging such improvements. For a very long time, cities were perceived as collections of physical objects: a fortified enclosure, houses, monuments. This is what Alberti mapped in his *Descriptio Urbis Romae* (*Description of the City of Rome*), what architects and engineers were tasked with building and maintaining.

At the beginning of the First Industrial Revolution, cities started to be addressed in terms of circulation and flow. The transformation of major capitals, such as Paris in the nineteenth century, was greatly inspired by this vision, which placed its emphasis on networks.[8] This perspective also gave birth to new cartographic representations of cities, such as those in Adolphe Alphand's *Les Travaux de Paris*, a lavish publication showing the development of the French capital's various networks during the nineteenth century, or indeed Bertillon's *Atlas*, which charts the flows channeled by those networks.[9]

We now tend to consider the city from the perspective of billions of elementary occurrences recorded digitally, more and more often in real time. It is as if the substance of the urban were made of billions of extremely small particles, moving dust, a cloud, or—even better—a massive swarm of pixels that allowed one to build a comprehensive picture of its inner workings. Images of what happens can be produced at different levels. From elementary occurrences, one can gain access to more noticeable events and situations. For instance, the geolocation of tens of thousands of vehicles enables the construction of instantaneous representations of automobile

7 Pierre Lévy, *La Machine univers: Création, cognition et culture informatique* (Paris: La Découverte, 1987), 124.

8 See Antoine Picon, *La Ville des réseaux: Un imaginaire politique* (Paris: Éditions Manucius, 2014).

9 See Antoine Picon and Jean-Paul Robert, assisted by Anna Hartmann, *Le Dessus des cartes: Un Atlas parisien* (Paris: Éditions du Pavillon de l'Arsenal, Picard, 1999).

traffic, which pinpoint congestions. Similarly, the recording of cell phone locations reveals use patterns of urban public spaces. As mentioned above, the city is no longer assumed to be in equilibrium, but the resulting potentialities find their counterpart in an abundant production of scenarios and other models that, feeding on the billions of recorded occurrences and on the multitude of events and situations they reveal, are meant to help control future developments as much as possible.

One way to understand what is truly radical in the rise of the smart city is to pay attention to this transformation in what matters today. The maps gathered in this atlas show how it will soon be possible to monitor many things in real time, and at all scales, and to simulate some of the trajectories that are likely to ensue. A new urban era is dawning. Smart cities will continue to accommodate flows and networks, but these will play only one part in the wider scheme of happenings: billions of occurrences, events, and situations that development scenarios will enable us to handle. Will we still need to consider the holistic figure of the flow when we have access to molecular descriptions of phenomena? Occurrences such as the transmission of information by a sensor, situations such as the state of automobile traffic, and scenarios that result from the simulations made possible by the massive production of data on how the city is functioning constitute a new urban reality.

Such dramatic change should enable us to better understand the true scope of the claim made by the advocates of a new urban science that our cities are becoming inexorably computable. This is actually part of an old debate. Since the age of rapid European urbanization in the nineteenth century, the approach to cities has oscillated between two extremes. On the one hand is what could be called a romanticist view, a belief in the city as fundamentally beyond the powers of human comprehension and thus best apprehended through qualitative means. On the other hand is a quantitative tradition committed to the belief that the structures, patterns, and dynamics of cities can be reduced to numbers.

Without a doubt, the smart city movement is the inheritor of the latter tradition, through the development of urban statistics at the end of the nineteenth and beginning of the twentieth centuries and attempts in the 1950s and 1960s to mobilize cybernetics and systems theory to model cities.[10] But the claim that cities are becoming *computable* which has accompanied the movement's rise should be properly understood. It does not mean that everything in the urban realm will actually become computable. Rather, it implies that what matters for the various constituencies in charge of steering cities has become more and more systematically apprehended via data gathering and quantitative simulation. It is also worth noting that computable does not necessarily mean predictable. As dynamic systems, cities may very well follow nonlinear and, by the same token, often unpredictable paths. In any case, there are limits to what big data, scenarios, and other models can tell us about the future. This points to a more circumscribed evolution than one leading to a fully controllable city, but its implications are probably as important as those of the rise of the networked metropolis during the First Industrial Revolution. Our atlas is inseparable from this essential transition.

10 On attempts to model and steer city development inspired by cybernetics and system theory, see Jennifer Light, *From Warfare to Welfare: Defense Intellectuals and Urban Problems in Cold War America* (Baltimore: Johns Hopkins University Press, 2003).

New Forms of Collective Intelligence

Another characteristic of the new type of city that is emerging before our eyes is due to new forms of collective behavior and consciousness. From Facebook to Twitter, social media are emblematic of this emergence. It is interesting to note that the combination of enthusiasm and fear they provoke is not without analogue in the mixed feelings experienced by the contemporaries of nineteenth-century revolutions before the rising phenomenon of the crowd, a phenomenon ultimately theorized by the French sociologist and psychologist Gustave Le Bon in his 1895 classic *Psychologie des foules*, translated in English as *The Crowd: A Study of the Popular Mind*. Social media are definitely in need of their own Le Bon, who can help us better understand the new ways of making friends and attracting followers but also the dangers of memes, fake news, and conspiracy theories.

These forms of collective behavior and consciousness should incite us to give a more literal meaning to *smart city*: *smart* as capable of thought, deliberation, and action. To this list of collective cognitive faculties, one should certainly add feeling and emotion. For social media and the maps that serve them can also be mobilized to share sensations and emotions, for better and for worse. On such maps, we can post impressions and feelings, restaurant and shop ratings, opinions about places. The logbook can thus be shared and contribute to other people's experiences.

Finally, on social media we may believe that we humans are only among ourselves. But we are in fact constantly interacting with algorithms and bots. Often perceived as entirely human because of the site's collaborative nature, Wikipedia's contributors are actually a collection of human and nonhuman actors.[11] More generally, the smart city will be based more and more on the coexistence of humans, algorithms, and robots, on the close association between organic intelligence and electromechanical intelligence that will form new types of collectives. Whole swaths of the economy, from industry to banking, are already functioning within this hybrid system as cyborgs, in the sense that they represent and operate as intimate and almost inseparable alliances between humans and machines capable of reason.[12] Being smart could also be described as being augmented. Since human cognitive capacity is now accompanied and supported by that of machines, difficult questions about political governance are raised by the resulting new type of city. Should a top-down decision-making model be applied to it, or, on the contrary, should we consider its intelligence to reside in the collaborative capacity of individuals, leading from the bottom up? Again, we should probably envisage a mixture of the two, with the proportions varying from one city to another. The smart city will be not a utopia that is rooted in the perfection of an unequivocal choice but rather the result of complex negotiations and adjustments between contradictory requirements.

Digital mapping is one of the preferred expressions of the dynamics of the smart city's emergence and the medium through which some of this city's characteristics will be firmly set in place. It reflects the inexorability of what

11 Aaron Halfaker and John Riedl, "Bots and Cyborgs: Wikipedia's Immune System," Computer 45, no. 3 (March 2012): 79–82; R. Stuart Geiger and Aaron Halfaker, "When the Levee Breaks: Without Bots, What Happens to Wikipedia's Quality Control Process?," accessed 14 June 2021, http://stuartgeiger.com/wikisym13-cluebot.pdf.

12 See on this question Matthew Gandy, "Cyborg Urbanization: Complexity and Monstrosity in the Contemporary City," *International Journal of Urban and Regional Research* 29, no. 1 (March 2005): 26–49; and Erik Swyngedouw, "Circulations and Metabolisms: (Hybrid) Natures and (Cyborg) Cities," *Science as Culture* 15, no. 2 (June 2006): 105–121.

is happening: the rise of a world populated by occurrences and events more than by objects, and of communication situations marked by the sending and receiving of ever-changing messages more than by semantic codes set in stone. From this point of view, the gradual blurring of the distinction between map and screen or between cartography, surveillance, and control takes on its full significance. But above all, digital maps allow top-down and bottom-up logics to come face to face and adapt to each other. Indeed, many of these maps refer to the new relationships that are being formed between large-scale sociotechnical measures and connected individuals. Digital maps are also instrumental in sharing more than raw information—that is, sensations, experiences, and ultimately emotions. It is in this context that the projects presented in this atlas should be considered. The visualization of physical and digital flows reveals the new importance of the events that shape urban life, from the arrival and departure of subway cars or railroad trains to major concerts by pop stars. The notion of urban metabolism and the question of lived experience are shown to be inseparable from the relationship between the city and the individual scale. In this framework, we prefer to use the term *senseable city* instead of *smart city*, to focus less on technology and more on human agency.

As databases, images, and infrastructure, maps are infiltrating every nook and cranny of urban reality. They have become an invaluable interface through which people can make sense of increasingly digital and (potentially) smarter urban areas. The size of contemporary digital urban maps is that of the city, or rather of what matters in the city today, and like Jorge Luis Borges's or Lewis Carroll's map they coincide almost point for point with the ground they cover.

INDEX

Note: Names of projects appear in bold.

Except for the images in each chapter's introductory sections,
all data viz are reproduced with courtesy of the MIT Senseable City Lab
http://senseable.mit.edu/

Chapter 1

Charles Joseph Minard, *Carte figurative des pertes successives en hommes de l'armée française dans la campagne de Russie 1812–1813,* in *Tableaux graphiques et cartes figuratives de Mr Minard* (Paris: École Nationale des Ponts et Chaussées, 1869), fol. 10975, tabl. 28. Reproduced from https://en.wikipedia.org/wiki/File:Minard.png.

Jacques Bertillon, *Paris 1888: Recettes kilométriques des lignes d'omnibus,* in *Seine, Service de statistique municipale, Atlas de statistique graphique de la ville de Paris,* vol. 1 (Paris: G. Masson, 1889), n.p. Reproduced from https://commons.wikimedia.org/wiki/File:Atlas_de_statistique_graphique_-_18._Paris_1888._Recettes_kilometriques_des_ligne_d%27Omnibus_-_David_Rumsey.jpg.

Paul-Henry Chombart de Lauwe, *Trajets pendant un an d'une jeune fille du XVIe arrondissement.* Reproduced by permission from Chombart de Lauwe, *Paris et l'agglomération parisienne* (Paris: Presses Universitaires de France, 1952), vol. 1, 106. © 1952 by Presses Universitaires de France.

Laura Kurgan, 50 minutes, 5 points (Storefront). Reproduced by permission of the artist from *You Are Here: Information Drift,* exhibited at the Storefront for Art and Architecture, 1994. Receiver location: Storefront for Art and Architecture. NAVSTAR Satellite constellation: 01, 05, 12, 15, 20, 21, 23, 25. 1,349 position records, acquired 25 January 1994: 16:41:06–16:51:06, 17:08:21–17:17:59, 17:19:05–17:29:06, 17:31:28–17:41:28, 16:56:13–17:05:53 (GPS time).

Waag, Esther Polak, and Jeroen Kee, *Amsterdam RealTime* (2002). Reproduced by permission.

Chapter 2

Jacques Bertillon, *Paris 1880–1889: Service télégraphique et postal,* in *Seine, Service de statistique municipale, Atlas de statistique graphique de la ville de Paris,* vol. 2 (Paris: G. Masson, 1891), n.p.

Neil C. Gustafson, *Average Number of Daily Telephone Messages per 100,000 Persons between New York and Selected Cities for April, 1958,* in Jean Gottmann, *Megalopolis: The Urbanized Northeastern Seaboard of the United States* (Cambridge, MA: MIT Press, 1962), 584. Reprinted courtesy of the MIT Press.

Buckminster Fuller, Geoscope illustration (1962). Courtesy The Estate of R. Buckminster Fuller.

Barrett Lyon, opte.org, *Map of the Internet* (2003). Reprinted by permission.

Mark A. Sicoli, *Consensus Network Summary of MCMC Run* (map of North American and Siberian languages; 2014). Reproduced under the Creative Commons Attribution 4.0 International Public License (CC BY 4.0), obtained from https://www.researchgate.net/figure/Network-summarizes-all-splits-with-at-least-10-support-in-3001-trees-sampled-Longer_fig3_260758349, and used here in unmodified form. The full text of the CC BY 4.0 license is available at https://creativecommons.org/licenses/by/4.0/legalcode.

Chapter 3

John Snow, map 1 in *On the Mode of Communication of Cholera*, 2nd ed. (London: John Churchill, 1855), insert after p. 44. Reproduced from https://commons.wikimedia.org/wiki/File:Snow-cholera-map-1.jpg.

R. P. Studley Company, *Richard's Illustrated and Statistical Map of the Great Conflagration in Chicago* (St. Louis: R. P. Studley, 1871). Reproduced from https://commons.wikimedia.org/wiki/File:1871_Richard%27s_map_of_the_great_conflagration_in_Chicago.jpg.

Jay Wright Forrester, fig. 15-18 from *Industrial Dynamics* (Cambridge, MA: MIT Press, 1961), 17. Reproduced by permission.

Buckminster Fuller, *Dome over Manhattan* (1960). Courtesy The Estate of R. Buckminster Fuller.

Chapter 4

Guy Debord, *Guide psychogéographique de Paris: Discours sur les passions de l'amour: Pentes psychogéographiques de la dérive et localisation d'unités d'ambriance* [sic] (1957). 59.4 × 73.8 cm. Lithography on paper. Museu d'Art Contemporani de Barcelona (MACBA) Collection. MACBA Consortium. © Guy Debord, 2019. Photo: Tony Coll. Reproduced by permission of MACBA.

Andre Bertrand, *Situationist International* (1967). Reproduced by permission from http://www.international-times.org.uk/ITarchive.htm#1968.

Constant Nieuwenhuys, *Symbolische kaart New Babylon nord* (1958). Reproduced by permission of Fondation Constant and Societa' Italiana Degli Autori ed Editori (SIAE).

Gordon Bell, photo collage from a talk given at the Institute for the Future's Health Horizons Conference, Sausalito, California, 5–6 June 2014. Reproduced by permission of the artist from https://www.dropbox.com/sh/t6sw29bbi1qofeh/AADrE6fgLFC9_RlI20zl1ZkVa?dl=0&preview=Bell_Lifelogging_technology_for_memory_recall_IFTF_2014-06-05.pptx.

This book would not have been possible without the contribution of the many people formerly or currently working at the MIT Senseable City Lab since its foundation almost 20 years ago. Together, they produced the many visuals and infographics that constitute the backbone of the *Atlas of the Senseable City*.

Leadership
Carlo Ratti *Director, Professor of the Practice*
Assaf Biderman *Associate Director*
Fábio Duarte *Principal Research Scientist*
Paolo Santi *Principal Research Scientist*
Umberto Fugiglando *Research Manager and Partnerships Lead*

Management
Erin Baumgartner *Assistant Director*
Jackie Dufault *Executive Director*
Erin Schenck *Assistant Director*

Support
Margaret Bryan, Lauren DeRusha, Jared Embelton, Julie-Paine Fajardo, Meaghan Jalbert, Caroline Moore, Jessica Ngo, Arthur Pesaturo, Prudence Robinson, Rachel Seavey, Rose Silva, Paulina Sterpe, Bettina Urcuioli

Past and present researchers
Timur Abbiasov, Marwa Abdulhai, Katherine Adler, Katherine Adler, Kwesi Afrifa, Rohit Aggarwala, Wahjeeha Ahmad, Wajeeha Ahmad, Myra Ahmad, Chaewon Ahn, Anwar Al-Khateeb, Alaa AlRadwan, Nikolas Albarran, Livingston Albritten, Eric Alm, Thomas Altmann, Brian Alvarez, Ricardo Alvarez, Alexander Amini, Clio Andris, Amin Anjomshoaa, Samuel Anklesaria, Afian Anwar, German W. Aparicio Jr., Mariana Arcaya, Ian Ardouin-Fumat, Burak Arikan, Anna Arpaci-Dusseau, Hiba Awad, Dima Ayyash, Dima Ayyash, Eric Baczuk, Matthew Baldwin, Natasha Balwit, Esmeralda Barreiro, Aline Barros, Seckin Basturk, Erin Baumgartner, Juan Bautista Hobin, Juan Nico Bautista Hobin, Fabio Bazzucchi, Keis Bejgo, Aliaksandr Bely, Alexander Belyi, Eran Ben-Joseph, Lorenzo Benedetti, Tom Benson, Antonio Berrones, Daniel Berry, Luis Berríos-Negrón, Assaf Biderman, Alice Birolo, Quentin Bitran, Lukas Block, Nick Boer, Iva Bojic, Christian Bongiorno, Michele Bonino, Soorajnath Boominathan, Paul Bouisset, John Bowler, Jorrie Brettin, Rex Britter, Aurimas Bukauskas, Aurimas Bukauskas, Amedeo Buonanno, Bill Cai, Francesco Calabrese, Francisco Camara Pereira, Riccardo Campari, Sarah Campbell, Alexander Campillanos, Nhat Cao, Cyndia Cao, Giulio Capolino, Luis Carli, Daniel Carmody, Alan Casallas, Blake Chambers, Patricia Chan, Colin Chaney, Louis Charron, Oleksandr Chaykovskyy, Caroline Chea, Xiaoji Chen, Vicky Chen, Zitong Chen Cristen Chinea, Justin Chiu, Sharlene Chiu, Carnaven Chiu, Jennifer Choi, Leigh Christie, Anya Christy, Clara Cibrario Assereto, Matthew Claudel, Fransheska Colon, Julian Contreras, Julian Contreras, Christopher Cook, Andrea Corti, Enrico Costanza, Theodore Courtney, Gillian Crampton Smith, Pedro Cruz, Hongyan Cui, Dominik Dahlem, Cheng Dai, Alyx Daly, Joseph Daly, Matthias Danzmayr, Neel Das, Zolzaya Dashdorj, Vincent Daub, Lorenzo Davoli, Antoine De Malprade, Elena De la Paz, Salvatore Di Dio, Giusy Di Lorenzo, Lei Dong, Talia Dorsey, Mélanie Droogleever Fortuyn, Guangyu Du, Fábio Duarte, Jacqueline Dufault, Sarah Dunbar, Jennifer Dunnam, Bradley Eckert, Benjamin Eysenbach, Greg Falco, Zhuangyuan Fan, Gracie Fang, Luigi Farrauto, Kelly Fang, Chris Fematt, Selena Feng, David Fernández, Joseph Ferreira, Reinaldo Figueroa, Lucie Boyce Flather, Edward Flores, Richard Florida, Logan Ford, Dennis Frenchman, Dennis Frenchman, Umberto Fugiglando, Andrea Galanti, Nadina Galle, Qiyun Gao, Rene Garcia Franceschini, Tomas Gast, Carolien Gehrels, Jamie Geng, Carlos Gershenson, Newsha Ghaeli, Banti Gheneti, Saba Ghole, Fabien Girardin, Emenike Godfrey-Igwe, Alejandro Gonzalez Garcia, Claire Gorman, Sebastian Grauwin, Carlos Greaves, Kael Greco, Christopher Green, Cale Gregory, Dana Gretton, Cesare Griffa, Virgil Griffith, Gabriel

Grise, Serena Grown-Haeberli, Benedikt Groß, Damiano Gui, Akshit Gupta, Joaquin Pischner Gutierrez, Daniel Gutierrez, Gary Hack, Niklas Hagemann, Dylan Halpern, Yoon Chung Han, Yoon Chung Han, Helena Hang Rong, Malgorzata Hanzl, Karen Hao, Karen Hao, Roy Zhang Haoqiang, Cesar Harada, Behrooz Hashemian, Shirin Hashim, Bartosz Hawelka, Shan He, Mengqi Moon He, Cate Heine, Pedro Henrique da Silva Alves, Chennah Heroor, Tylor Hess, Guy Hoffman, Thomas Holleczek, Teerayut Horanont, Lindsey Hoshaw, Anyang Hou, Katherine Huang, Kuan Wei Huang, I-yang Huang, Alexander Huang, Sonya Huang, William Hunter, Faith Huynh, Hiroshi Ishii, Elyud Ismail, Oluwaferanmi Issachar, Kee Moon Jang, Lenna Johnsen, Robert Johnson, Robert Johnson, Michael Joroff, Holly Josephs, Samuel Judd, Yuhao Kang, E Roon Kang, Chaogui Kang, Erkan Kayacan, Ryan Kelly, Benjamin Kettle, Muhammad Khairul, Anuj Khandelwal, Eunsu Kim, Tiasa Kim, Haeri Kim, Cameron Kleiman, Nikita Klimenko, Michael Klinker, Kristian Kloeckl, Aaron Koblin, Jan Kokol, Fabio Kon, Dániel Kondor, Jeevesh Konuru, Gautier Krings, Sriram Krishnan, Kevin Kung, Evie Kyritsis, Flavien Lambert, Vincent Lamoureux, Bruno Latour, Eugene Lee, Hanna Lee, Namju Lee, David Lee, Joey Lee, Deborah Lefosse, Lesian Lengare, Pietro Leoni, Frank Levy, Tracey Li, Maddy Li, Lezhi Li, Xiaojiang Li, Qianhui Liang, Xiongjiu Liao, Alyson Liss, Charles Liu, Tingyu Liu, Charles Liu, Kevin Liu, Liang Liu, Shiyang Liu, Davor Ljubenkov, Sunny Long, Sunny Long, Iñigo Lorente, Jia Lou, Amanda Lowery, David Lu, Ruixian Ma, Meaghan MacDonald, Yuki Machida, Martina Maitan, Nick Malleson, Matteo Mandrille, Diego Maniloff, Vincenzo Manzoni, Nic Marchesi, Nahom Marie, Cristina Marquez, Claudio Martani, Damien Martin, Mauro Martino, Emanuele Massaro, Thomas Matarazzo, Luis Mateos, Andrea Mattiello, Dian Mattingly, David Mayo, Sabrina Mazer, Martina Mazzarello, Noah McDaniel, Anil Menon, Drew Meyers, Sebastiano Milardo, Stephen Miles, Dimitrios Milioris, Sey Min, Justin Moe, John Mofor, Mohamed Mohamed, Mahsan Mohsenin, Franco Montalvo, Caroline Moore , Simone Mora, Eugenio Morello, Pietro Morino, Merry Mou, Gabriele Musella, Nashid Nabian, Brandon Nadres, Brandon Nadres, Nazanin Naeini, Till Nagel, Pooja Nair, Marina Neophytou, Otto Ng, Jessica Ngo, Uyen Nguyen, Linh Nguyen, Leonardo Nicoletti, Walter Nicolino, Alexandra Nwigwe, Marguerite Nyhan, Stephanie O'Brien, Kevin O'Keeffe, Dietmar Offenhuber, Gonzalo Ortega, Christine Outram, Oluwatobi Oyinlola, Levent Ozruh, Sebastian Palacios, Andrea Paraboschi, Shinkyu Park, Bahar Partov, Paolo Patelli, James Patten, Sanjana Paul, Tao Pei, Wenzhe Peng, Alexander Penn, David Perez, David Perez, Arthur Pesaturo, Dang Pham, Dang Pham, Santi Phithakkitnukoon, Antoine Picon, Francesco Pilla, Fabio Pinelli, Natasha Plotkin, Christine Pourheydarian, Riki Pribadi, François Proulx, Adam Pruden, Riccardo Maria Pulselli, Pietro Pusceddu, Yuan Yuan Qiao, Isabel Quispe, Juan Rached Viso, Rahul Rajagopalan, Rahul Rajagopalan, Martin Ramos, Yaseem Rana, Amish Rasheed, Punit Rathore, Carlo Ratti, Lea Rausch, Jon Reades, Daan Rennings, Bernd Resch, Tim Robertson, Prudence Robinson, Stephane Roche, Adam Rodriguez, James Rodriguez, Francisca Rojas, Larissa Romualdo Suzuki, Abraham Rosenfeld, Miriam Roure Parera, Daniela Rus, William Ruschel, Sadegh Sabouri, Soheil Sadeghi Eshkevari, Basant Sagar, Basant Sagar, Oleguer Sagarra, Arianna Salazar Miranda, Darshan Santani, Paolo Santi, Lorenzo Santolini, Adele Santos, Daniele Santucci, Saskia Sassen, Katja Schechtner, Erin Schenck, Markus Schlapfer, Leonard Schrage, Philipp Schmitt, Marc-Edouard Schultheiss, Rachel Seavey, Stefan Seer, Ian Seiferling, Susanne Seitinger, Oliver Senn, Richard Sennett, Andres Sevtsuk, Anna Shafiro, Mohit Shah, Tixiao Shan, Kyuha Shim, Youjin Shin, Alastair Shipman, Aaron Siegel, Rose Silva , James Simard, Sara Sime, Luca Simeone, Dhiraj Sinha, Louis Sirota, Michelle Sit, Michelle Sit, Izabela Sitko, Ramprasad Sivaprakasam, Bram Smolenaars, Jessica Snyder, Wonyoung So, Stanislav Sobolevsky, Christian Sommer, Hyemi Song, Zhenyu Song, Alberto Speroni, Mayuri Sridhar, Paulina Sterpe, Harihar Subramanyam, Maoran Sun, Jonathan Sun, Larry Susskind, Kristopher Swick, Kristopher Swick, Michael Szell, Remi Tachet Des Combes, Jialu Tan, Yue Tang, Fiona Tanuwidjaja, Ye Tao, Louis Tao, Najeeb Marc Tarazi, Surat Teerapittayanon , Aurora Terzani, Iacopo Testi, Pierrick Thebault, You Xuan Thung, Ye Tian, Meghan Timmons, Musstanser Tinauli, Aldo Treville, Vlad Trifa, Aashish Tripathee, Jesse Triplett, Raymond Tse, Wei Tu, Yaniv Turgeman, Samuel Udotong, Sebastian Uribe, Tamanna Urmi, Andrea Vaccari, Abhiti Vaish, Lawrence Vale, Anthony Vanky, Nancy Vargas, Mohammad Vazifeh, Abhitha Vegi, Titus Venverloo, Kenny Verbeeck, Alphonse Vial, Kayla Villa, Nathan Villagaray-Carski, Nathan Villagaray-Carski, Pablo Villegas, Amy Vogel, Jamie Voros, Behram Wali, Erica Walker, Brandon Wang, Yin-Jen Wang, Angela Wang, Yao Wang, Wei Wang, Michelle Wang, Rui Wang, An Wang, Mattie Wasiak, Tyler Wasser, Marshall Wentworth, Cody Wero, Geoffrey West, Andrew Whittle, Sarah Williams, Saul Wilson, Malima Wolf, Jared Wong, Priscilla Wong, Tien-Chun Wu, Mike Xia, Yang Xu, Wenfei Xu, Vasco Xu , Eddie Xue, Edward Xue, Ritwik Yadav, Li Yan, Longxu Yan, Katherine Yang, Karen Yegian, Mark Yen, Mark Yen, Wings Yeung, Fernando Yordan, Fernando Yordan, Dustin York, Yuji Yoshimura, Lylla Younes, Caitlin Zacharias, Çağrı Hakan Zaman, Mirko Zardini, Ostin Zarse, Snoweria Zhang, Hongmou Zhang, Fan Zhang, Xiaohu Zhang, Ann Zhang, Siyi Zhang, Pei Zhao, Siqi Zheng, Qinmin Zheng, Isabelle Zheng , Shaocong Zhou, Xiao Zhou, Chris Yulun Zhou, Diane Zhou, Siqi Zhu, Ziyuan Zhu, Rui Zhu, Ophelia Zhu, Davide Zilli, Tawanda Zimuto, Tawanda Zimuto, Filippo dal Fiore, Giovanni de Niederhausern, Irene de la Torre, Priyanka deSouza, David van der Leer